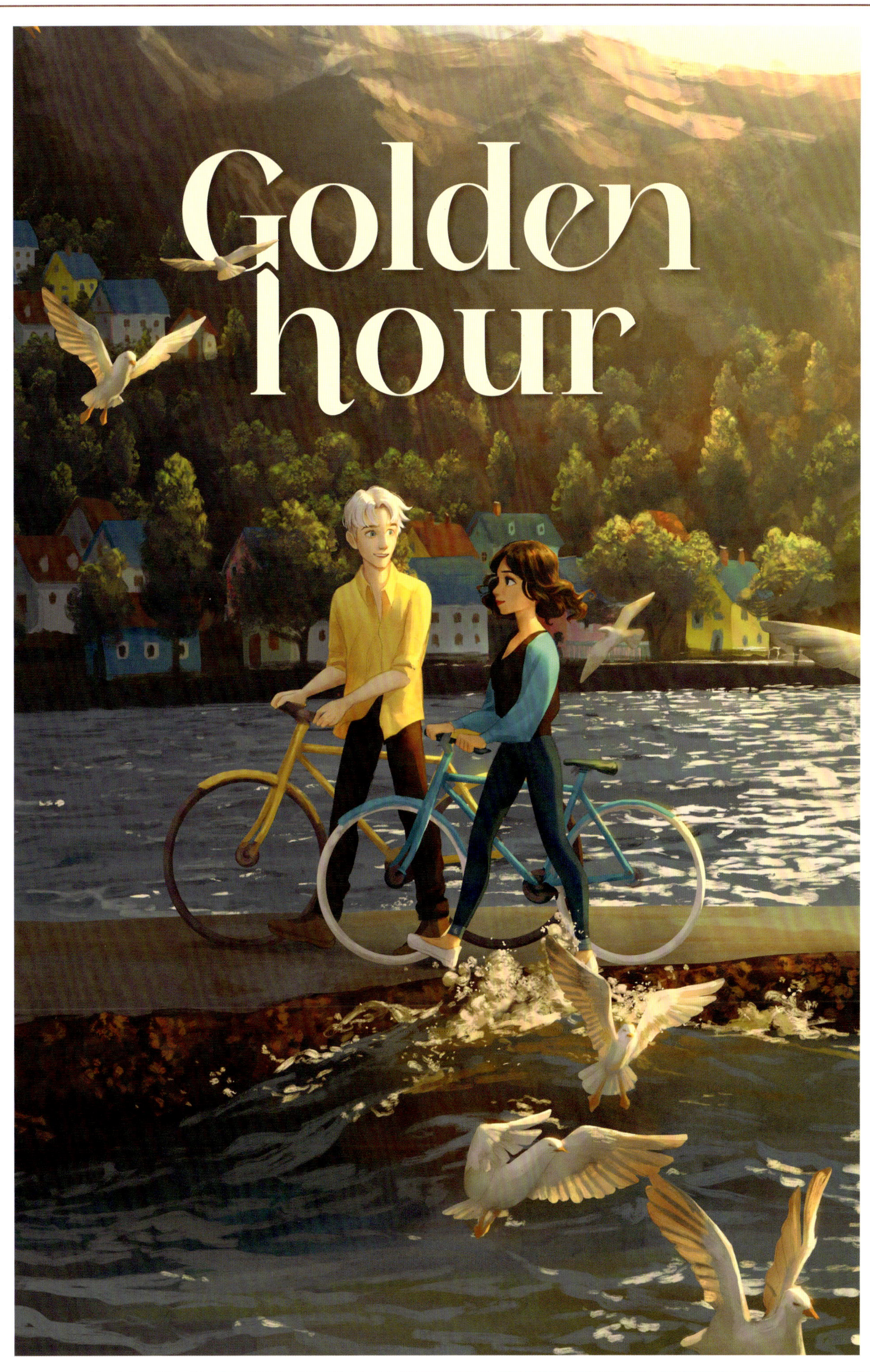
Golden
hour

3dtotal Publishing

Correspondence: publishing@3dtotal.com
Website: store.3dtotal.com

First published in the United Kingdom, 2024, by 3dtotal Publishing.

Address: 3dtotal.com Ltd, 29 Foregate Street, Worcester, WR1 1DS, United Kingdom.

Hard cover ISBN: 978-1-912843-82-4

Printed and bound in China by C&C Offset Printing Co., Ltd

Visit store.3dtotal.com for a complete list of available book titles.

Editorial Project Manager: Rhiannon Joseph
Lead Editor: Samantha Rigby
Lead Designer: Joseph Cartwright
Studio Manager: Simon Morse
Managing Director: Tom Greenway

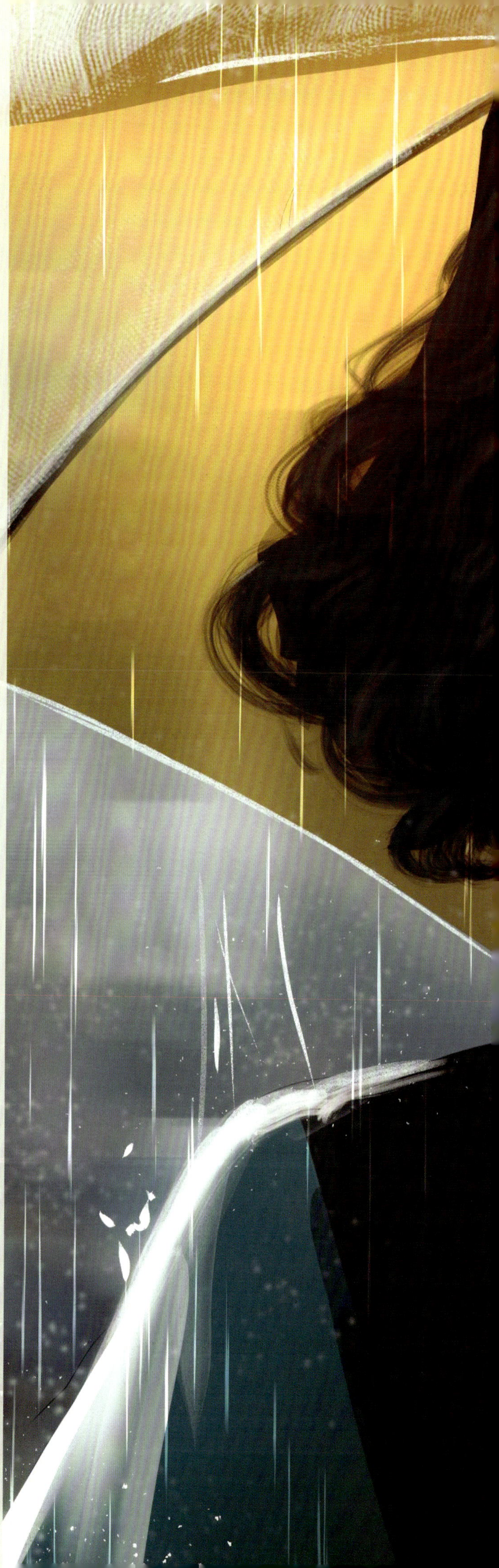

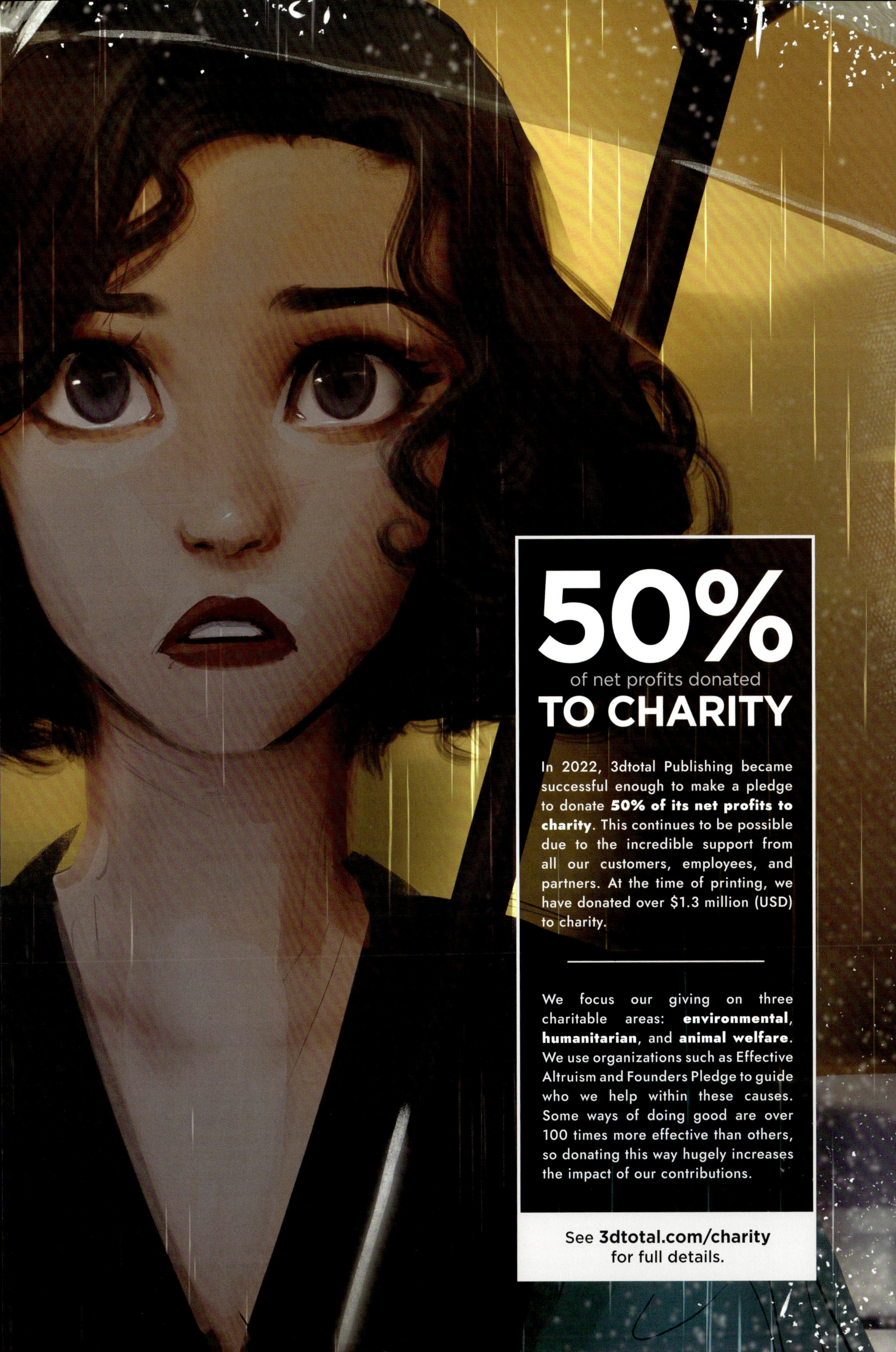

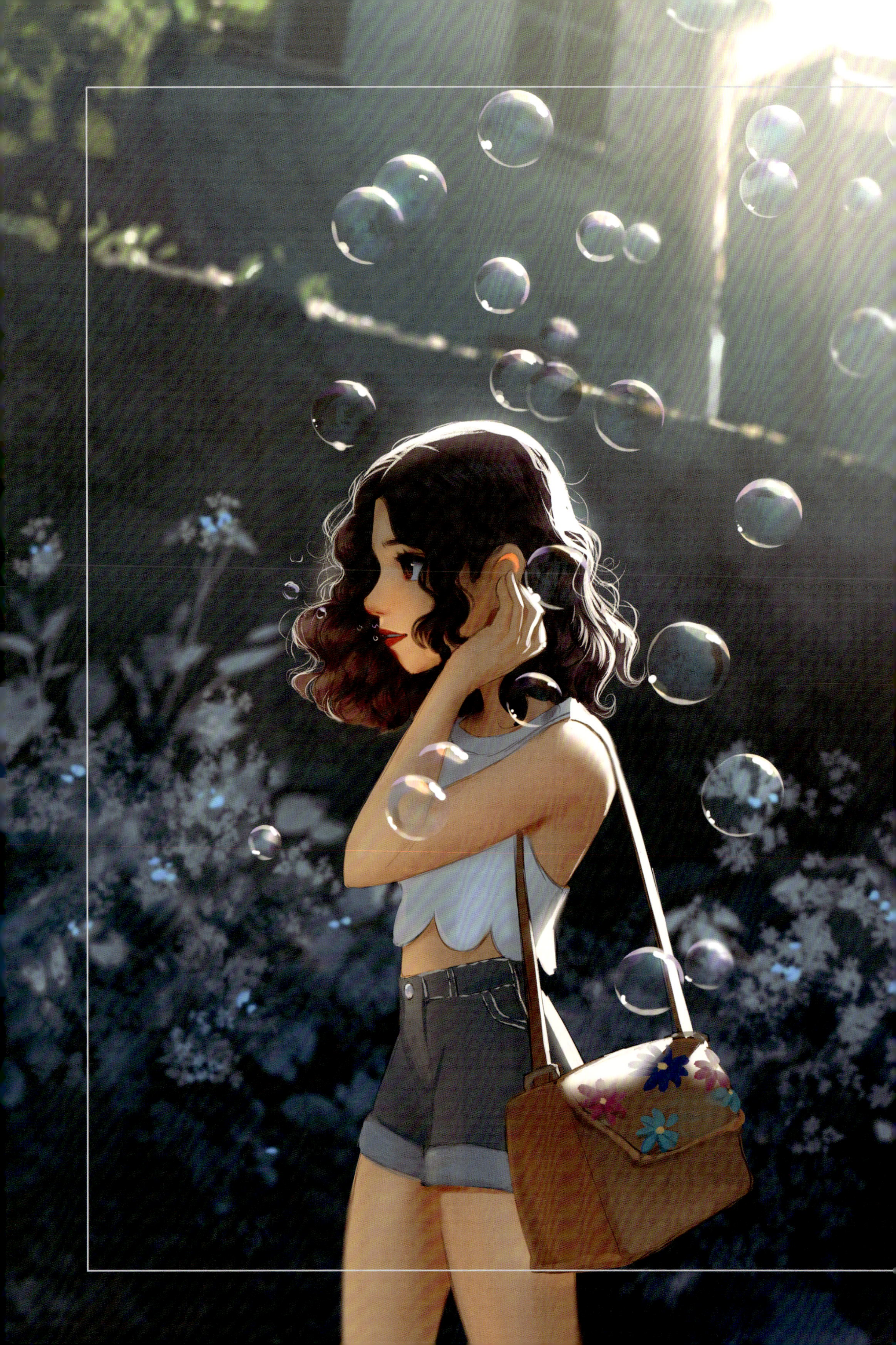

CONTENTS

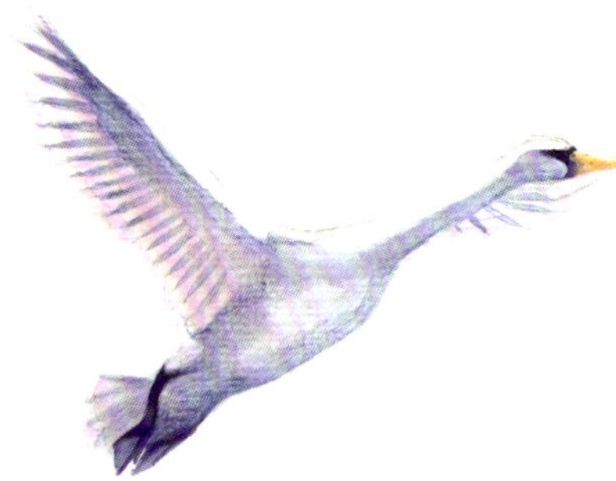

FOREWORD

Inevitably, my biggest source of inspiration will always be my twin sister, Raide. I watched her art evolve from the very beginning; our upbringing was identical and yet our styles have developed quite differently. While I shifted towards cartoons and animation, Raide seemed mesmerized by the tiniest of details. For years, I witnessed her carefully replicating images and paying close attention to rendering. I have always respected the amount of patience she has for her art, especially in those early years, when we drew with a computer mouse.

I'm very lucky to have a close bond with a person who shares my passion for art. It's very important to connect with people who will praise your work but also give you constructive feedback with little hesitation. When I was younger, I didn't quite understand this. However, as we both matured and our styles began to take form, I noticed that our strengths also evolved. Every artist flourishes in the area they feel passionate about. I noticed this the most when we began collaborating – Raide drew the backgrounds while I made the characters. We created a new type of illustration that was only possible when we both took advantage of our strengths.

Raide gets out of her comfort zone quite a lot and I admire the way she uses references. She doesn't just copy photos; she uses them as a guide to create something refreshing. While much of what I draw is from my imagination, Raide has always reassured me that there's nothing wrong with relying on a reference. She's also taught me to be mindful of my compositions. She'll always take a step back to evaluate, carefully planning the thumbnails of her pieces to see if the elements are in harmony.

What you'll see in this book is the result of hundreds of hours of practice – an evolution into an original style. I find it quite difficult to summarize her work in a few words because it's so diverse; from backgrounds to cinematic scenes, lighting studies, and character sheets, Raide always attempts to learn as many aspects of art as possible. I always wanted to hold a book of my sister's work and I am so proud that it became a reality! I hope that Raide will inspire you as much as she has me.

– Leffie

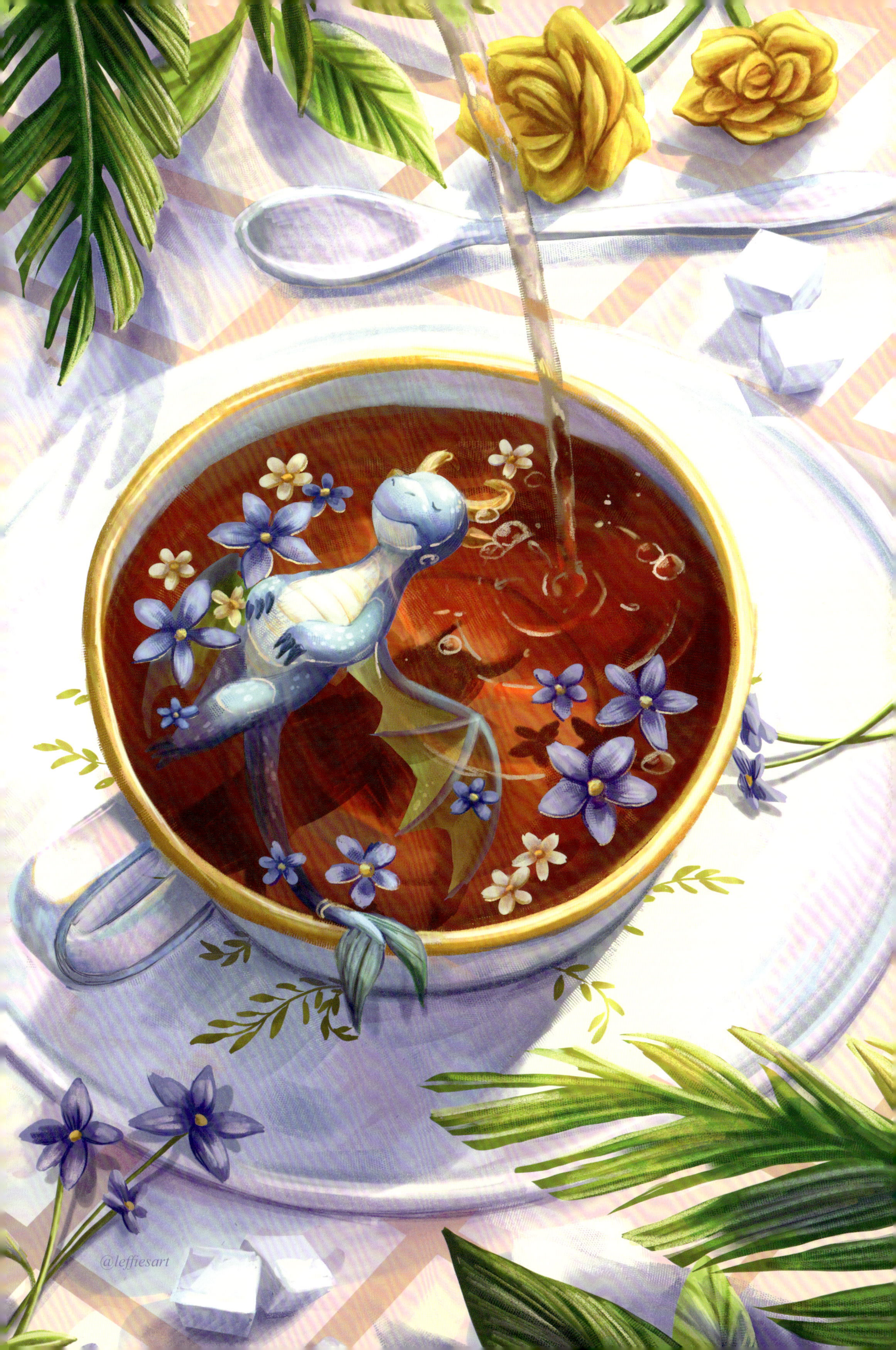
@leffiesart

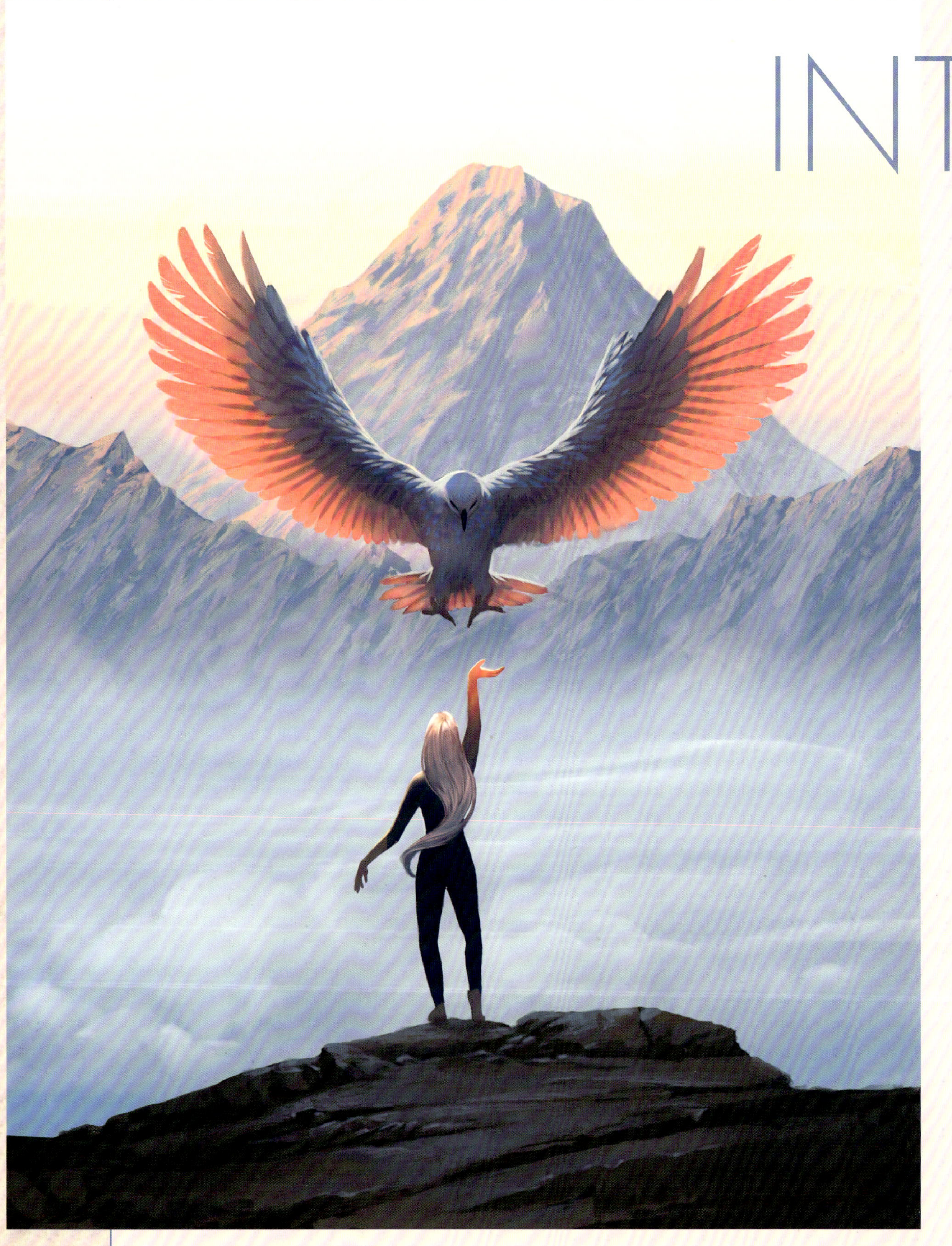

INT

ODUCTION

As a child, I vividly remember watching animated movies and being pulled into their colourful stories. *Spirited Away*, *Fantasia*, *Aladdin*, and *Corpse Bride* were some of my favourites, and I would be glued to the screen when they were on the television.

Although I live in Germany, most of my family live in Portugal, and during our annual three-day-long car rides to visit my relatives, my sisters and I would take a portable DVD player and our favourite animated movies along with us. All snuggled together in the back seats, we'd play the same movie over and over again. Once we arrived in Portugal, however, the movies were replaced with paper and pens supplied by our mother. The three of us loved drawing the characters and sceneries from the movies we'd been watching, taking turns with the few coloured pencils that were at our disposal.

After watching all of these movies, I soon became interested in what went on behind the scenes. I gradually invested my time into learning about the creative pipeline and started exploring anything related to the making of my favourites. At this time, I also developed a deeper interest in drawing and creating my own characters, always imagining what they would look and act like.

In my late teens, I watched *How to Train Your Dragon* for the first time and I was absolutely mesmerized. The animation, storytelling, music ... I'd never connected with something so deeply. Every ounce of passion was visible on the screen. Each detail was so carefully planned. I was absolutely hooked. I knew after watching the first movie that I wanted to pursue illustration. I thought that one day, maybe, just *maybe*, I could become a professional illustrator and create my own incredible stories. That was the dream!

Now here we are, about to take a deep dive into my first art book. After almost fifteen years of creating digital art, I'm so proud to share my experiences with you all. As you can see from my work (and the cover, no doubt), lighting and colour play such important roles when it comes to evoking a sense of nostalgia, wonder, and atmosphere in my pieces – that's why I've called this book *Golden Hour*, after the time of day when the sun covers everything in a warm, magical glow.

I hope you enjoy this book as much as I enjoyed making it. Maybe it will even spark some inspiration in you.

Raide

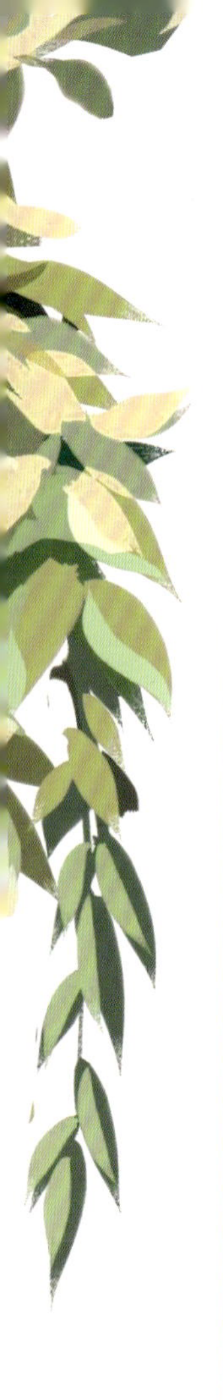

CREATIVE JOURNEY

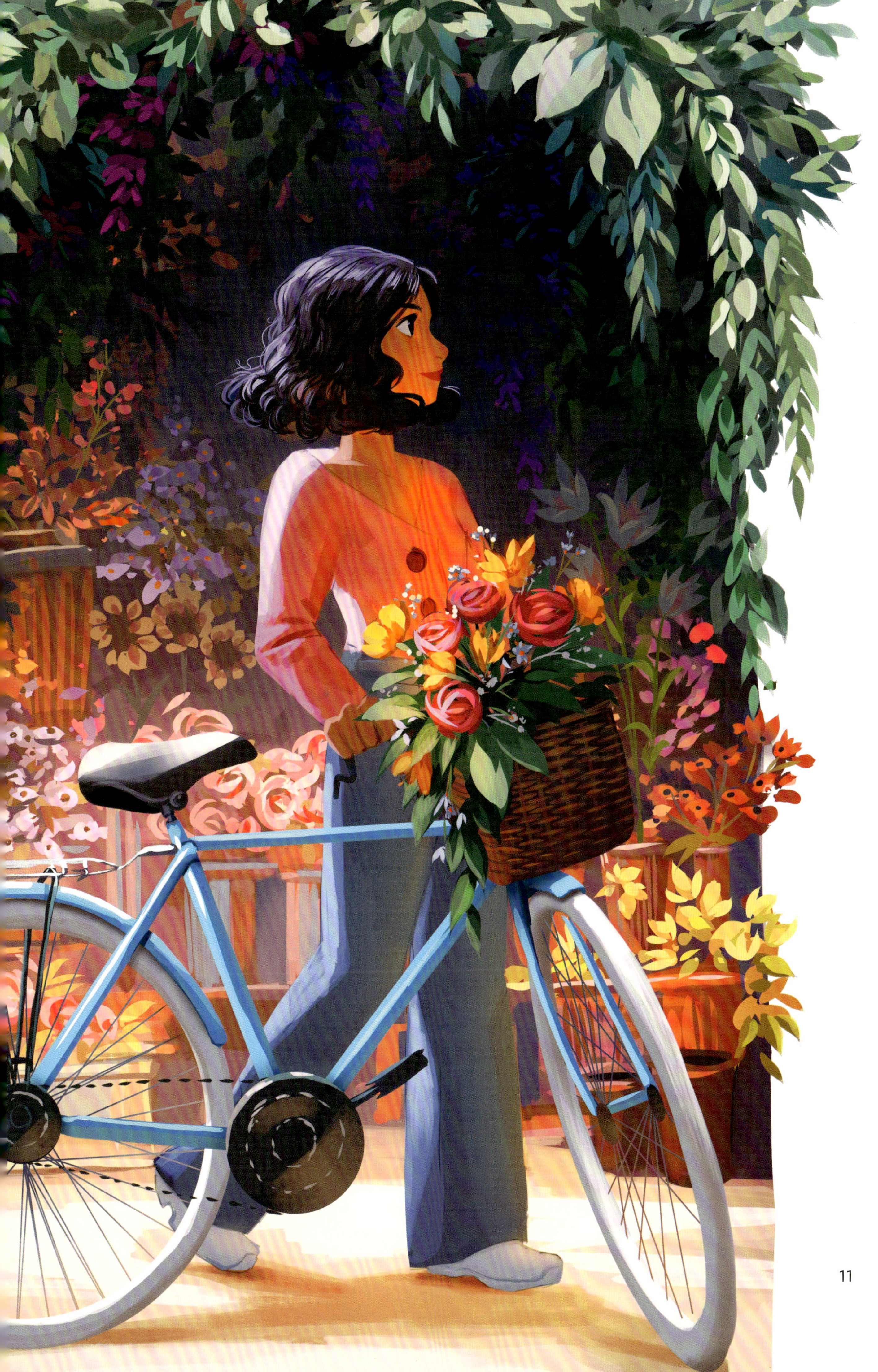

INFLUENCES IN CHILDHOOD

It almost seems impossible to talk about my creative journey without mentioning my family's positive impact. Having two creative sisters by my side made my childhood so fun! We used to draw silly characters and made (friendly) fun of each other's designs. Since our parents noticed that we loved drawing so much, they encouraged us to join after-school art activities in primary school. In the 'unARTtig' workshops, led by Verona Herzschuh, we created all sorts of artworks and crafting projects, from castles made of sugar cubes to acrylic paintings featuring some really wacky designs.

While my older sister eventually found interests elsewhere, my twin sister and I never let go of that passion. In secondary school, we stopped going to the after-school art club and became the typical quiet art kids. We used to doodle all over our notebooks and couldn't wait for art classes to begin. We started earning artsy reputations at school, and our peers would always ask if we could draw things for them. I was a shy bag of nerves whenever they watched me, but I always appreciated the positive comments.

When we were around eleven years old, our parents bought us ArtRage, which is the art program that I still use to this day. At that time, my sister and I shared a computer and we'd take turns drawing. Since we didn't have a tablet yet, we used to carefully (and very slowly) illustrate using a regular computer mouse.

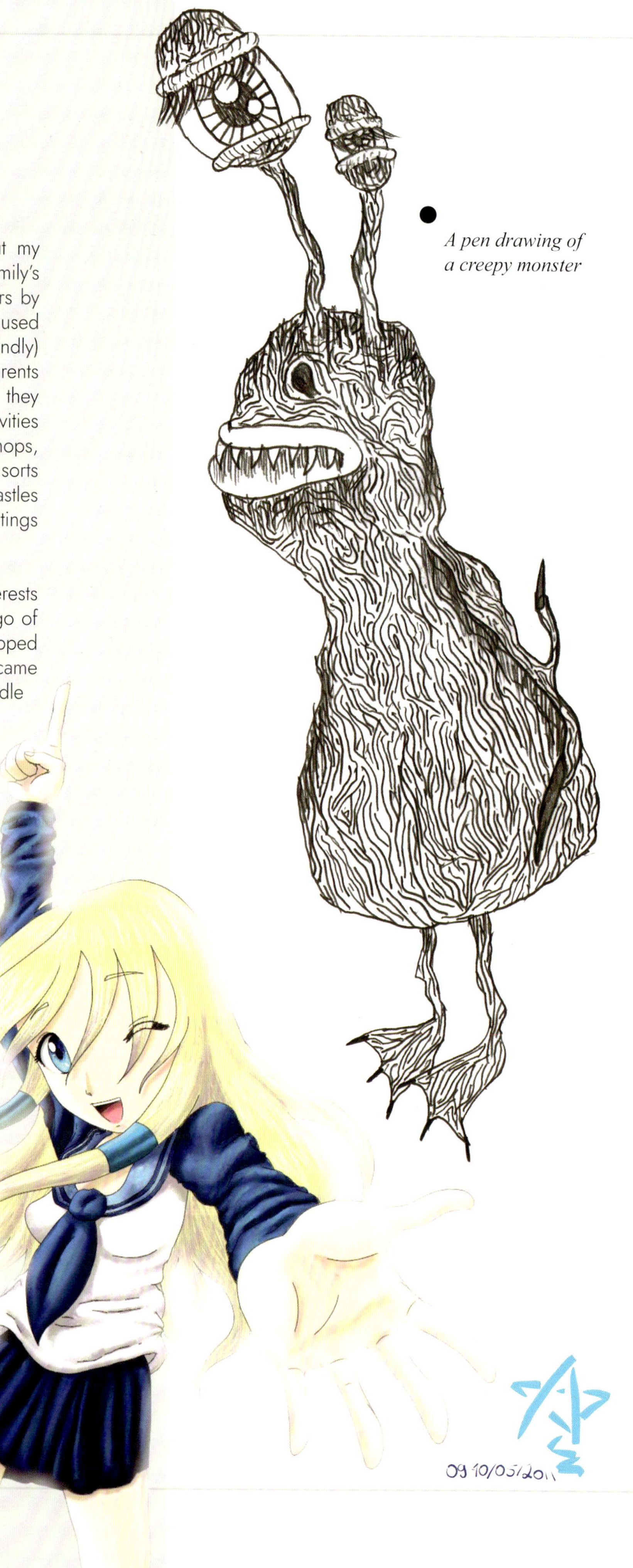

A pen drawing of a creepy monster

This is one of the first drawings I ever made in ArtRage. One of my classmates asked me to draw her in a manga style

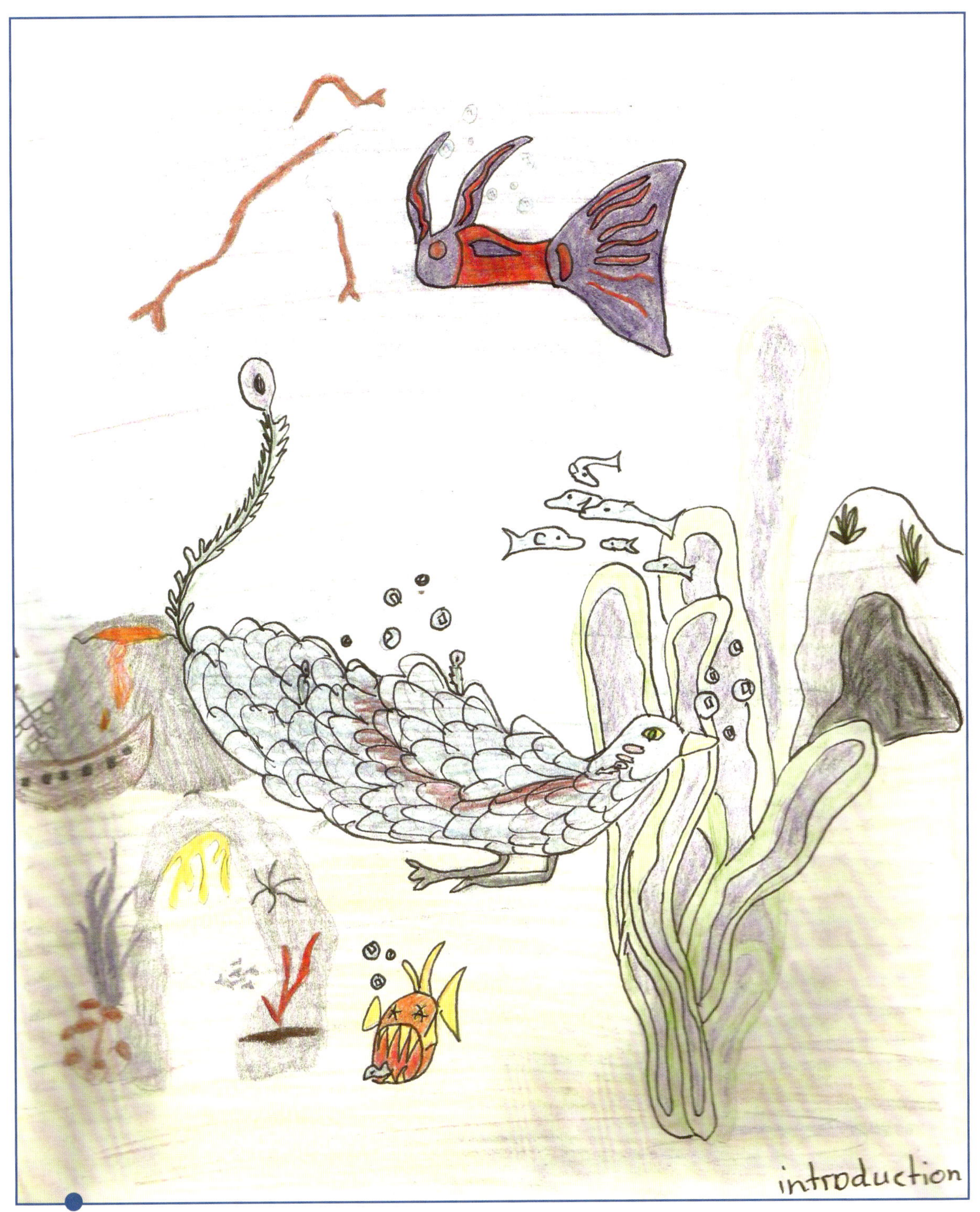

In fourth grade, I was tasked with creating and illustrating a story. I invented the 'fishbar', a mix between a fish and a large bird

ART IN HIGH SCHOOL

Like many young artists at the time, my sister and I were largely inspired by the different manga art styles that were popular online. We also developed a big interest in anthropomorphic characters inspired by *Sonic the Hedgehog*, and were amazed by the incredible number of artists we'd discovered on the social platform DeviantArt. In 2015, we both decided to start our own public art accounts on DeviantArt as 'RaideDeviant' (later RaidesArt) and 'LeffieDeviant' (later LeffiesArt), and the influence of the styles just mentioned soon grew very apparent in my own work.

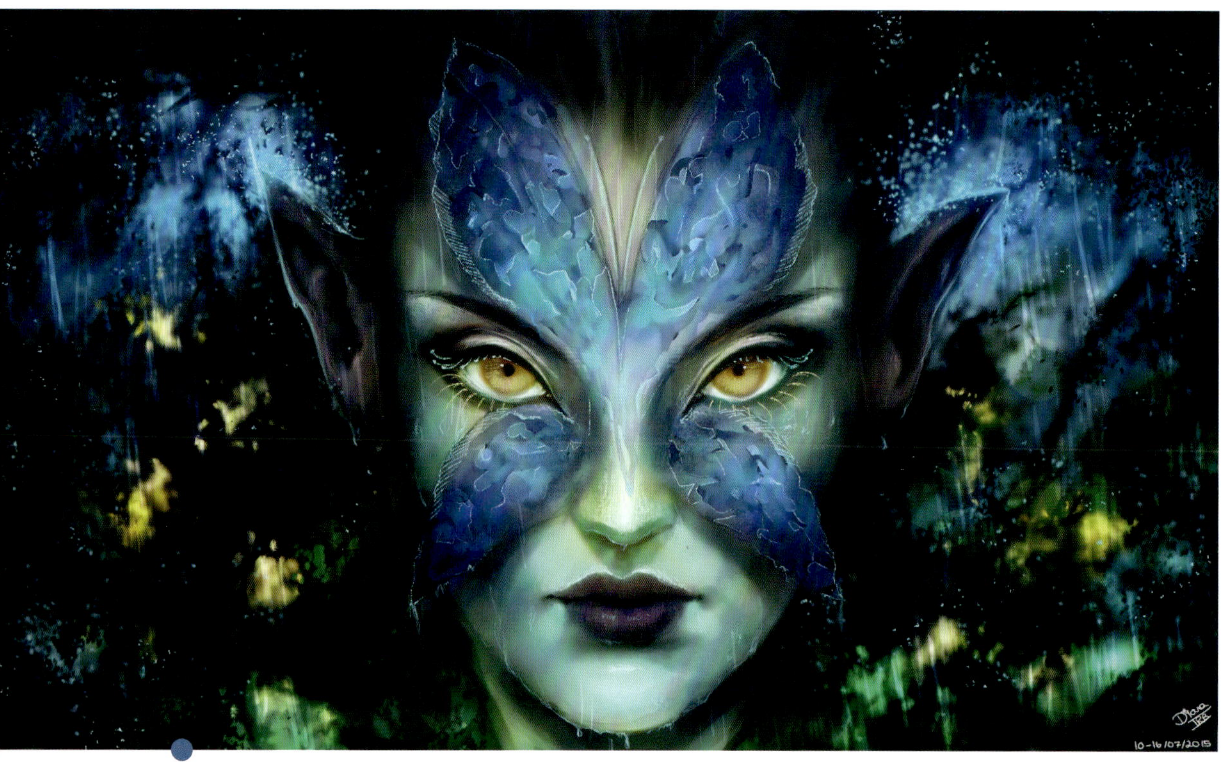

I've always enjoyed adding elements of nature into my pieces, even back in 2015!

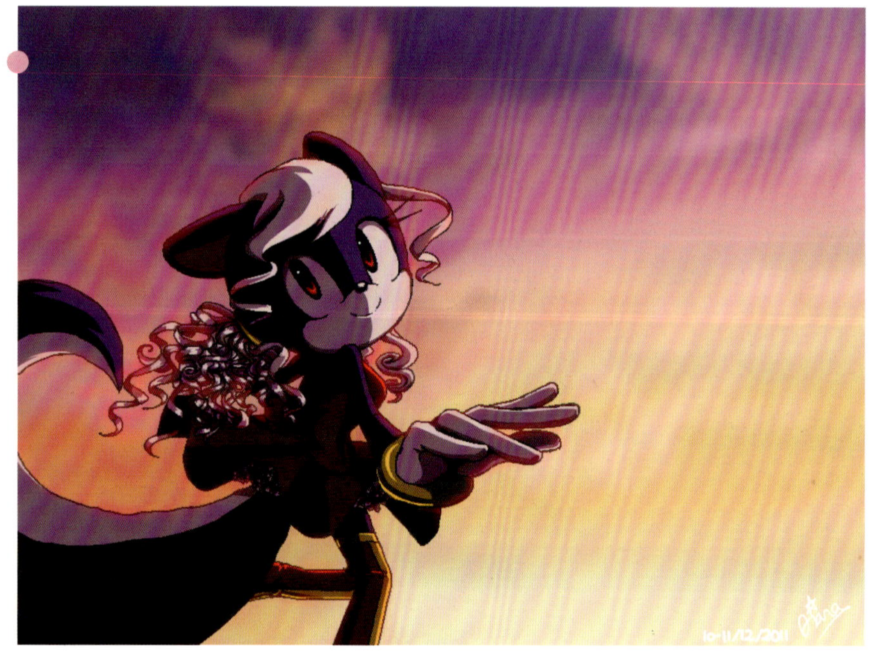

I experimented with the Watercolour tool in ArtRage to create the outlines of this anthropomorphic character

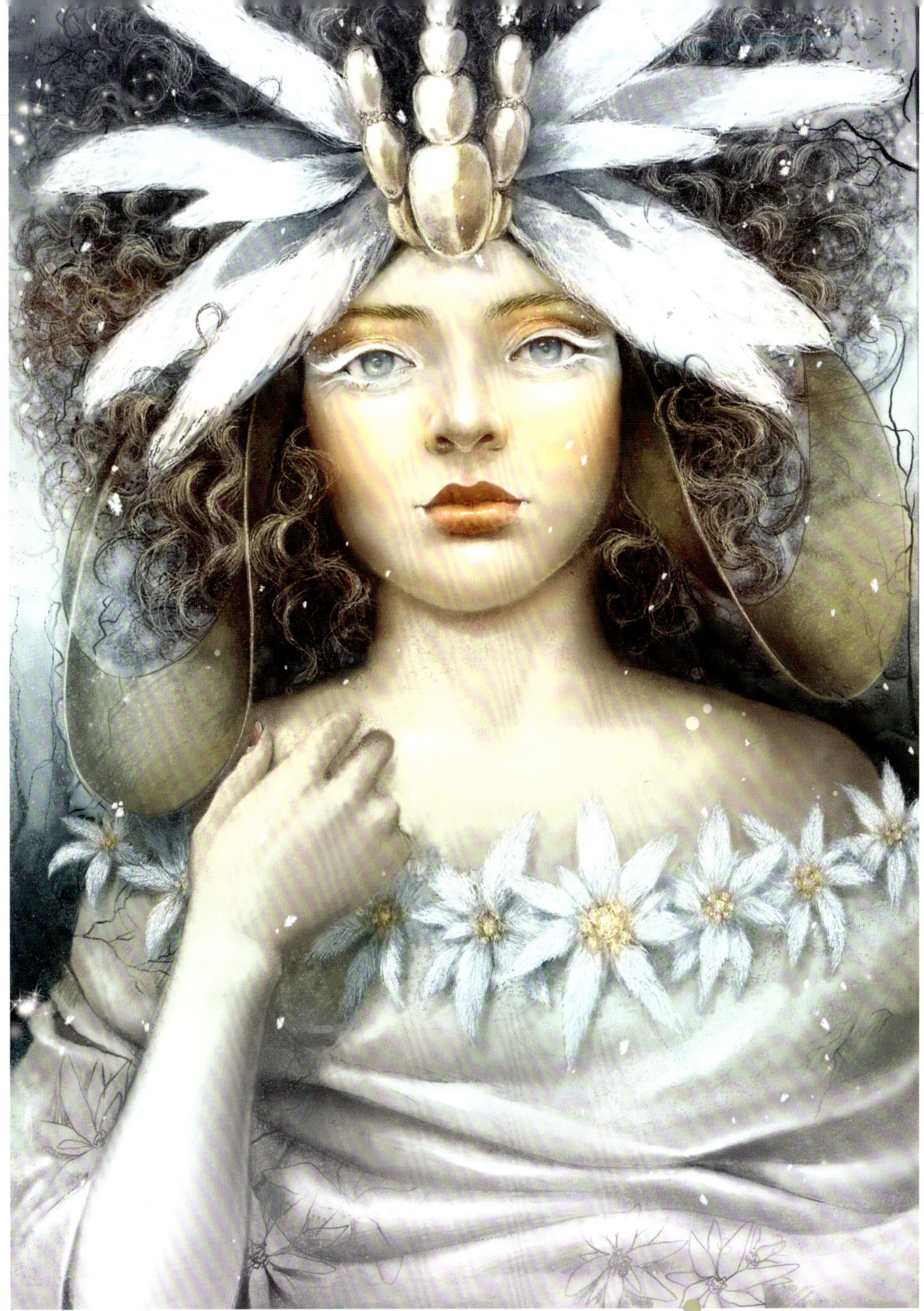

Since Mucha's work was a big inspiration for me, I started creating aesthetic female portraits like this one

In high school, my art teacher, Steve Lewis, saw potential in both me and my sister. Under his tutelage, we continued to improve our traditional drawing skills and ended up choosing art as a higher-level subject for our IB diploma. While the manga-inspired art we drew in class sometimes left some question marks on my teacher's face, he never stopped encouraging us to continue pursuing our artistic goals.

Steve introduced me to Alphonse Mucha, a Czech artist who is famous for his art-nouveau style, and I was amazed by his work. Many of the artists I looked up to seemed to be influenced by Mucha, so I began creating artwork inspired by him too.

I was devastated by the rejections from art schools, and started seriously rethinking what I wanted to do with my life. But I was only eighteen, and drawing brought me so much joy. My parents reassured me that other opportunities would come, so I started reworking my applications and switched my focus from traditional art schools to design universities. I went to portfolio courses, watched videos of other students who successfully applied, and tried my luck again the following year. This time, each course I'd applied to sent me an acceptance letter. It definitely gave me a great motivational boost!

It seemed like anything digital, especially simple aesthetic portraits, were not popular among German art professors. That's why I invested so much of my time revisiting traditional tools to create my new portfolio. Although I enjoyed stepping outside of the digital realm, I stuck to digital painting in my free time.

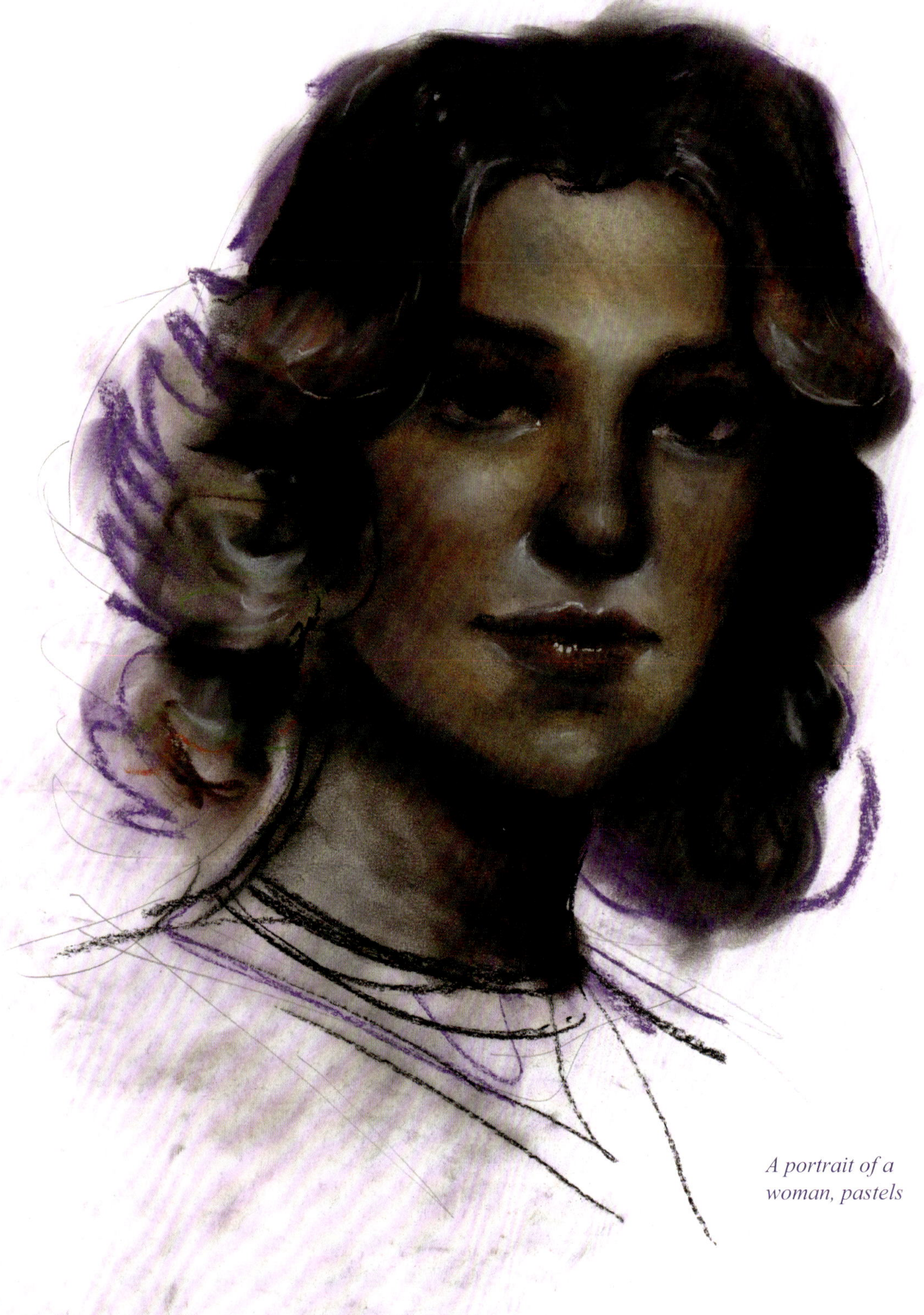

A portrait of a woman, pastels

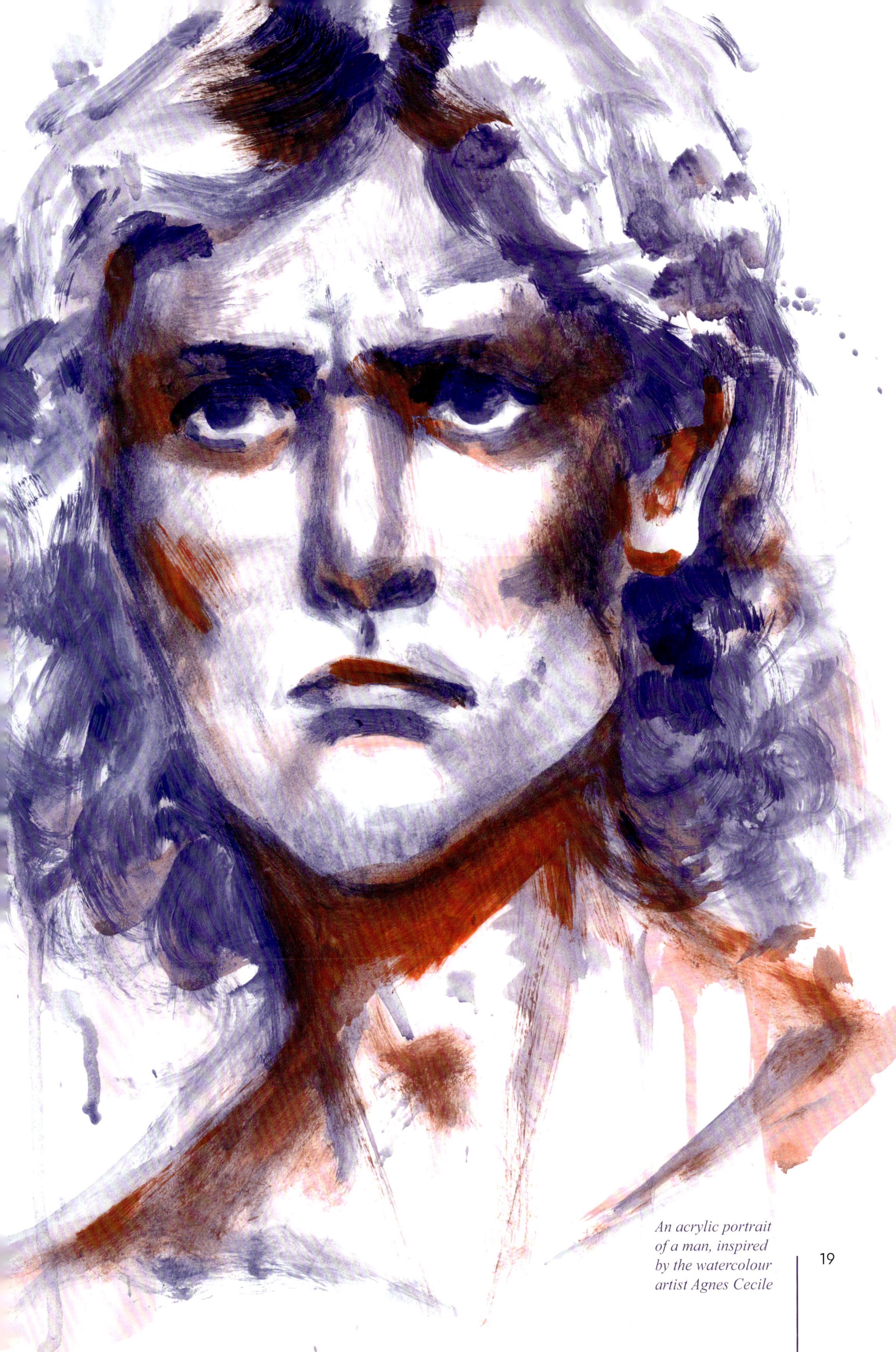

An acrylic portrait of a man, inspired by the watercolour artist Agnes Cecile

STUDYING INTEGRATED & INTERMEDIAL DESIGN

After much deliberation over where to study, my sister and I decided to pursue Integrated Design at the Hochschule Anhalt together. The course offered a wide spectrum of design disciplines, including graphic design, product design, and animation/film. Due to the range of courses available, I was mostly able to choose projects where I could improve my illustration skills. But I also really enjoyed exploring different aspects of design, which would not have been possible if I had studied graphic design or animation directly.

My course went smoothly until the beginning of 2020, when the pandemic arrived in Germany. I was in my sixth semester, almost done with my studies, when I had to change all my plans. Initially, I wanted to work as a full-time artist and/or designer after graduating, but with social life being on hold and the world's financial situation shaken up, I thought it would be a smart idea to continue on to my master's degree. As we all know, those were turbulent times.

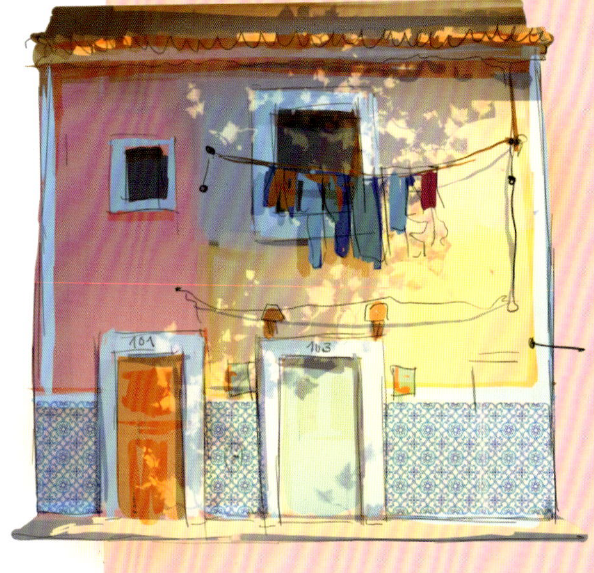

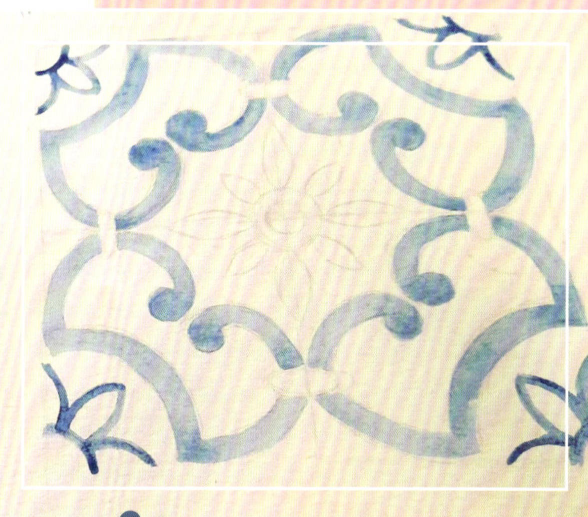

Process of creating a Portuguese tile. I edited this azulejo *pattern that I created using watercolours combined with my digital-painting techniques*

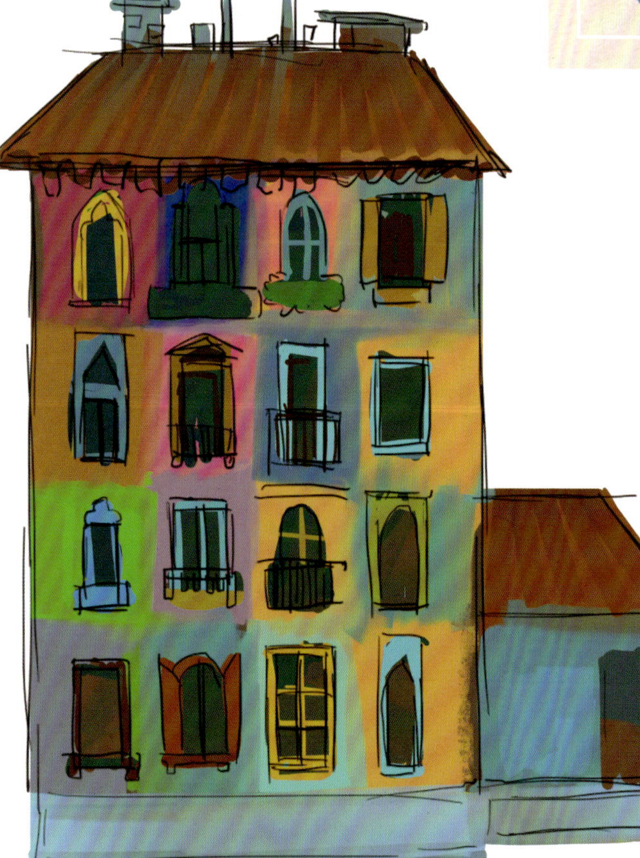

For the image on the right, I started with a dark base, then added some variation to the shadow colours by mixing different tones and hues together. Then, I layered the lighter colours on top of each other to add depth

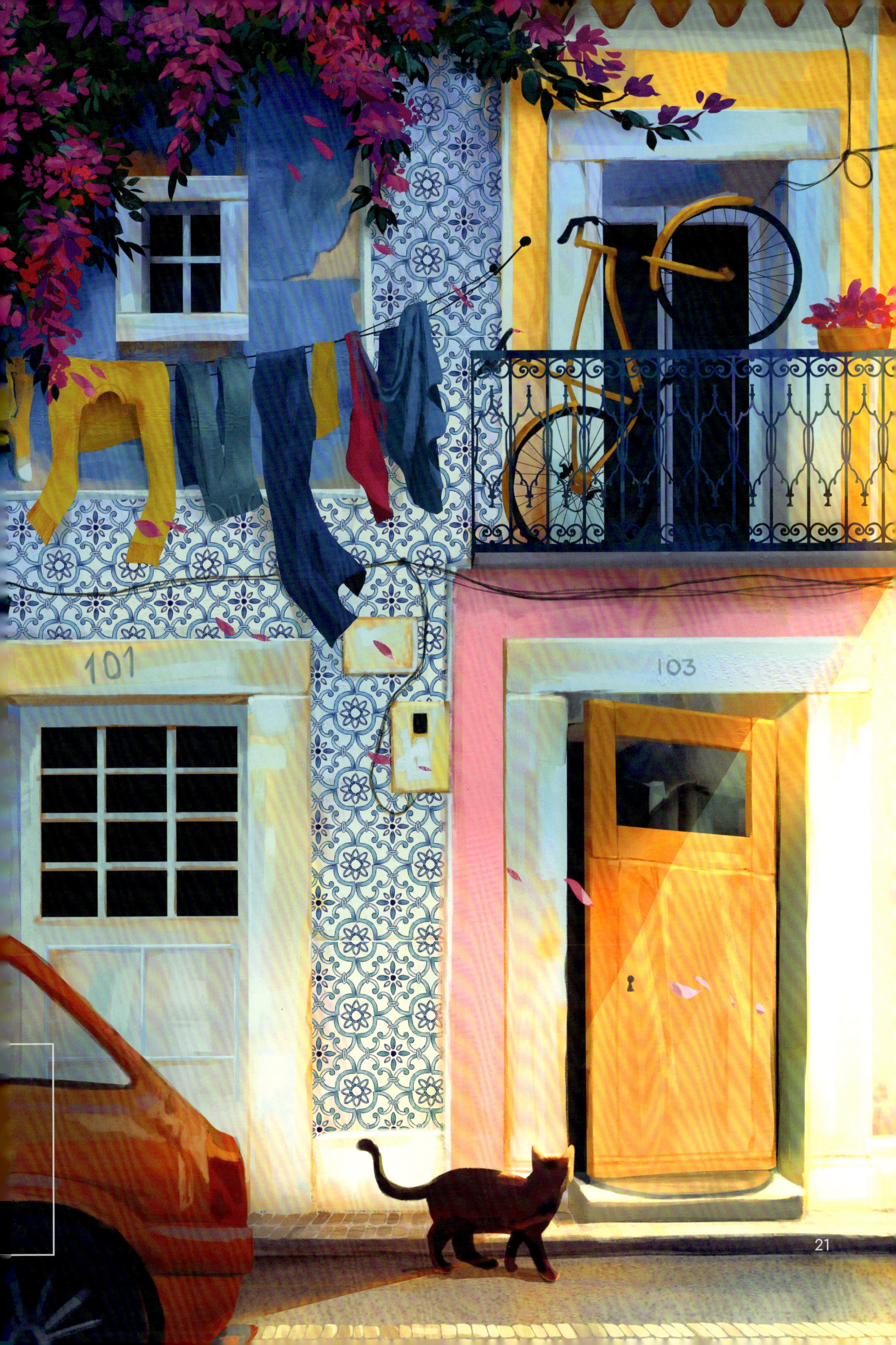
101
103

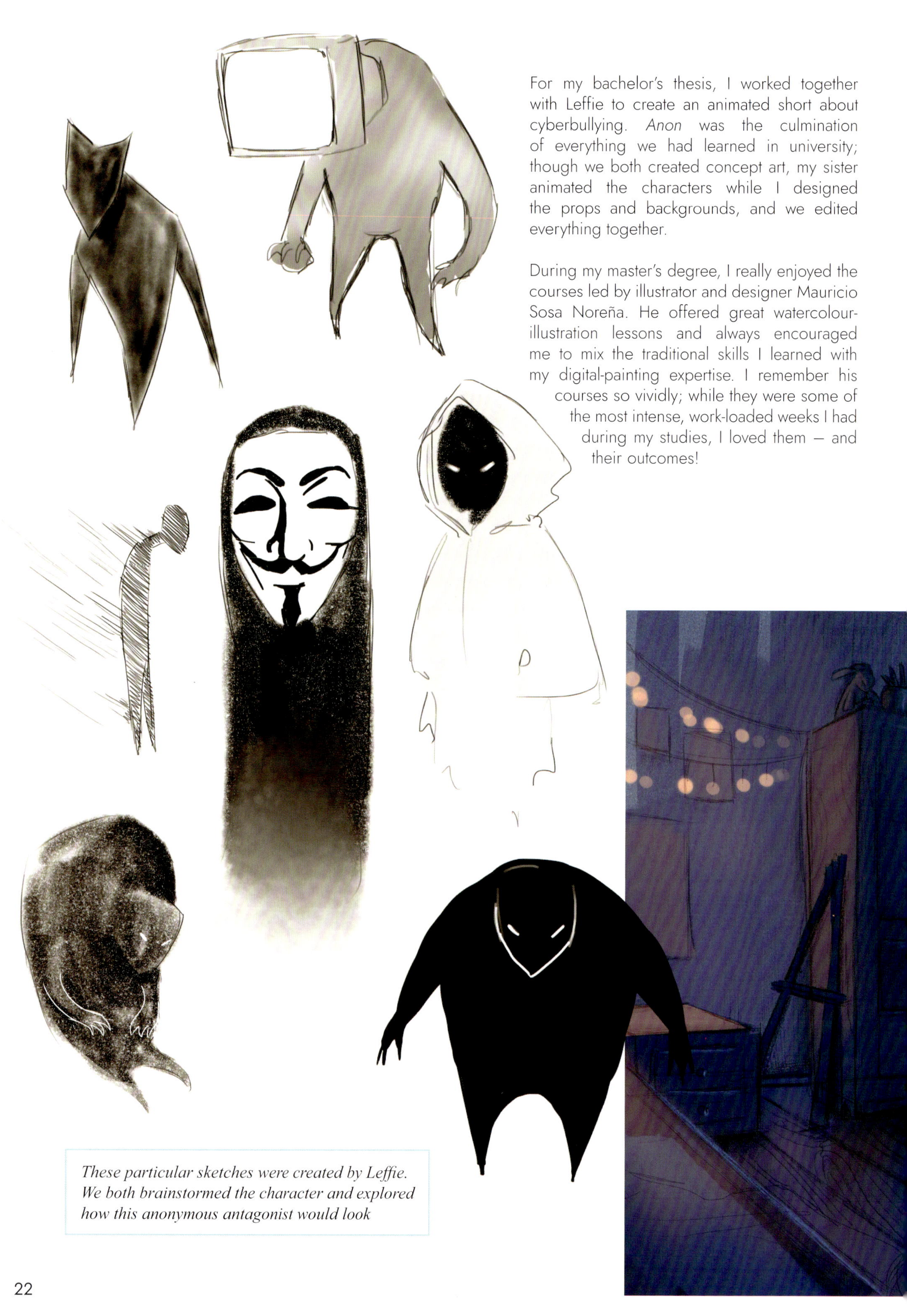

For my bachelor's thesis, I worked together with Leffie to create an animated short about cyberbullying. *Anon* was the culmination of everything we had learned in university; though we both created concept art, my sister animated the characters while I designed the props and backgrounds, and we edited everything together.

During my master's degree, I really enjoyed the courses led by illustrator and designer Mauricio Sosa Noreña. He offered great watercolour-illustration lessons and always encouraged me to mix the traditional skills I learned with my digital-painting expertise. I remember his courses so vividly; while they were some of the most intense, work-loaded weeks I had during my studies, I loved them – and their outcomes!

These particular sketches were created by Leffie. We both brainstormed the character and explored how this anonymous antagonist would look

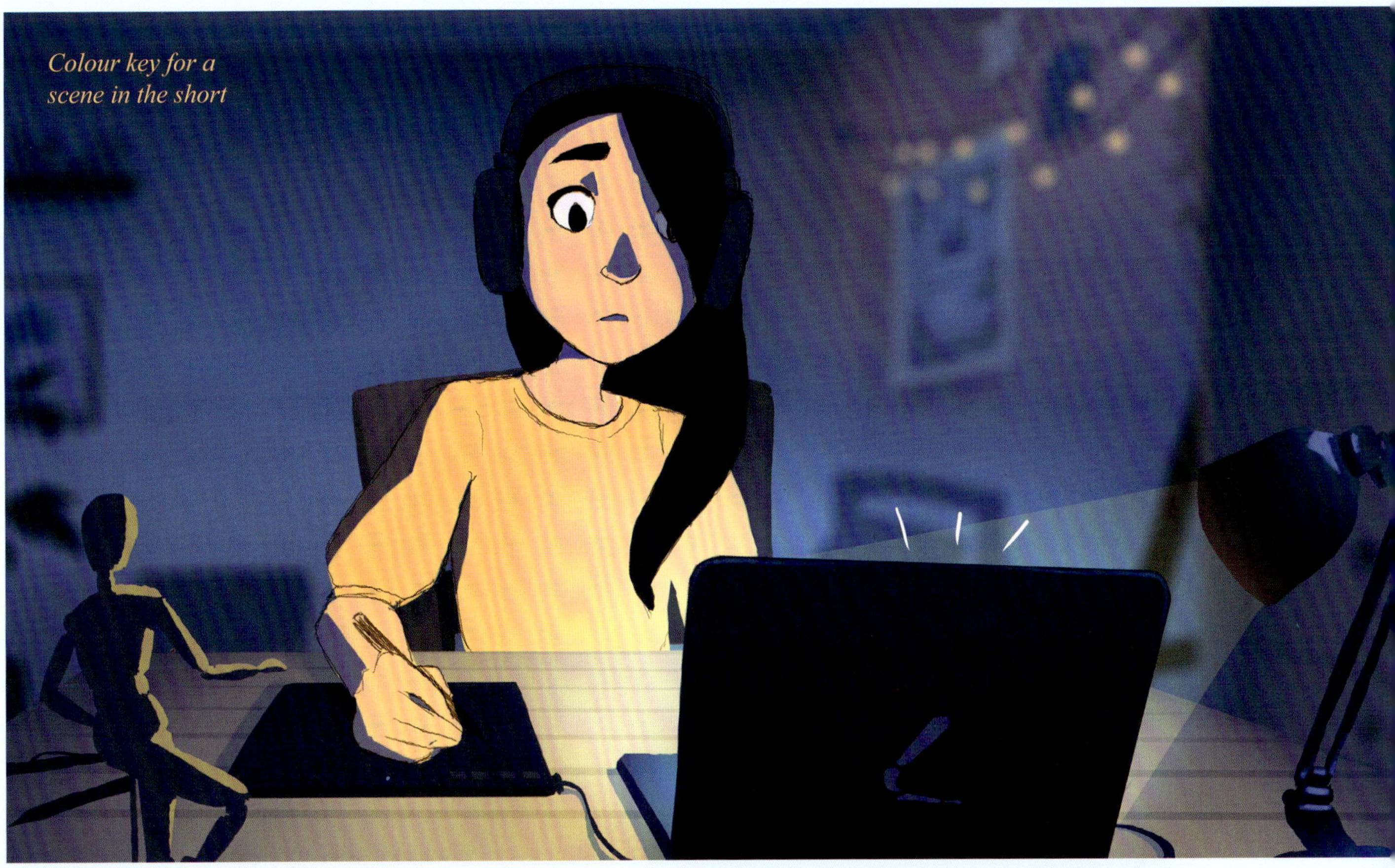

Colour key for a scene in the short

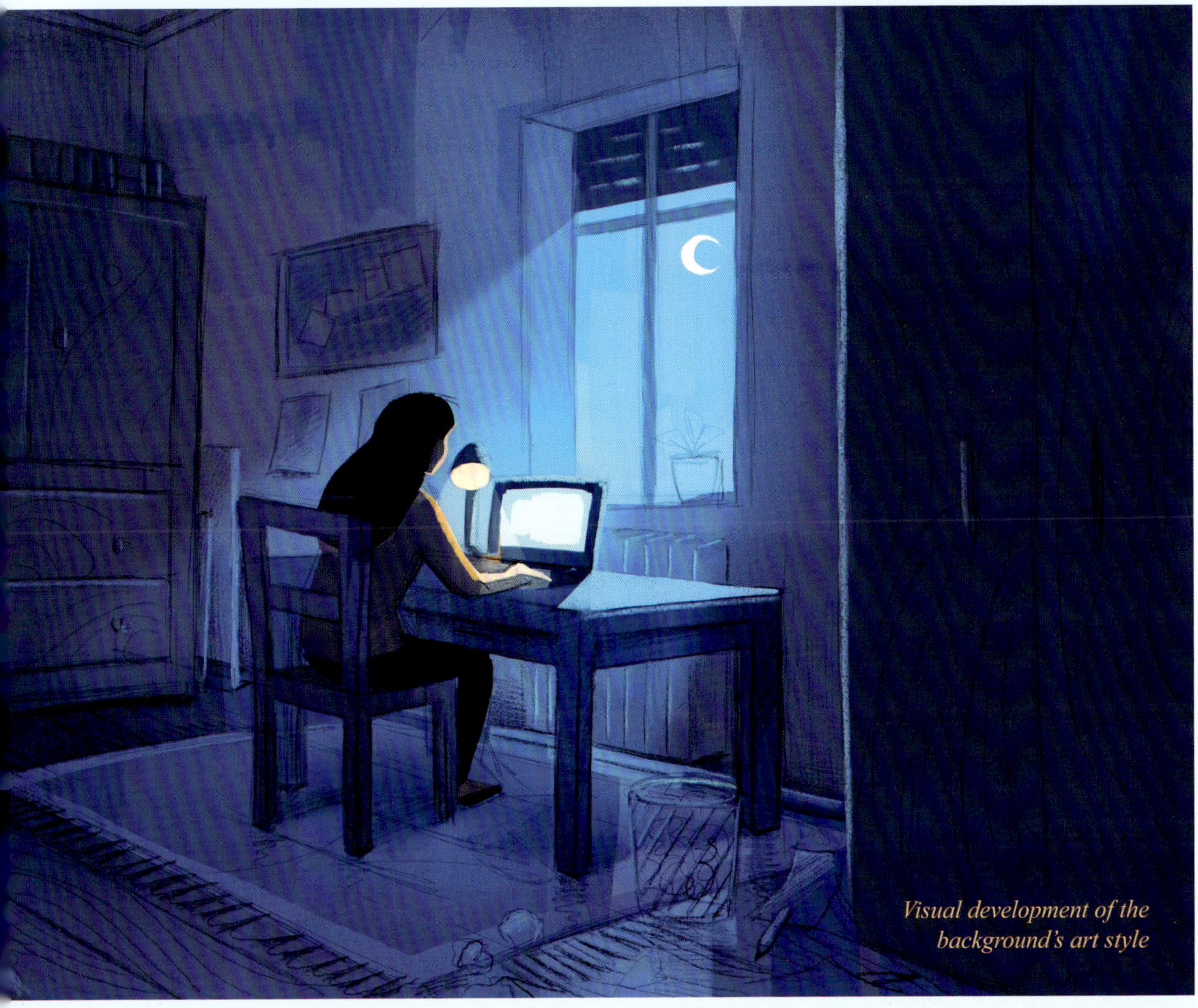

Visual development of the background's art style

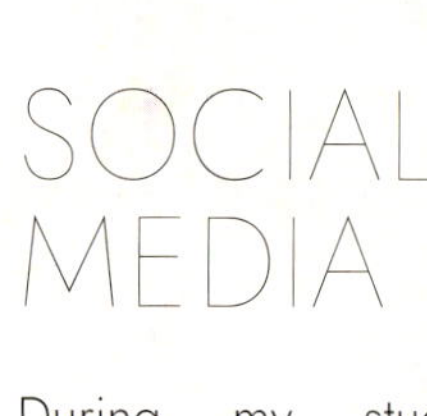

SOCIAL MEDIA

During my studies, I stuck closely to social media. Since starting that journey on DeviantArt back in 2015, I created several accounts on different platforms. In 2016, I made my first Tumblr account, which was mainly dedicated to my love of different media, especially *How to Train Your Dragon*. From 2016 to 2018, I created fan art of movie characters I liked and learned so much about anatomy, lighting, and composition. Seeing my art drastically improve in such a short amount of time motivated me to draw even more!

As my skills quickly improved, a good portion of my Tumblr and DeviantArt followers also decided to follow me on Instagram when I made an account in 2018. While browsing through the app's 'explore' feature, I noticed that many artists were participating in art challenges – specifically *Draw This In Your Style* (DTIYS). I had a lot of fun partaking and getting to know so many other artists.

As I was joining multiple challenges and making more art than ever before, I made sure to have a consistent posting schedule. Uploading artwork regularly boosted my account and I started to be more active online as a result.

While I received many amazing opportunities by having a social-media presence, it's important to also acknowledge that my experience with these apps didn't come without its flaws. In the early days of having an Instagram account, social media greatly dictated what I drew – I'd naturally create content that earned more engagement from my followers. At the time, this mainly included female portraits and art-challenge entries. Obviously, I still enjoyed what I painted and I was so thankful for all the positive feedback. But looking back, I feel like I let the numbers influence me more than I liked to admit.

I'm glad I didn't start my social-media presence earlier, so I could develop my art style away from the public eye. Art is something that is so incredibly personal, so drawing solely to please others – especially as a beginner – is not advisable.

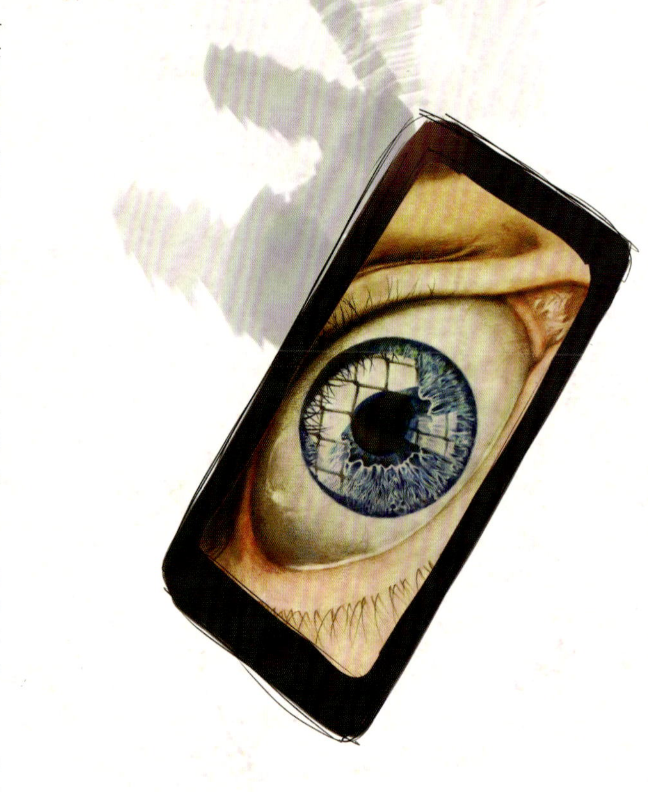

This watercolour and pencil drawing of an eye was one of the very first posts I ever published on social media. It was part of some coursework I made for my IGCSE art exam. I posted it to DeviantArt in January 2015

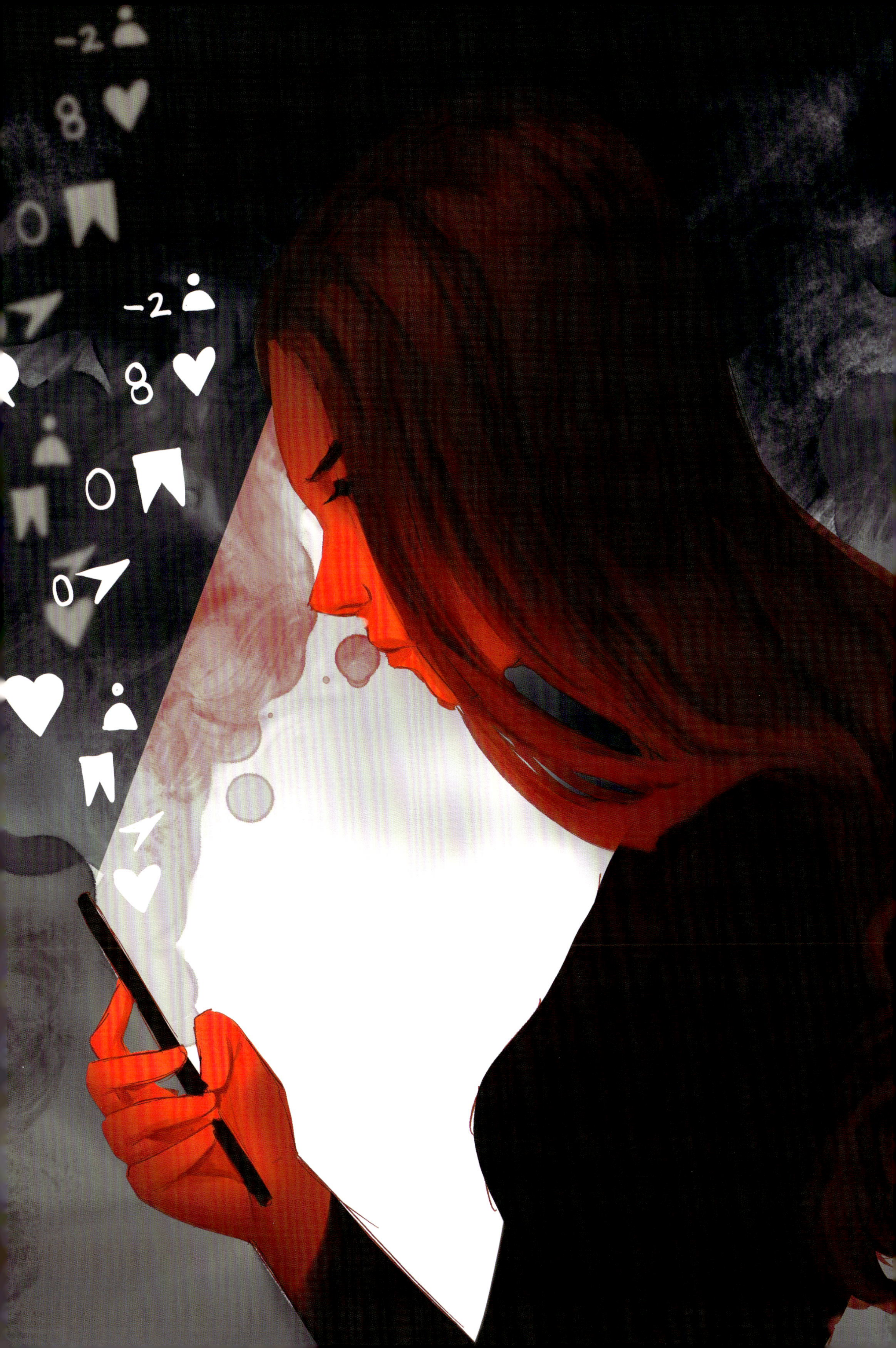
-2
8
0
-2
8
0
0

WORKING WITH CLIENTS

My first commercial client

Many years ago, I was asked to work on a project for a well-known name. Though it didn't pay the best, I felt honoured to have been offered the opportunity. I'd never worked on a large project before and I was excited to be a part of it.

Although I won't elaborate on this particular commission, I will say that I was glad once the work was over. My invoices remained unprocessed for months, but despite that, I continued the work. At the time, the worth of this project was directed to my portfolio instead of my pocket.

In hindsight, I can say this: yes, I was undervalued, but I was also inexperienced. Working for minimum wage is sadly something that many artists do in order to gain experience, especially if no other offers are coming in. But I'm glad to be able to say that I learned so much about myself and the industry.

What I want to deliver

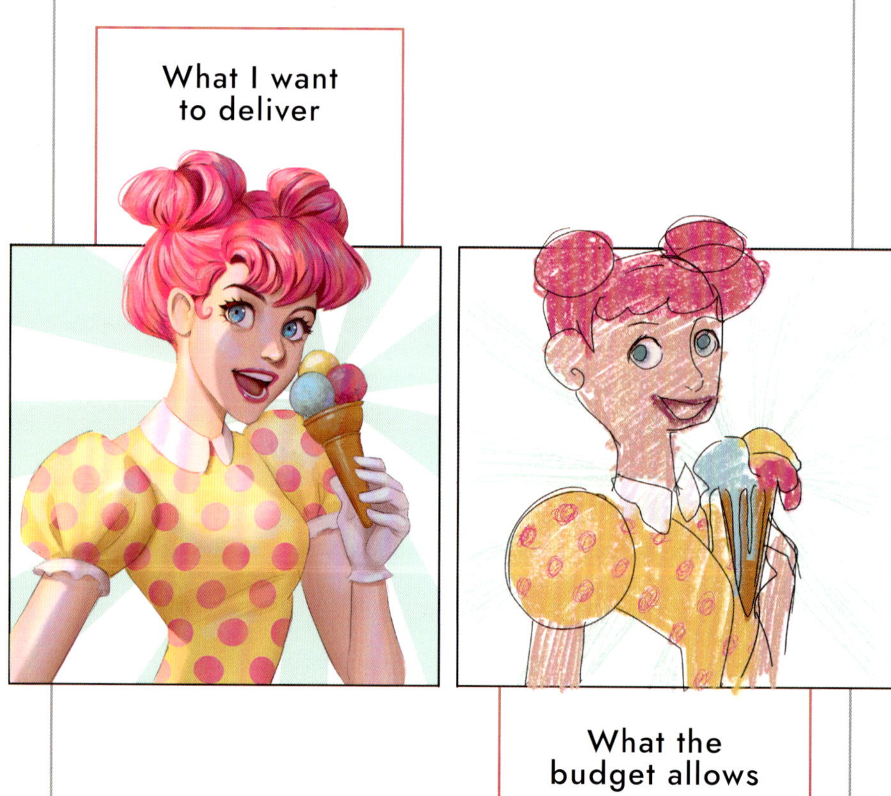

What the budget allows

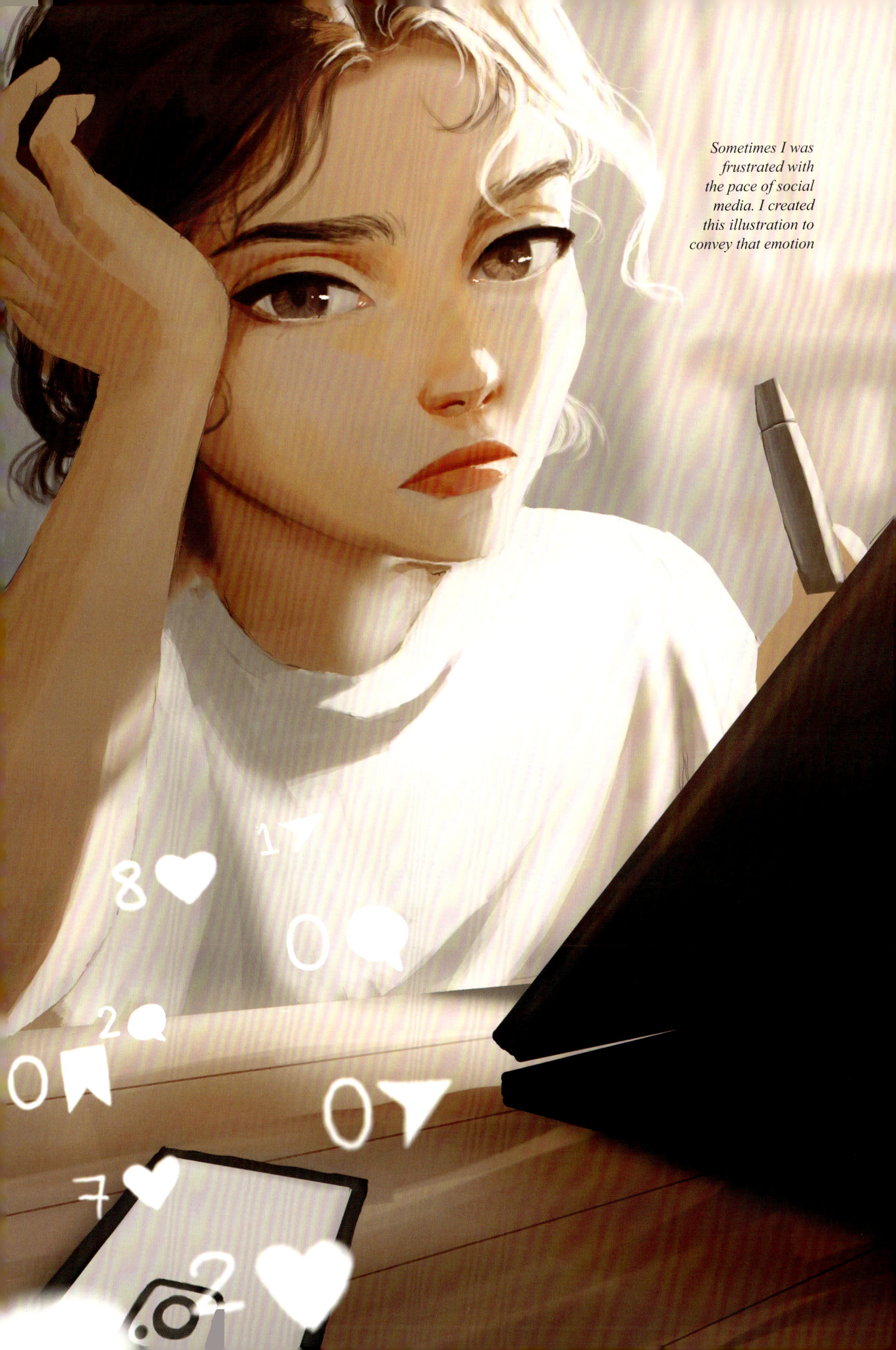

Sometimes I was frustrated with the pace of social media. I created this illustration to convey that emotion

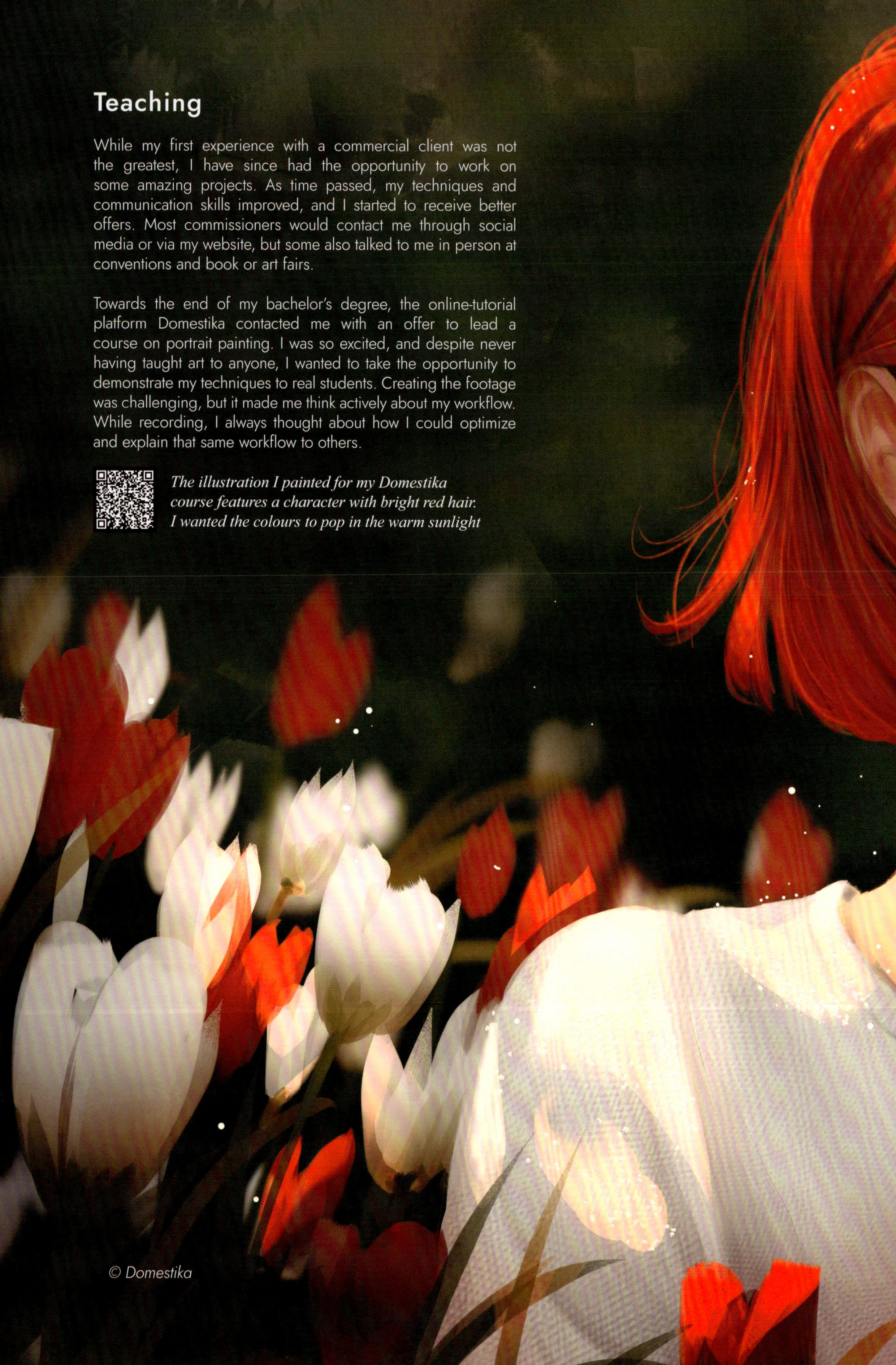

Teaching

While my first experience with a commercial client was not the greatest, I have since had the opportunity to work on some amazing projects. As time passed, my techniques and communication skills improved, and I started to receive better offers. Most commissioners would contact me through social media or via my website, but some also talked to me in person at conventions and book or art fairs.

Towards the end of my bachelor's degree, the online-tutorial platform Domestika contacted me with an offer to lead a course on portrait painting. I was so excited, and despite never having taught art to anyone, I wanted to take the opportunity to demonstrate my techniques to real students. Creating the footage was challenging, but it made me think actively about my workflow. While recording, I always thought about how I could optimize and explain that same workflow to others.

The illustration I painted for my Domestika course features a character with bright red hair. I wanted the colours to pop in the warm sunlight

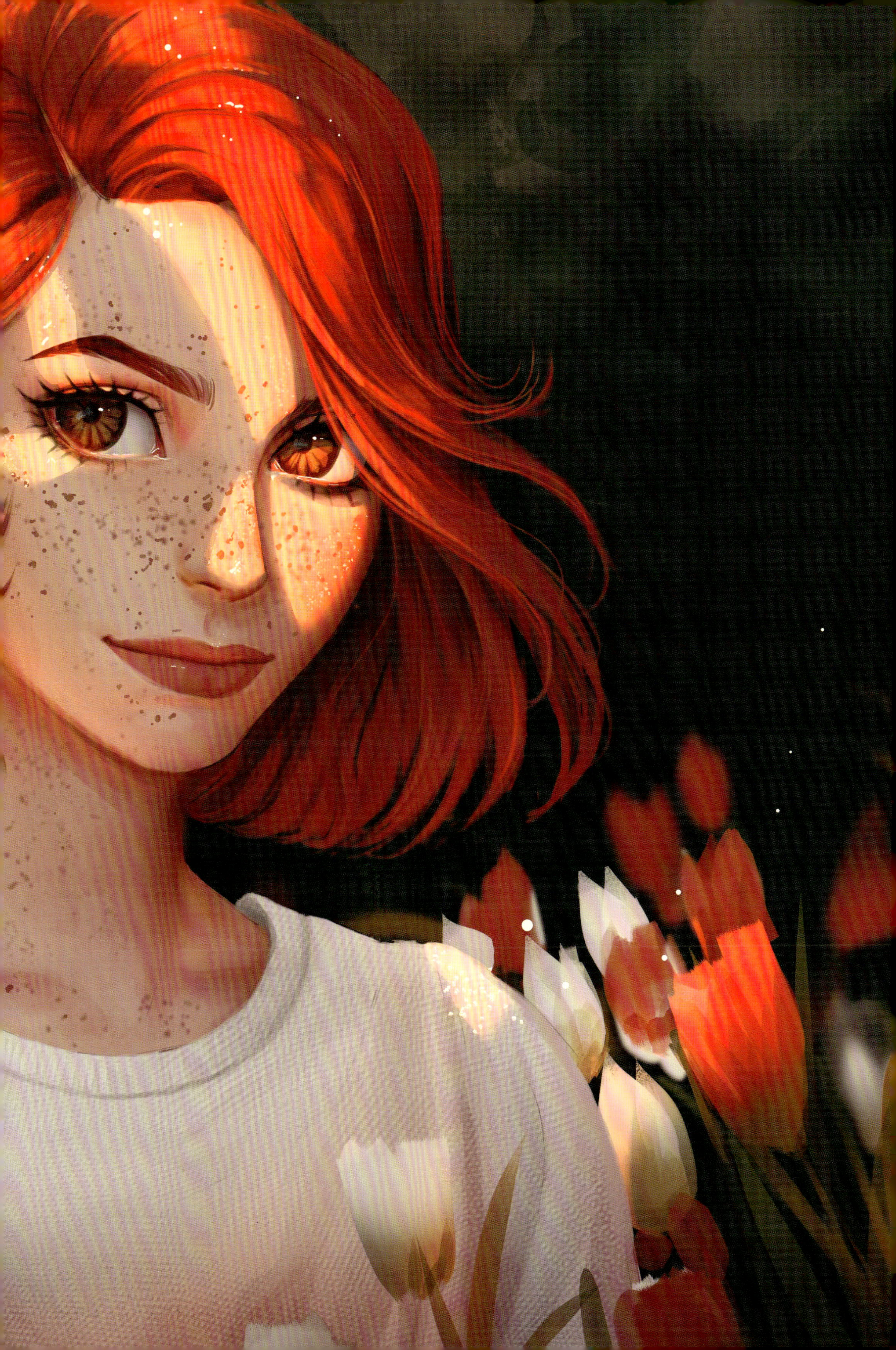

Creating book illustrations

Over the course of my studies, I also had the opportunity to create various cover artworks and interior illustrations for the prequels of *The School for Good and Evil* and the *Percy Jackson* series. For *Percy Jackson*, I was tasked with creating six new colourful covers for the Spanish series editions. For *The School for Good and Evil*, I had the opportunity to create two cover artworks, as well as fourteen black-and-white illustrations, which were interspersed throughout the books.

I had so much fun diving into these stories and making artworks of all the characters. Holding the books while knowing I contributed to them is such an amazing feeling! I can't wait to tell more stories with my art in the future, and I hope more projects like these are on the horizon for me.

These are the covers for the The School for Good and Evil *series by Soman Chainani. They both feature the book's main characters, Rhian and Rafal. I had so much fun designing and painting them*

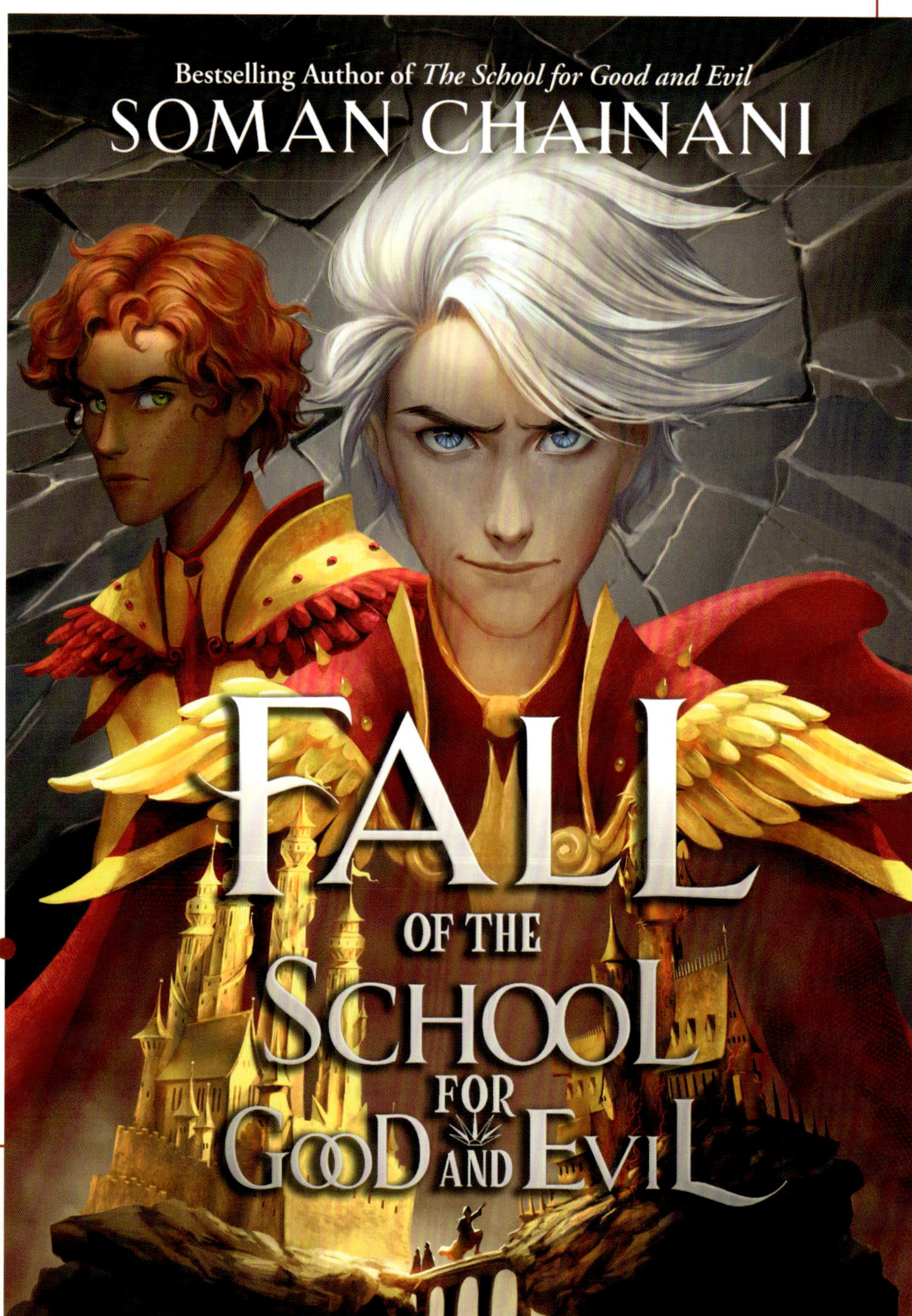

Bestselling Author of *The School for Good and Evil*

SOMAN CHAINANI

RISE OF THE SCHOOL FOR GOOD AND EVIL

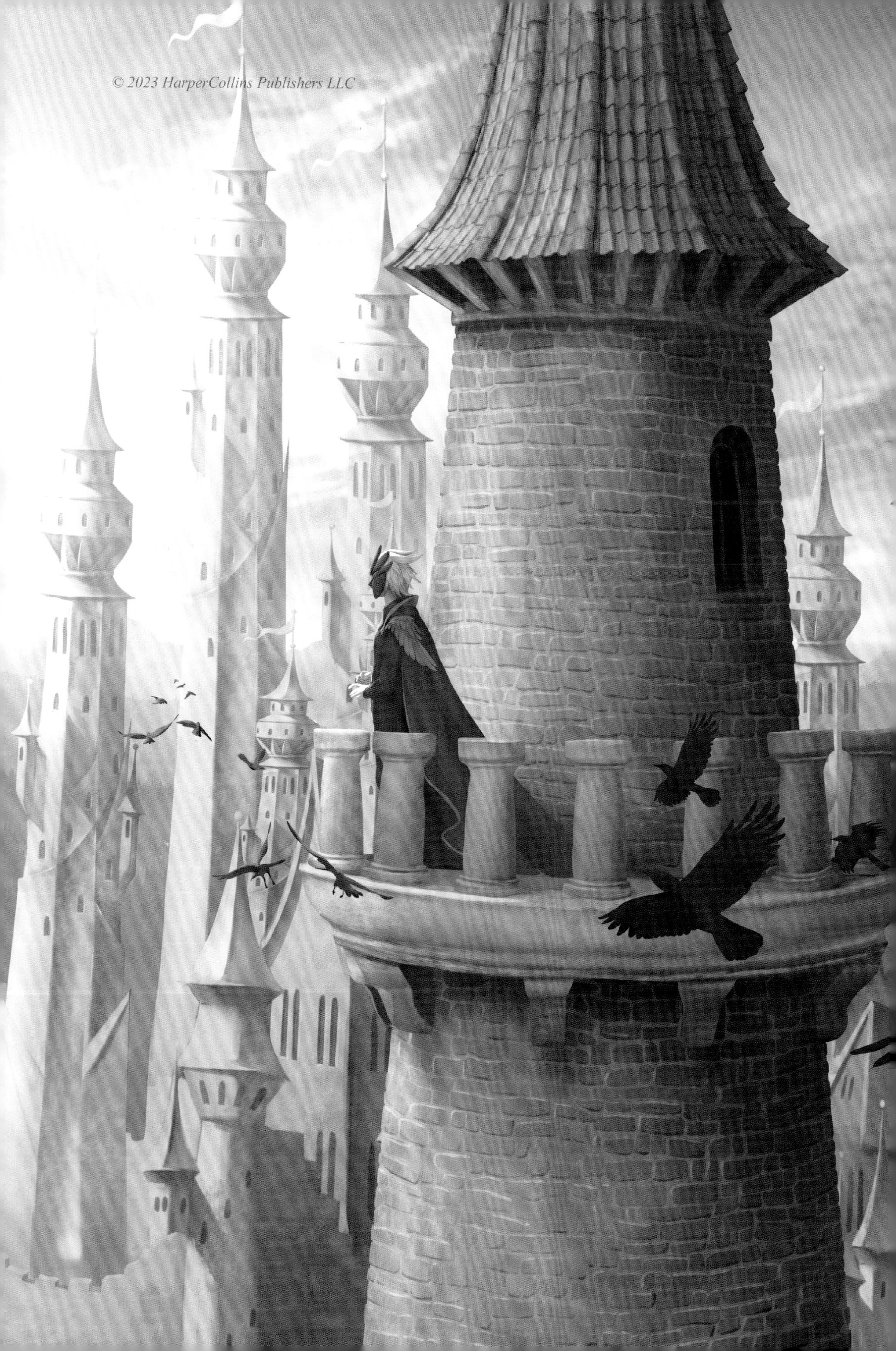

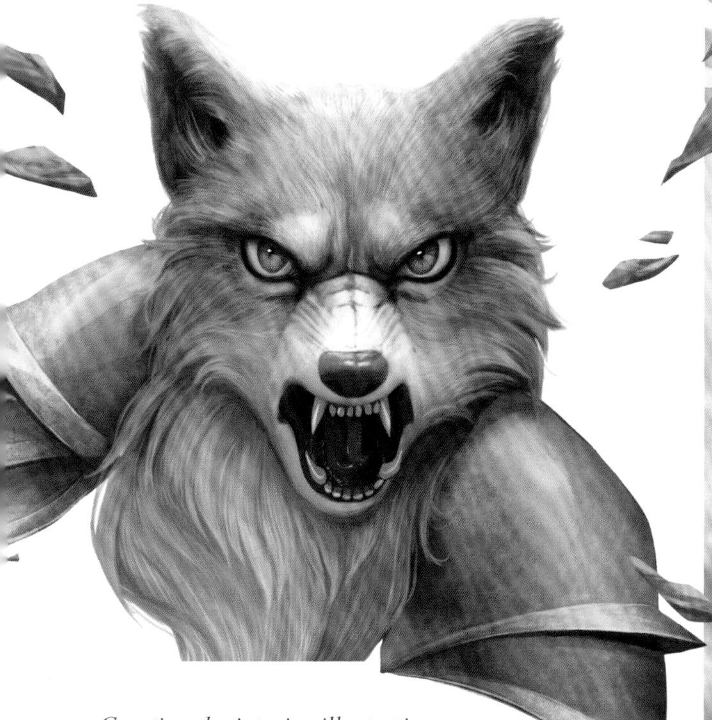

Creating the interior illustrations was interesting for me.I always love to work with colour, but these illustrations had to work in black and white, so I mostly played with value contrast and composition in order to guide the viewer's eye

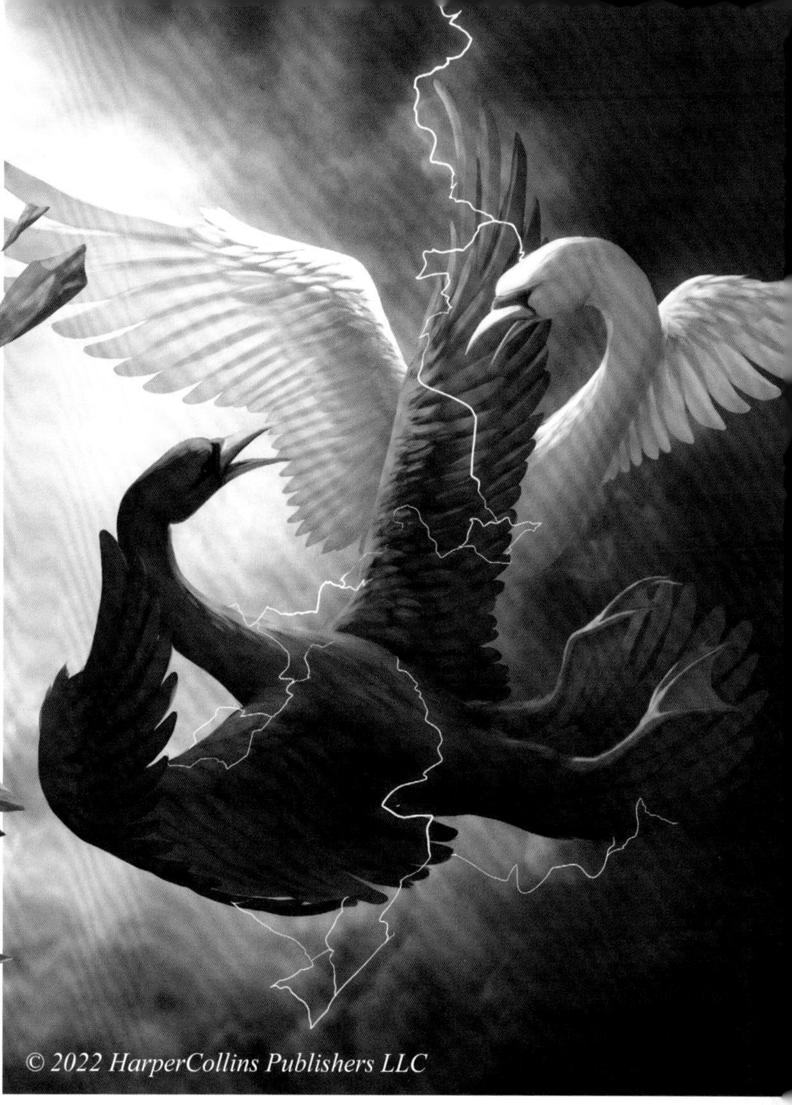

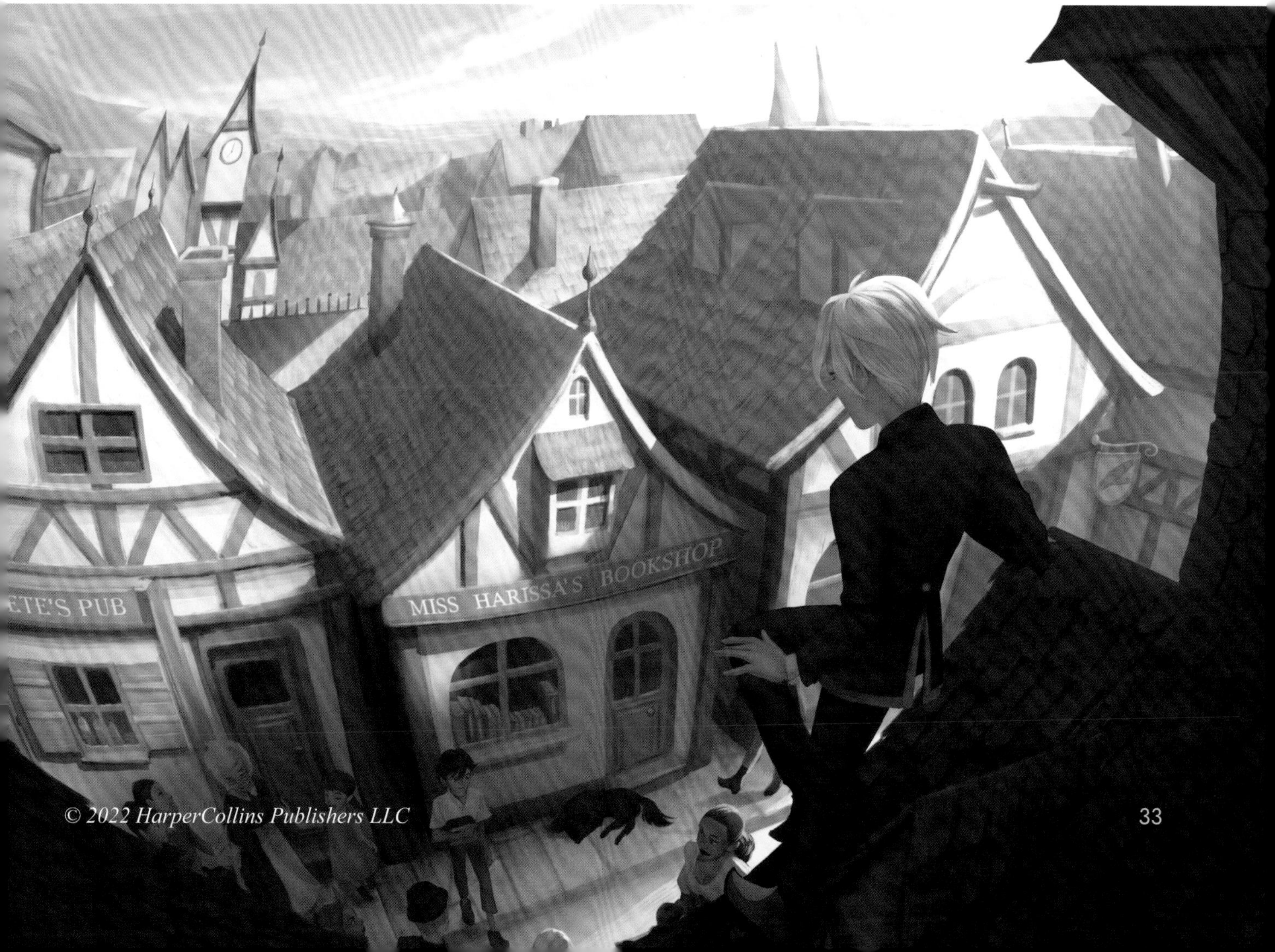

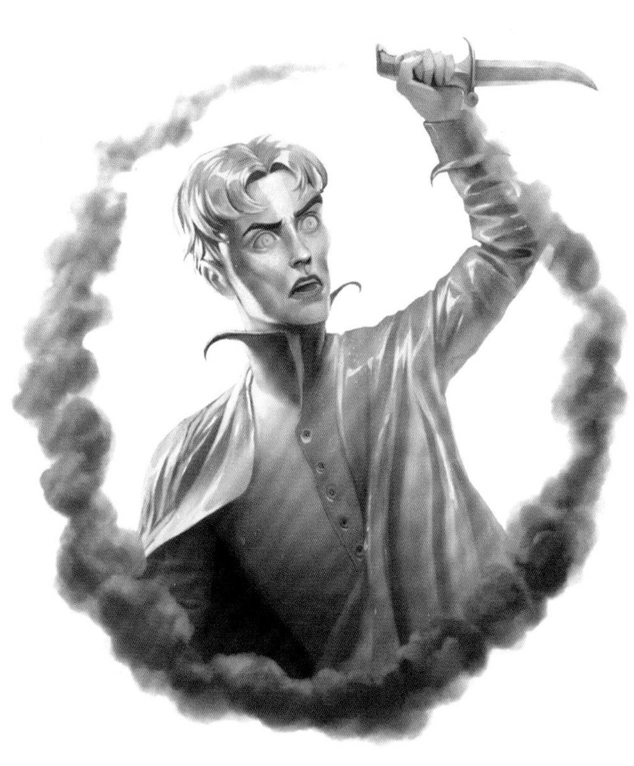

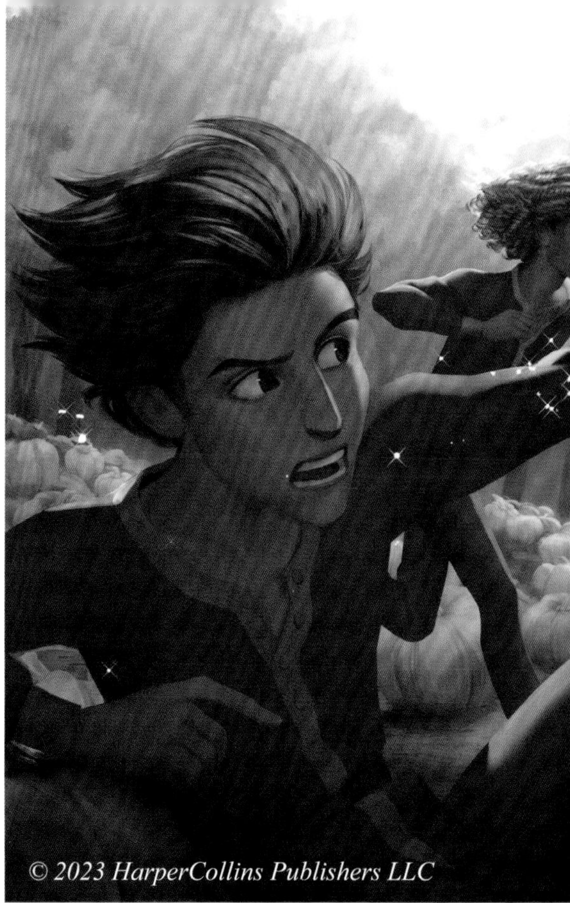

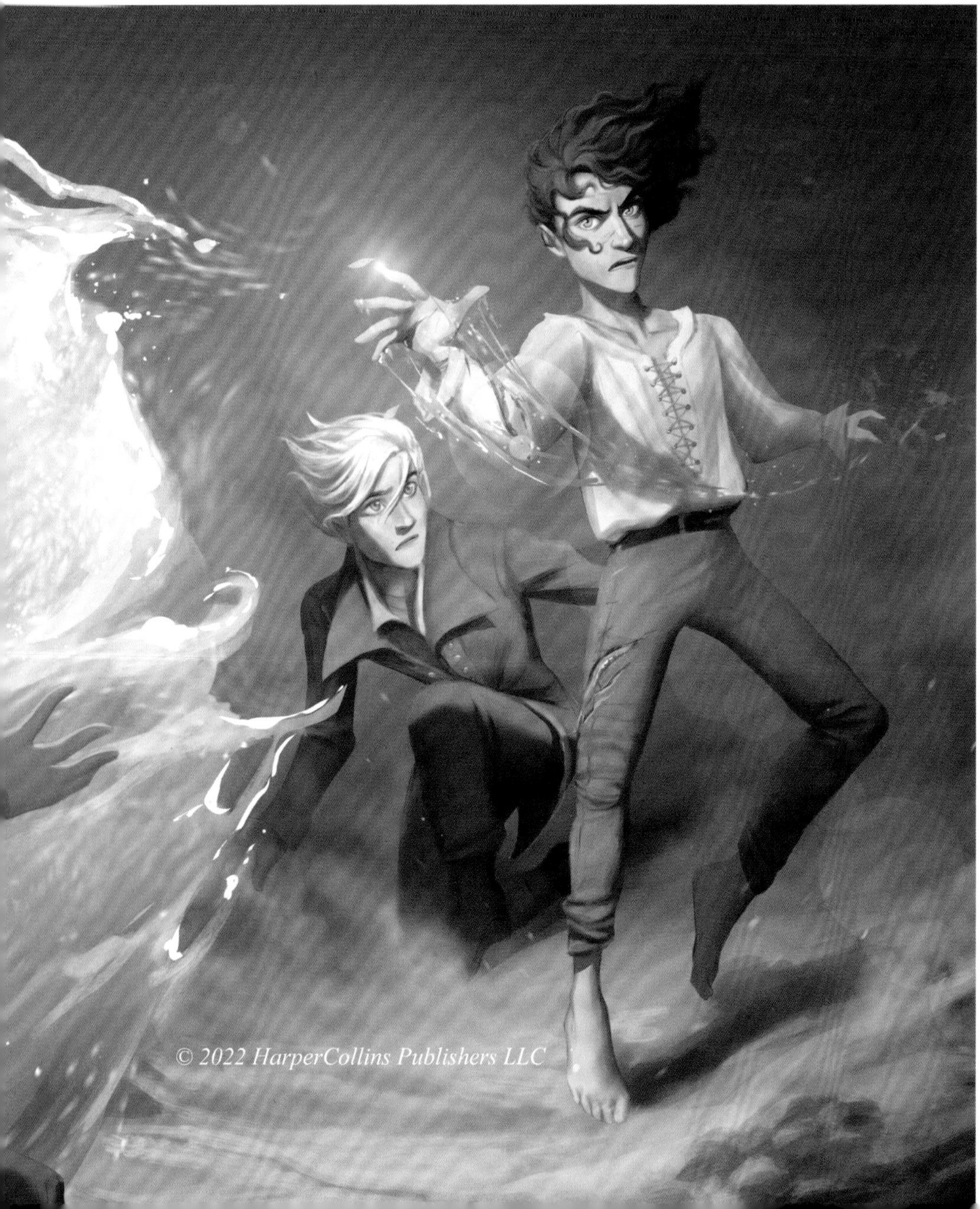

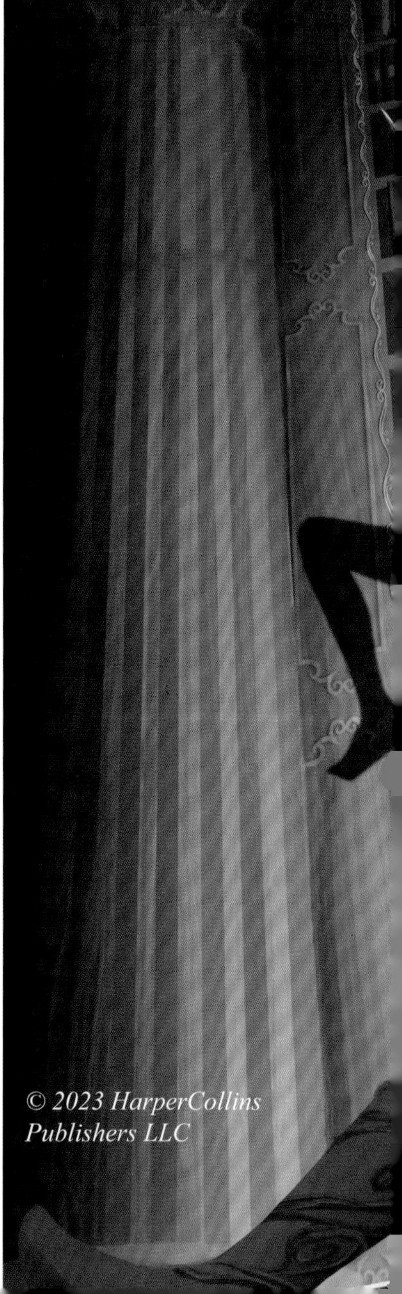

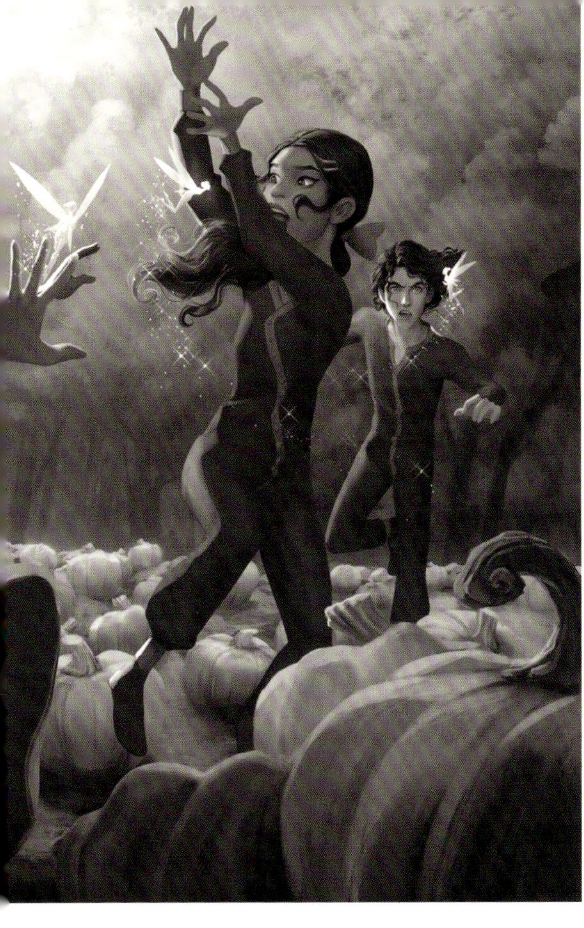

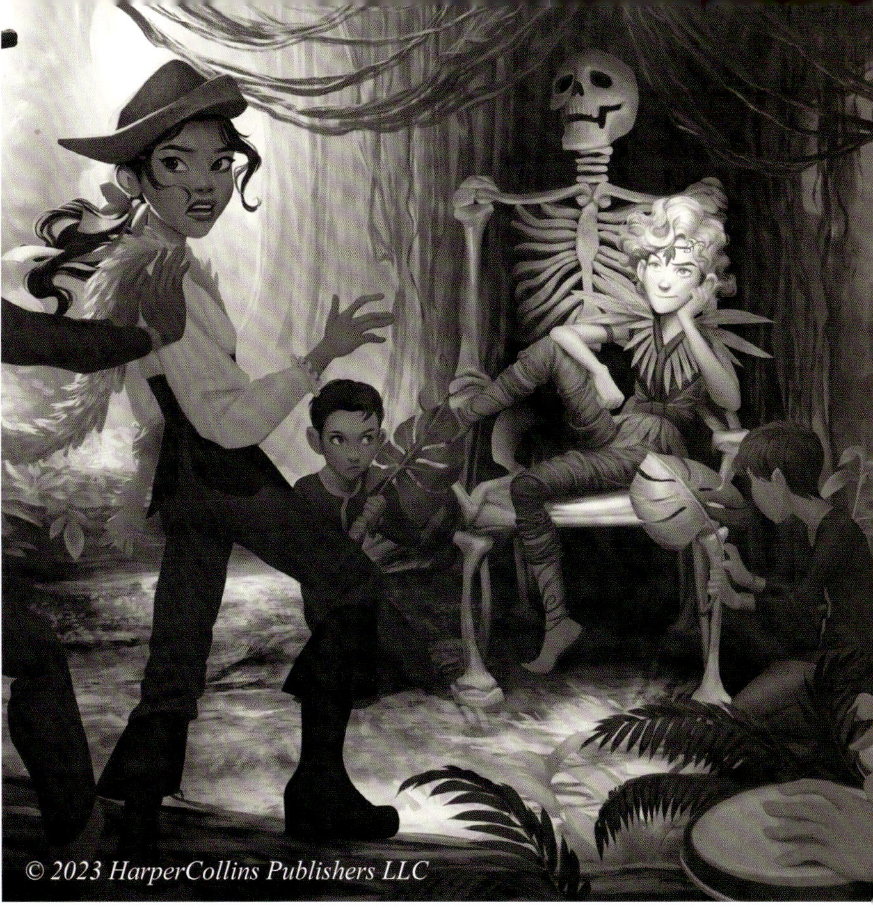

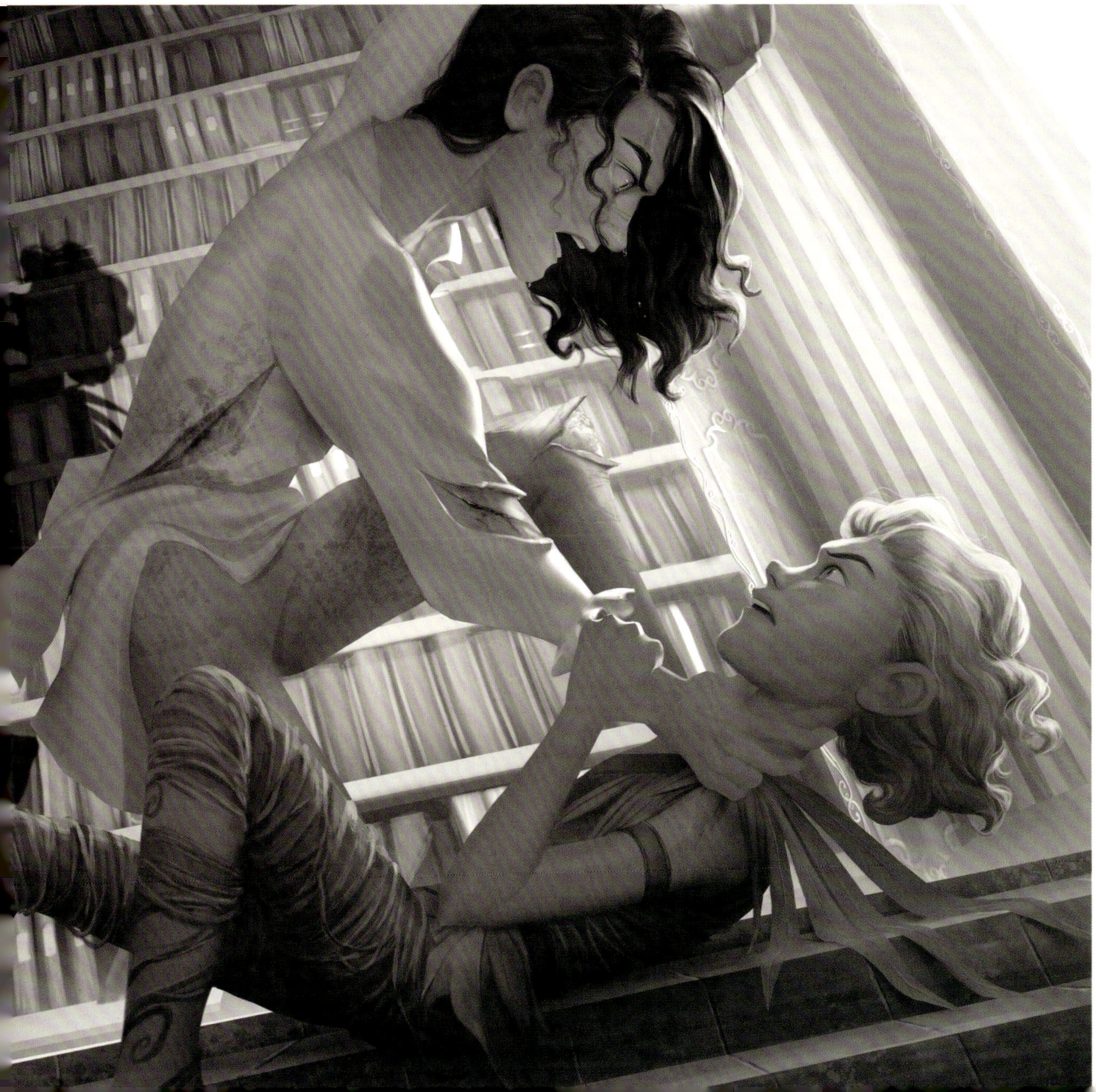

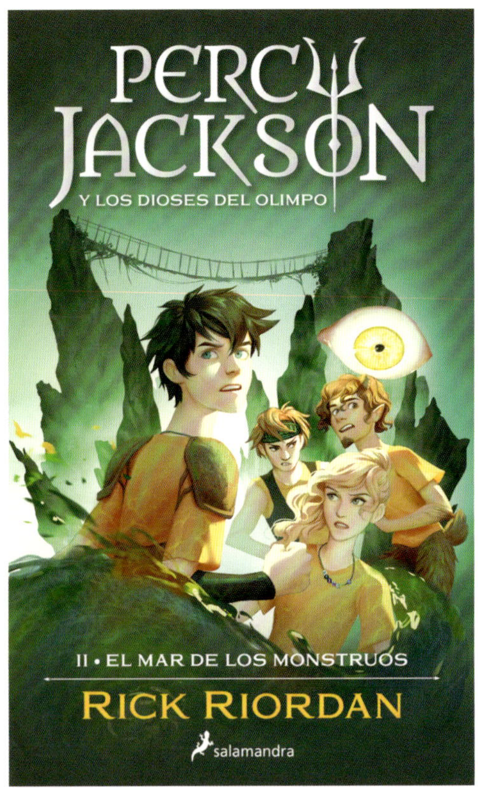

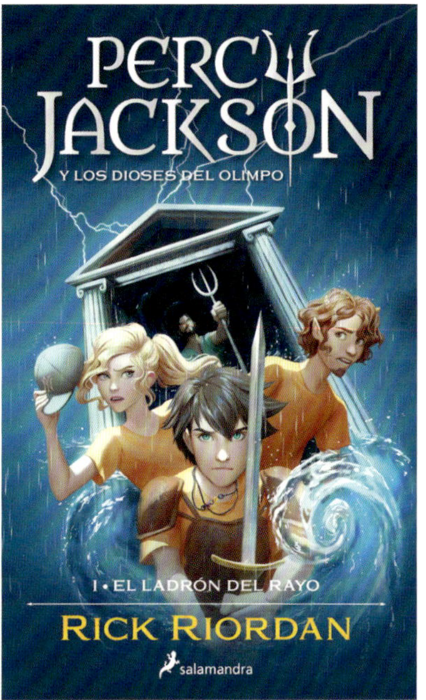

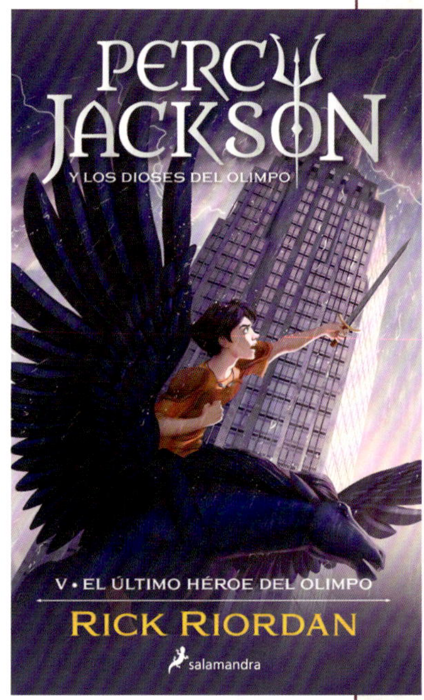

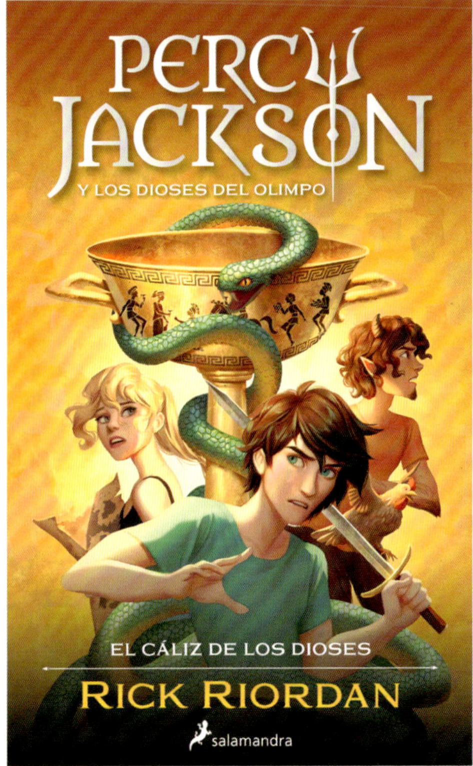

These are the six covers I made for Rick Riordan's Percy Jackson *series. I took inspiration from previous books in order to come up with these concepts; all the covers had to be somewhat similar to the older ones. They also needed to feature a main base colour to give each one a unique look. I always took the background colour as a starting point for the mood*

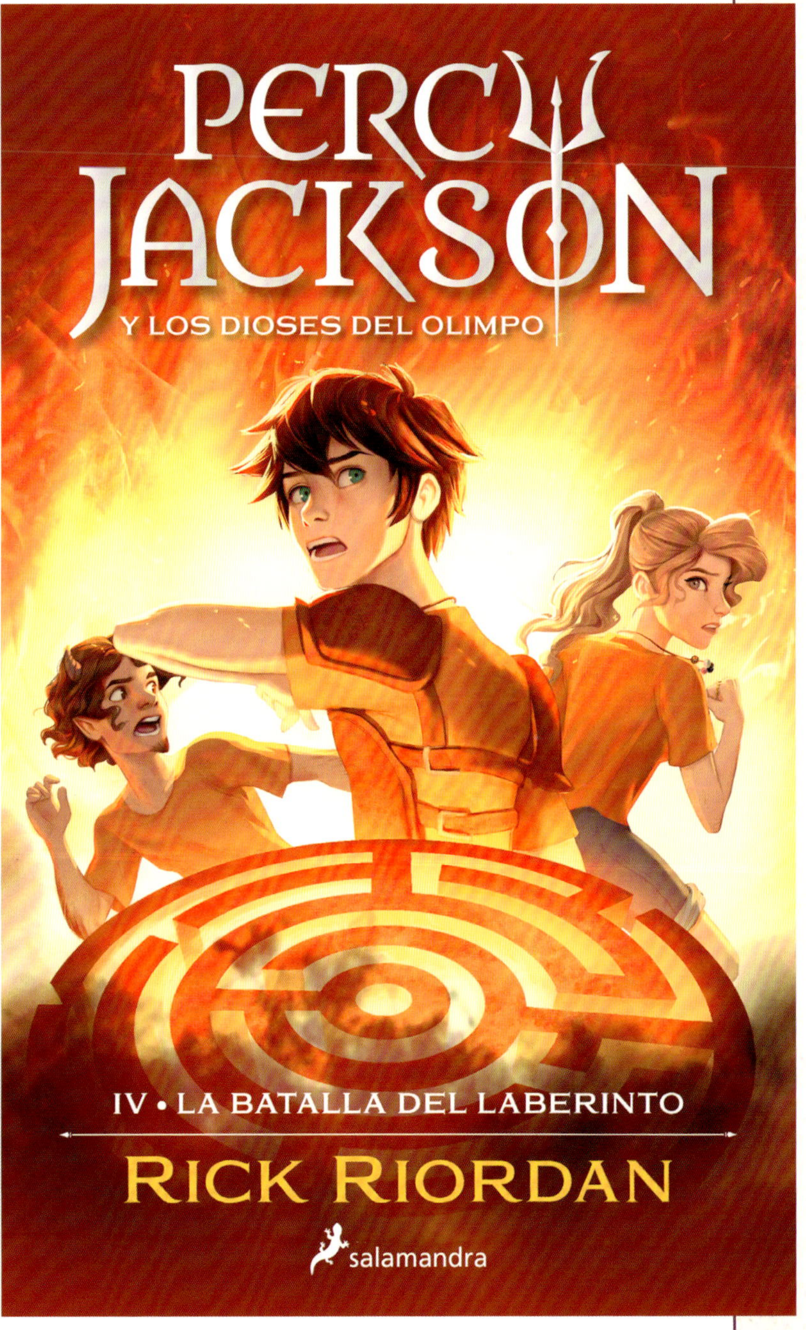

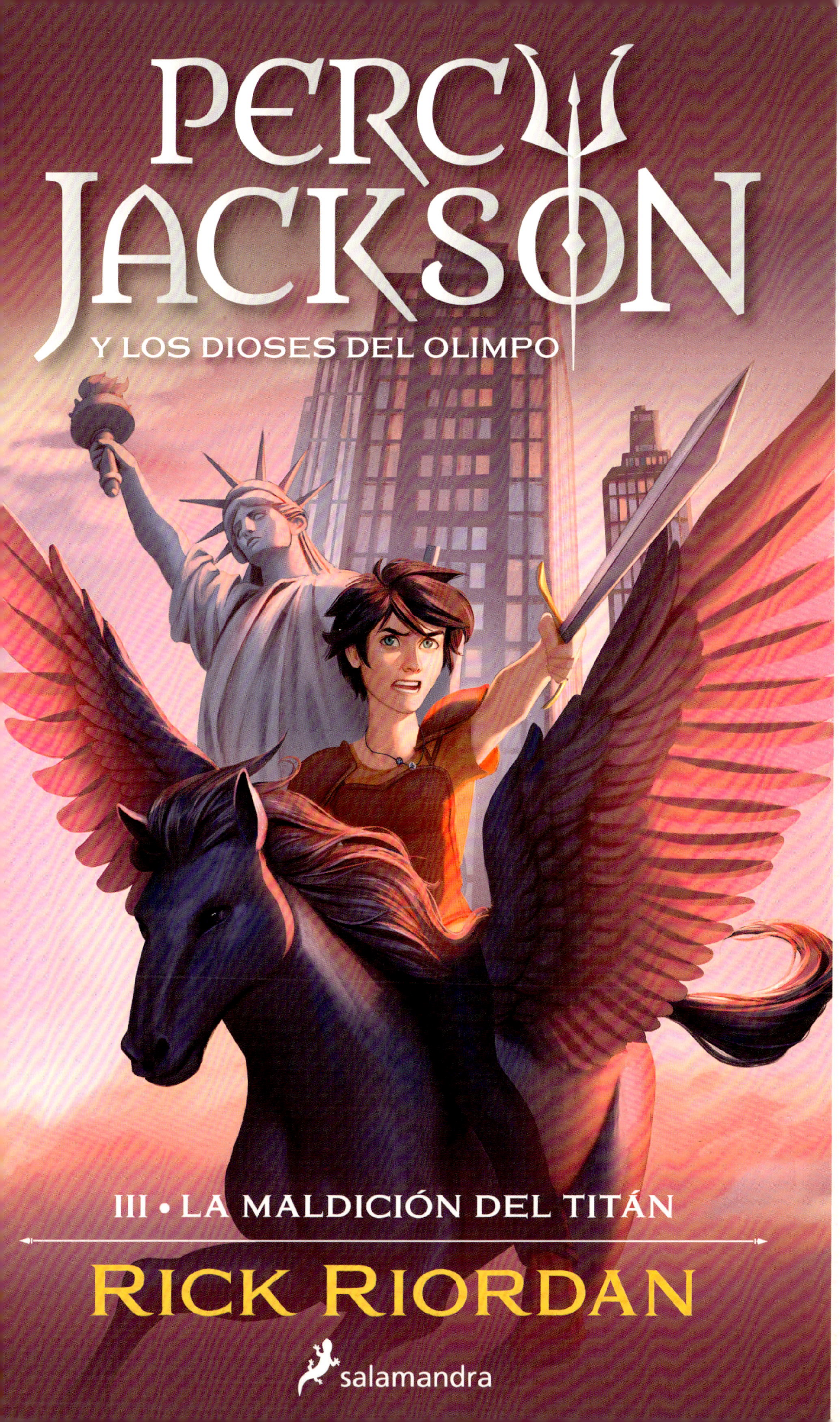

PERCY JACKSON

Y LOS DIOSES DEL OLIMPO

III • LA MALDICIÓN DEL TITÁN

RICK RIORDAN

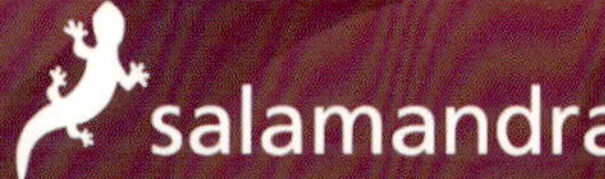

LOCATIONS

Germany

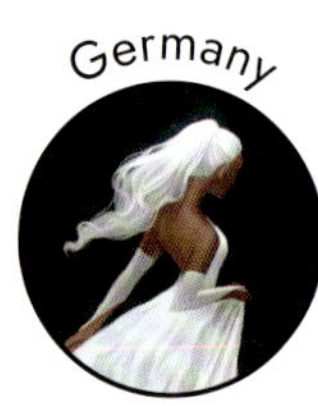

Manga-Comic-Con .... Leipzig
Leipzig Art Days .... Leipzig
NovaCon .... Leuna OT Günthersdorf
MAG-C .... Erfurt
German Comic Con Stuttgart .... Stuttgart
German Comic Con Dortmund .... Dortmung
DoKomi .... Düsseldorf
SPIEL .... Essen
ShiroCo .... Chemnitz
DeDeCo .... Dresden

Switzerland

Fantasy Basel .... Basel
Polymanga .... Montreux

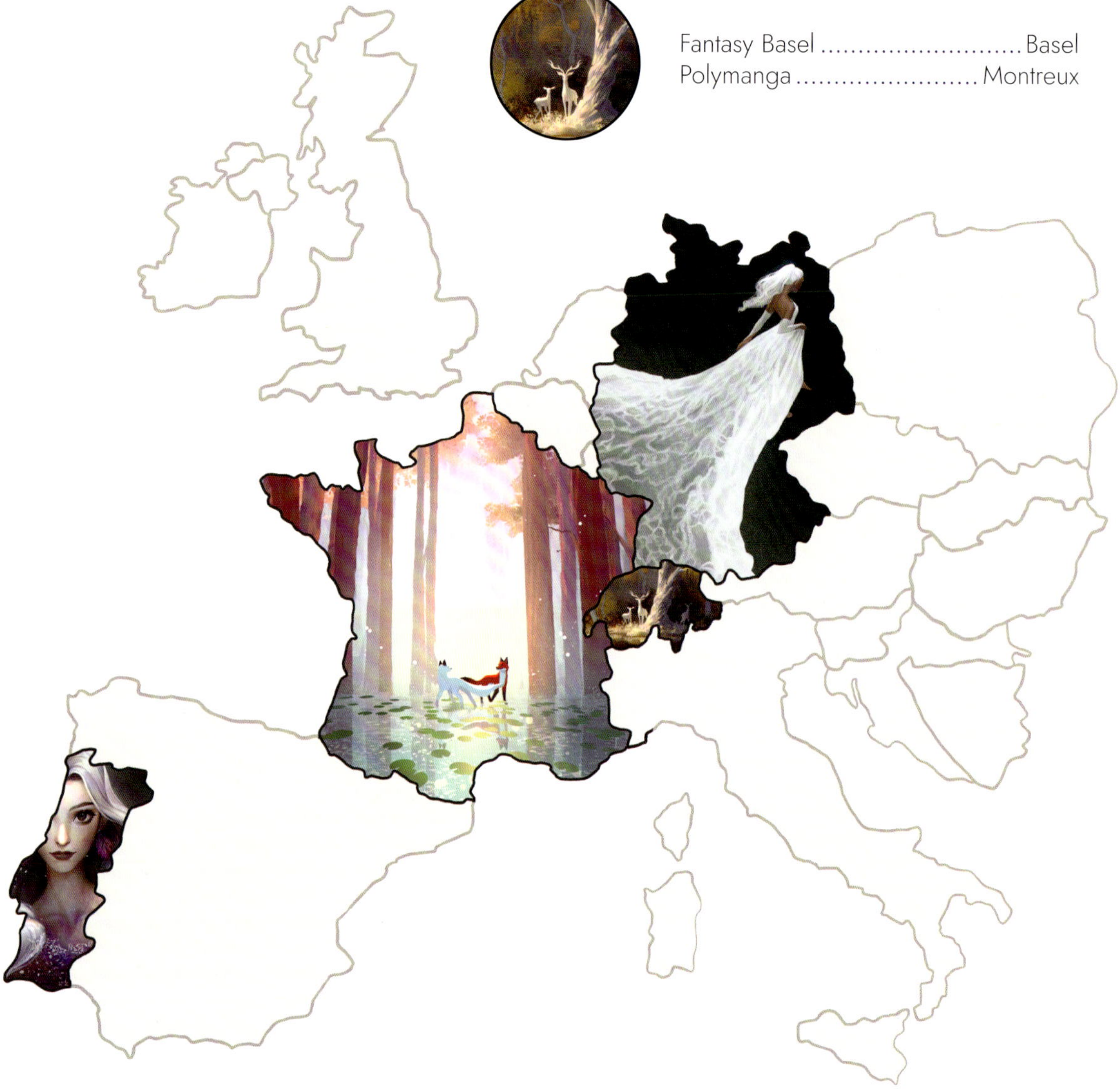

Portugal

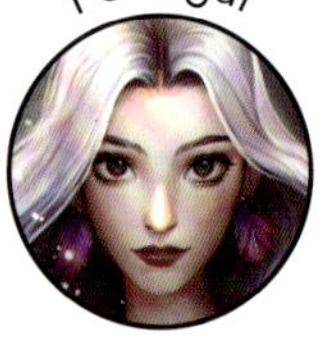

Comic Con Portugal .... Lisbon

France

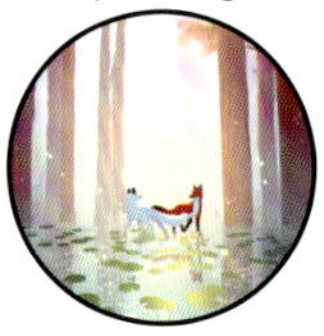

Paris Manga .... Paris

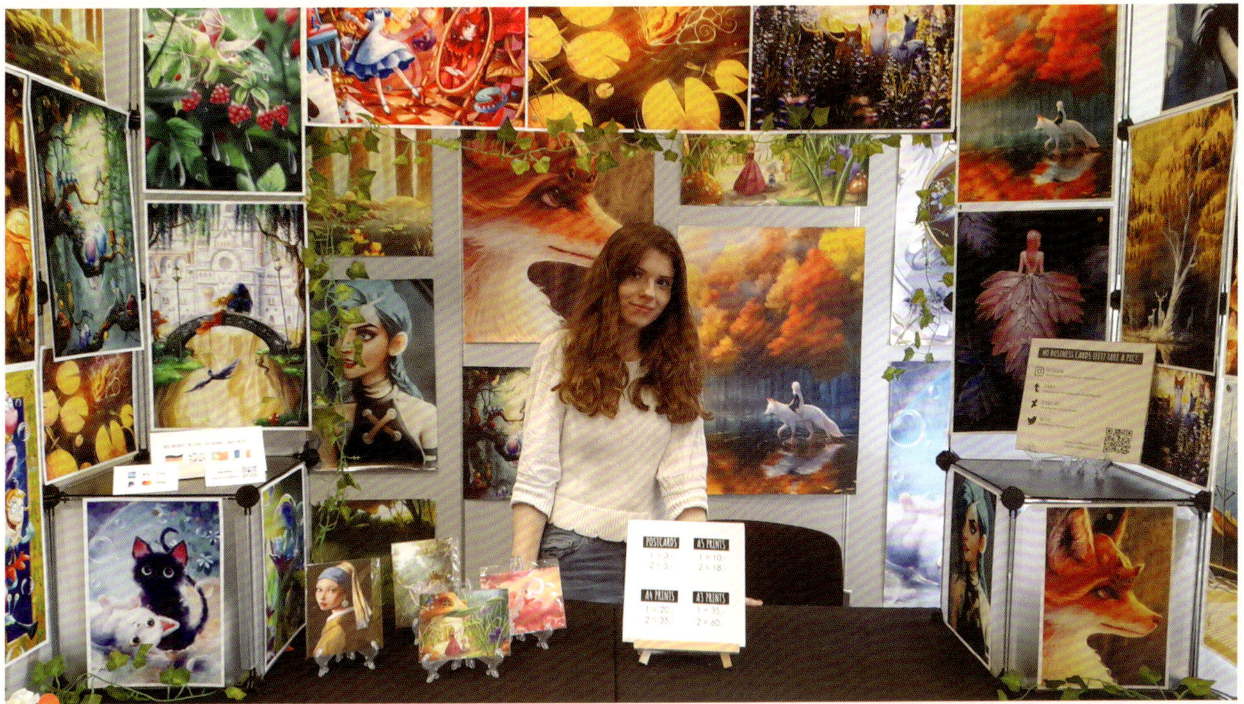

This was my colourful booth at Polymanga in 2022. I make sure to change my booth setup at almost every convention I go to in order to experiment with different displays. Doing this helps me figure out what display options work best for my artwork

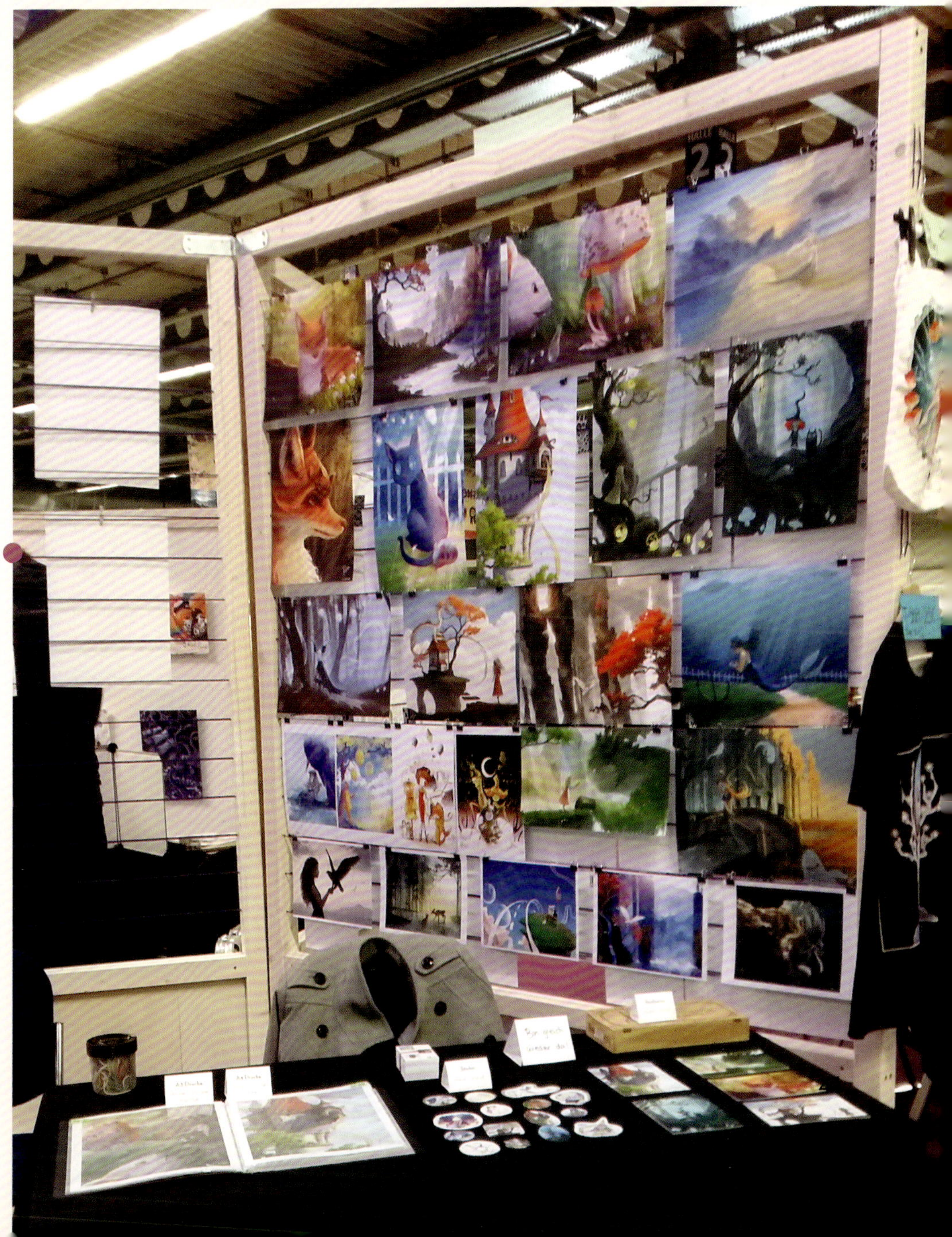

The display you can see on the right is the one I had at the second show I ever attended back in 2018. I didn't have any proper display on the table to raise anything up. Additionally, I only hung up small-sized prints (A4 and A3 formats) on the back wall. Even though it's pricey to order larger sizes, it's definitely worth it! Having even one large A2-or-A1 sized centre print or banner makes your booth more visible from afar

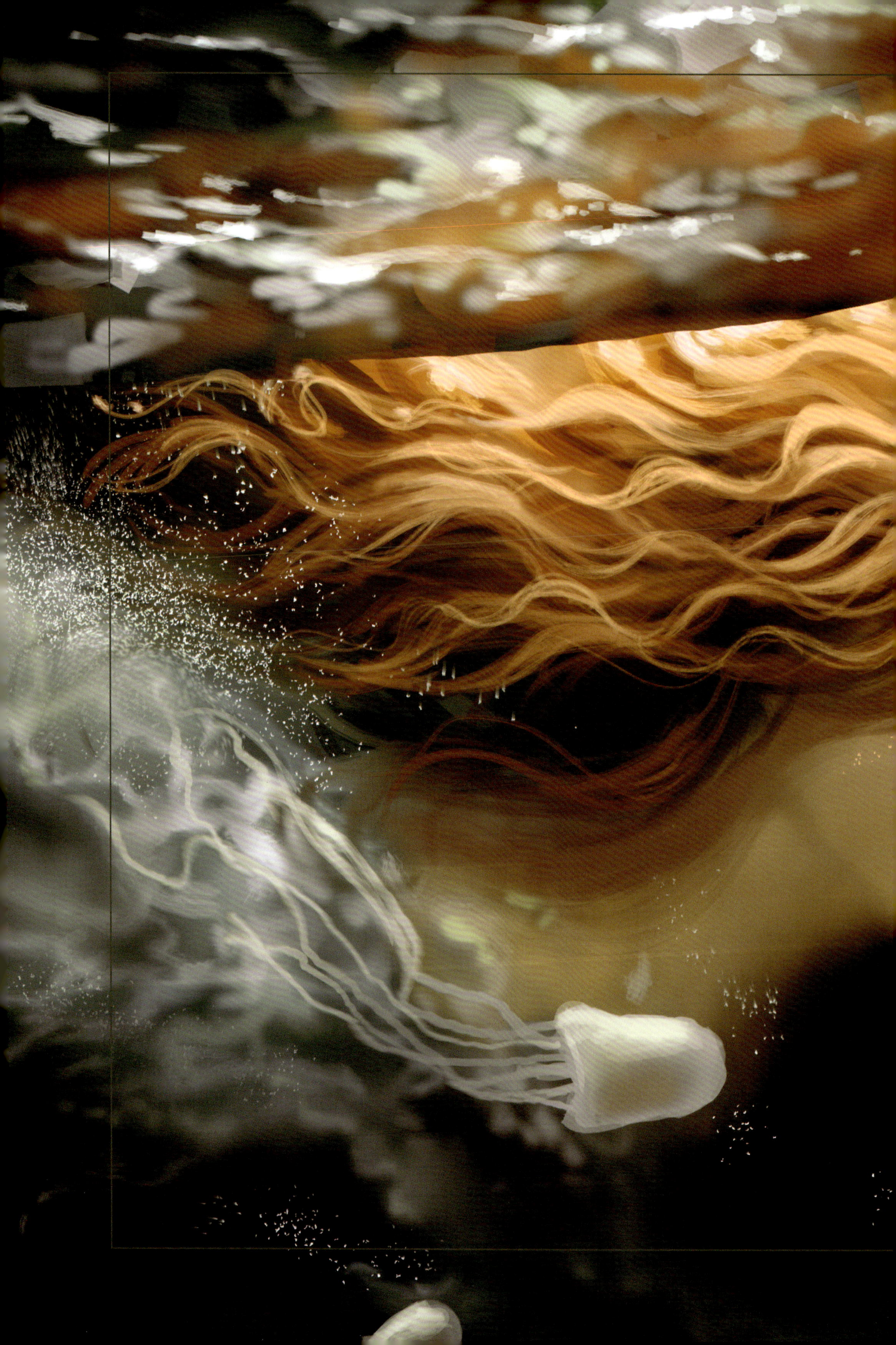

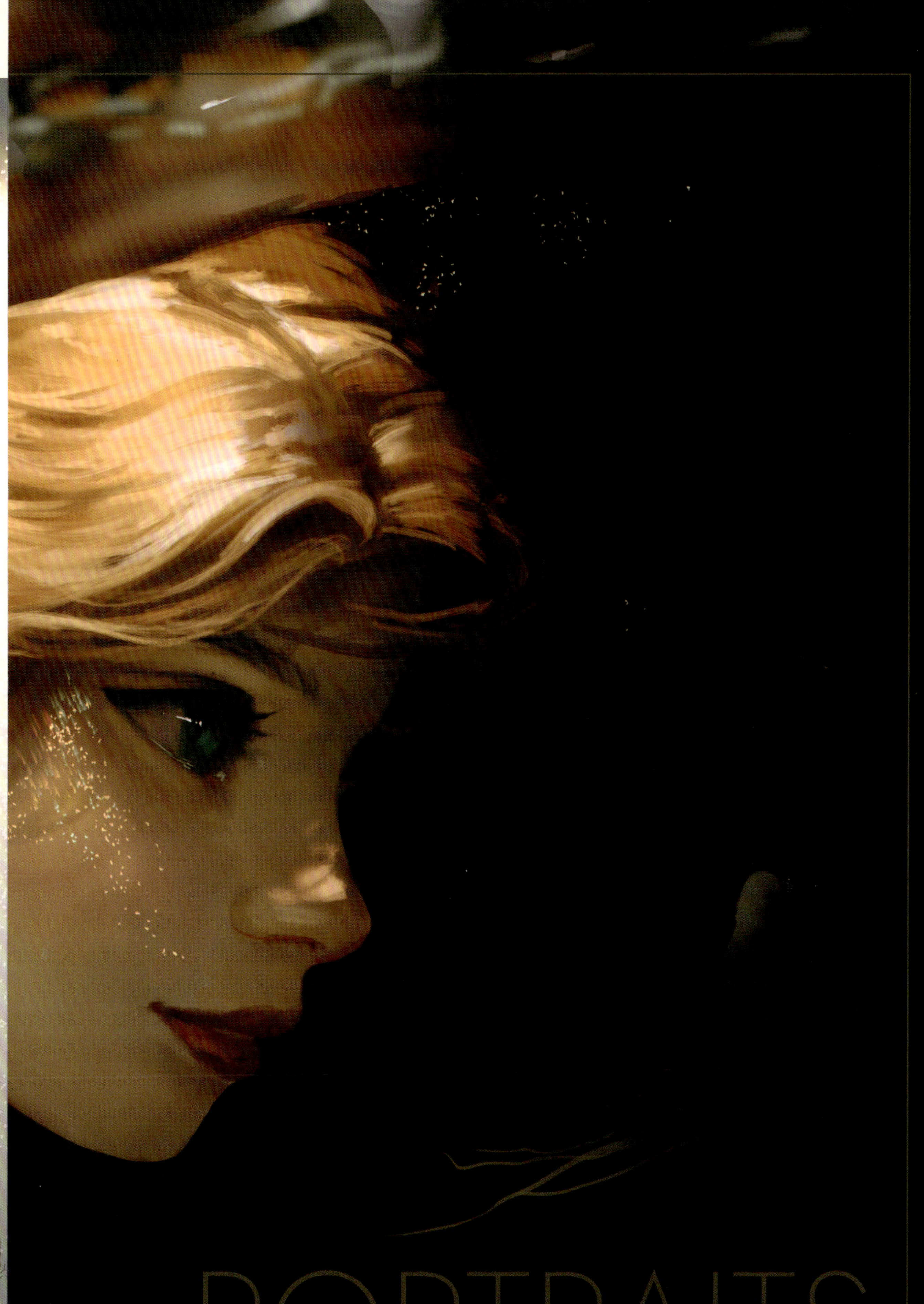

PORTRAITS

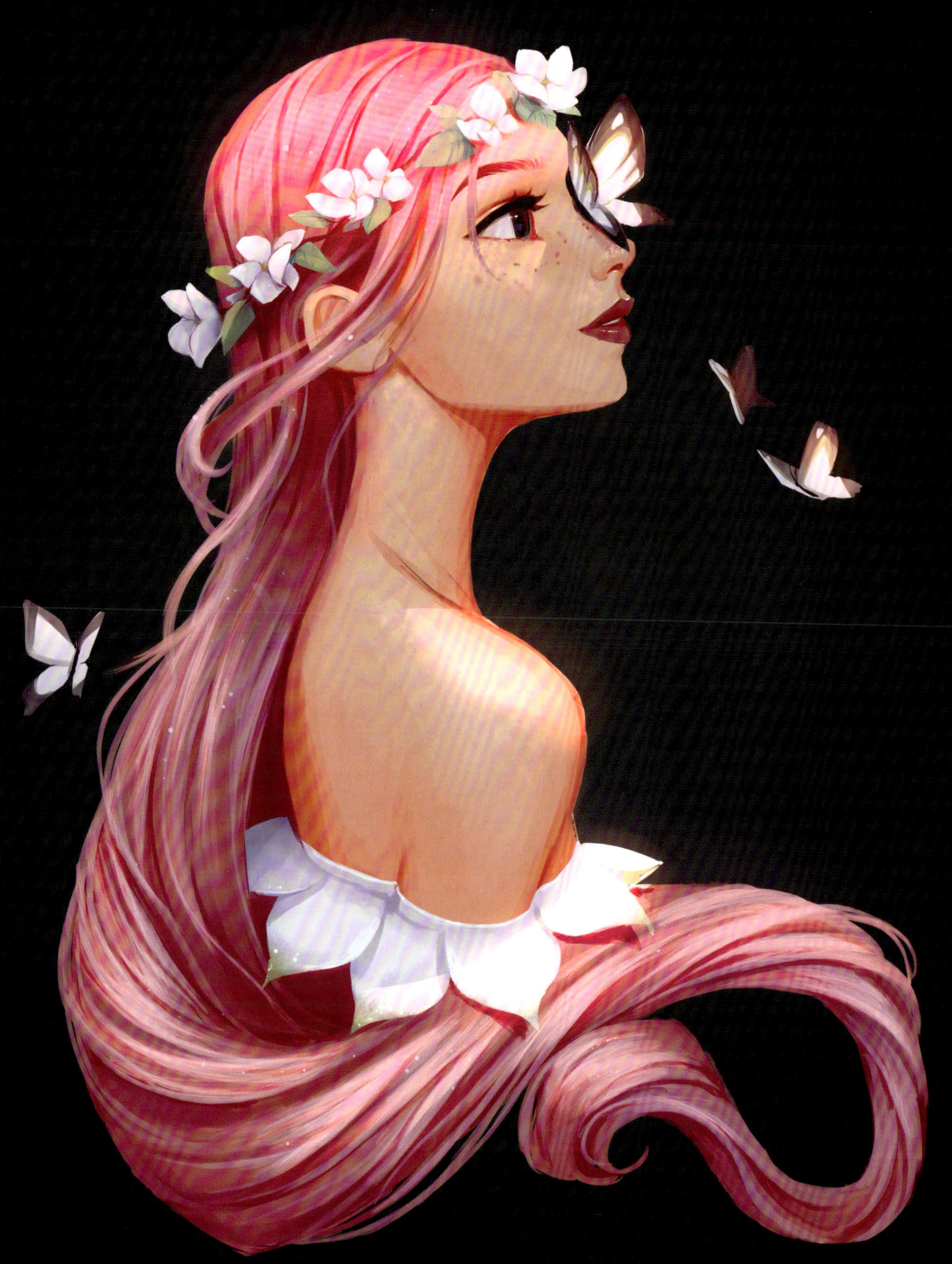

This is the image I created for my Butterfly Challenge. I teamed up with Clip Studio Paint to offer my three favourite entries a free licence of Clip Studio Paint Pro for two years. Over 1,500 artists participated in the challenge, and on the following pages you'll find some of my favourite interpretations

DRAW THIS IN YOUR STYLE

I greatly improved my drawing skills when I began focusing on portraits. As I briefly mentioned in my section on social media, I participated in many *Draw This In Your Style* challenges when I first joined Instagram. They mainly featured portraits of women with various designs, and like the name suggests, the challenge objective was to recreate the character in your own art style.

As a reward for joining these challenges, some of the hosting artists shared their favourite entries on their Instagram stories or on their page. Getting noticed by these well-known artists drew more people to my work, and some of them even followed me as a result. Not only were these challenges fun, they helped to grow my account.

While I absolutely loved painting these portraits, my entries didn't show a wide range of facial features. I mostly focused on accurately recreating faces and adding interesting light sources. Looking back, it's easy to see how much these artists and their challenges greatly influenced my work. While I wanted to give these characters my own spin, I didn't want to completely erase their original features. Therefore, I always stuck to the designs, but experimented with posture, composition, and lighting.

Since I loved these challenges so much, it didn't take me long to host my own! To celebrate reaching certain milestones, I hosted one or two DTIYS challenges per year, each featuring a new original character. I loved browsing through the entries and exploring so many talented, underrated artists. My Butterfly Challenge, as I like to call it, had some amazing results and showcased the wide variety of styles among the art community.

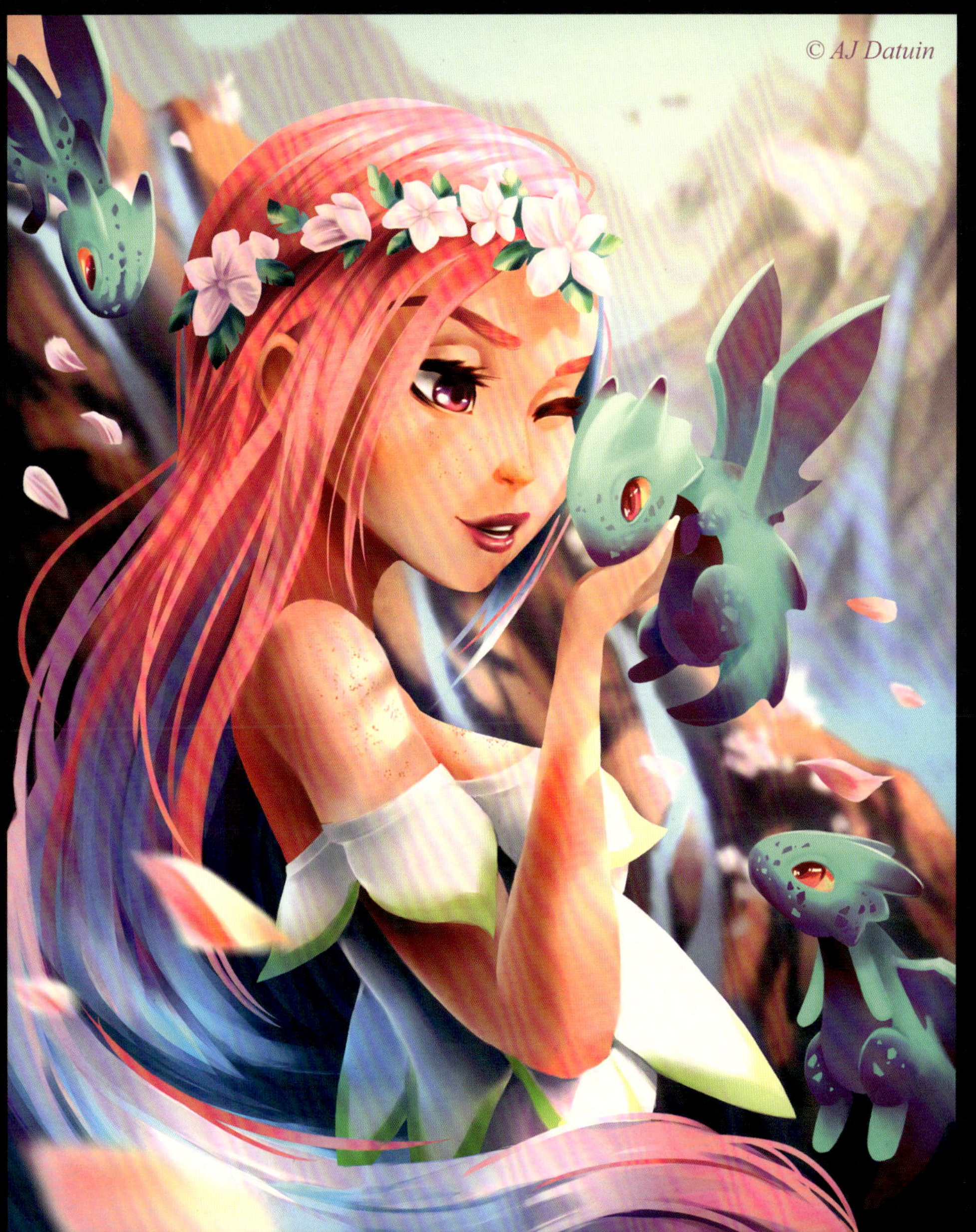

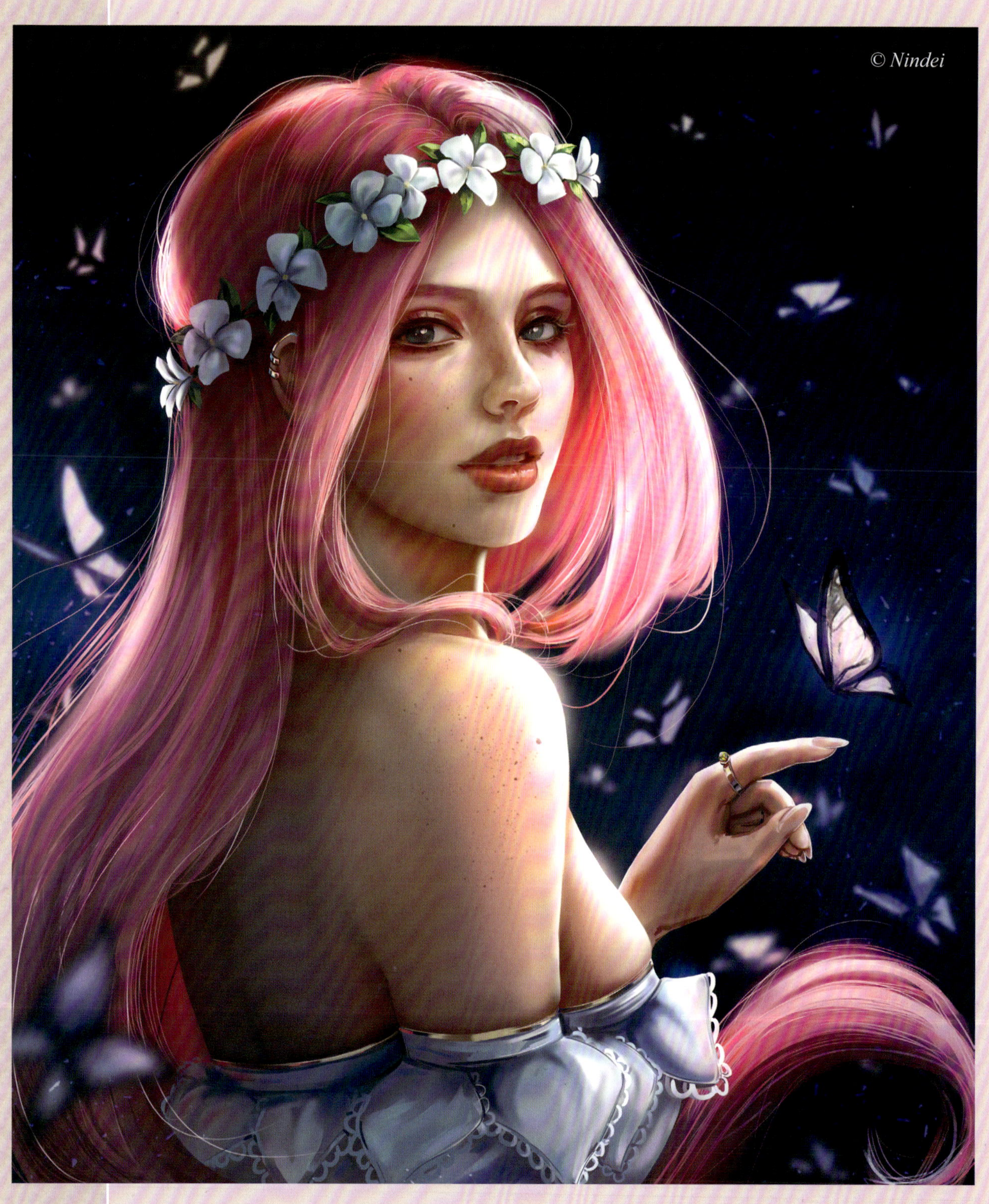
© Nindei

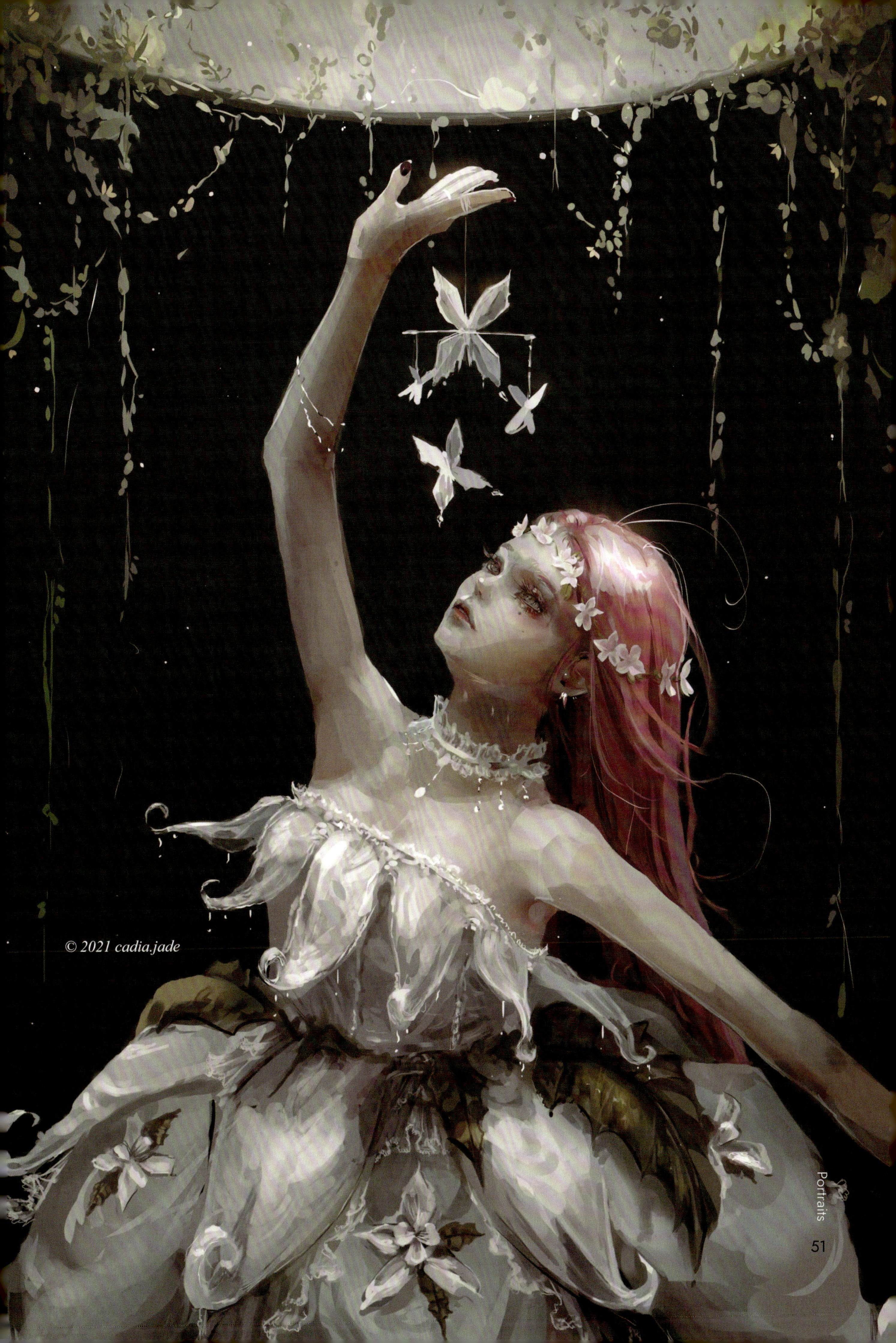
© 2021 cadia.jade

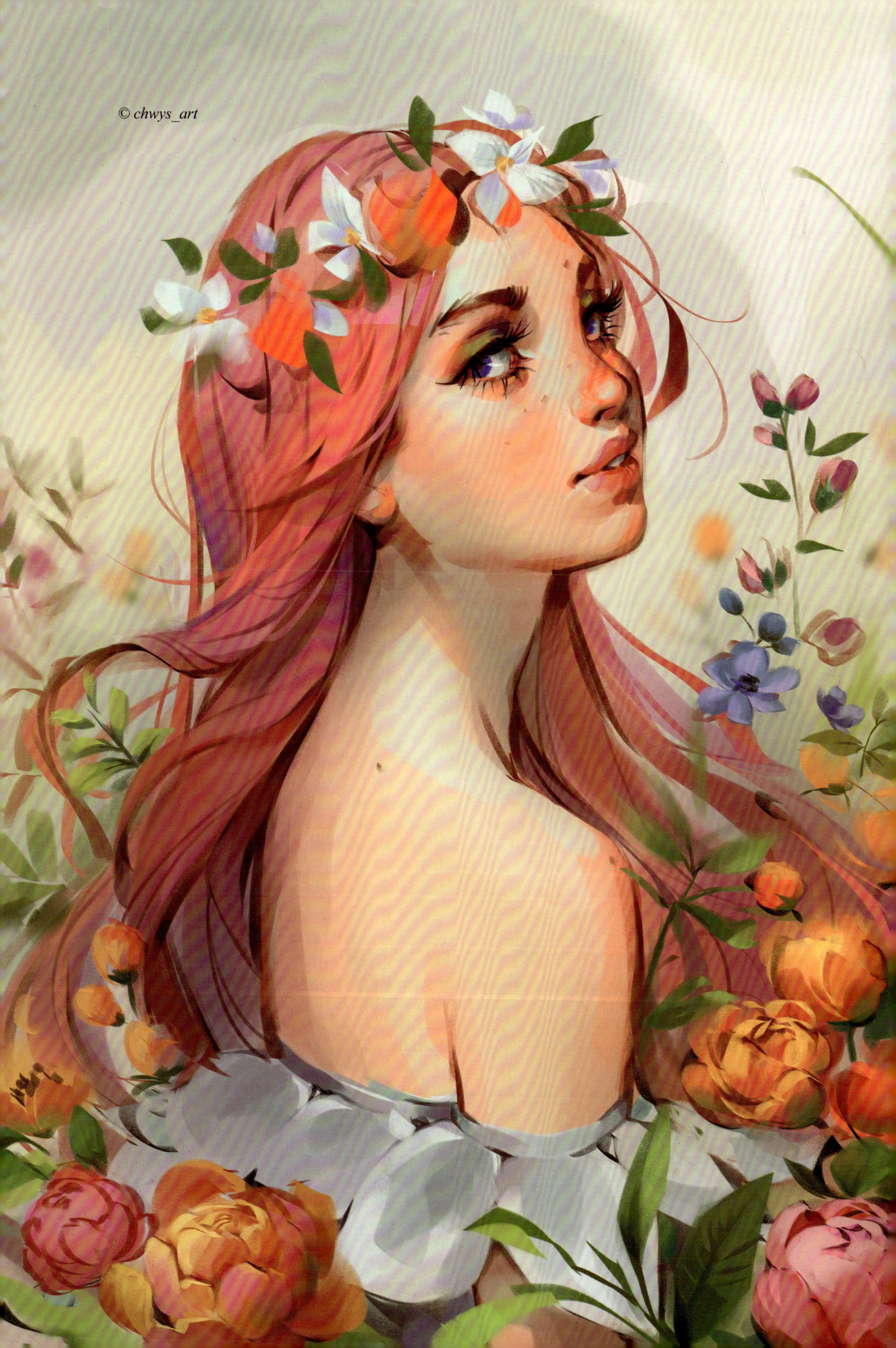
© chwys_art

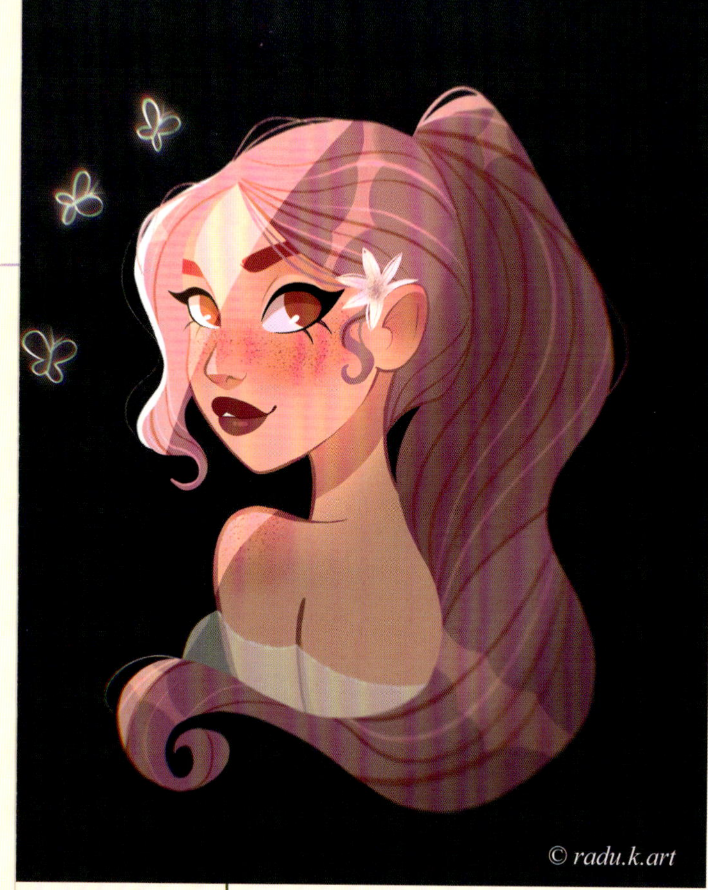
© radu.k.art

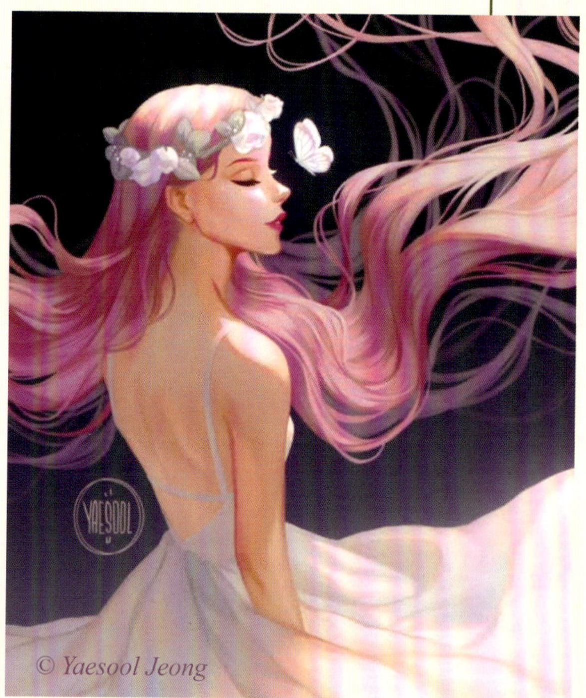

© Yaesool Jeong

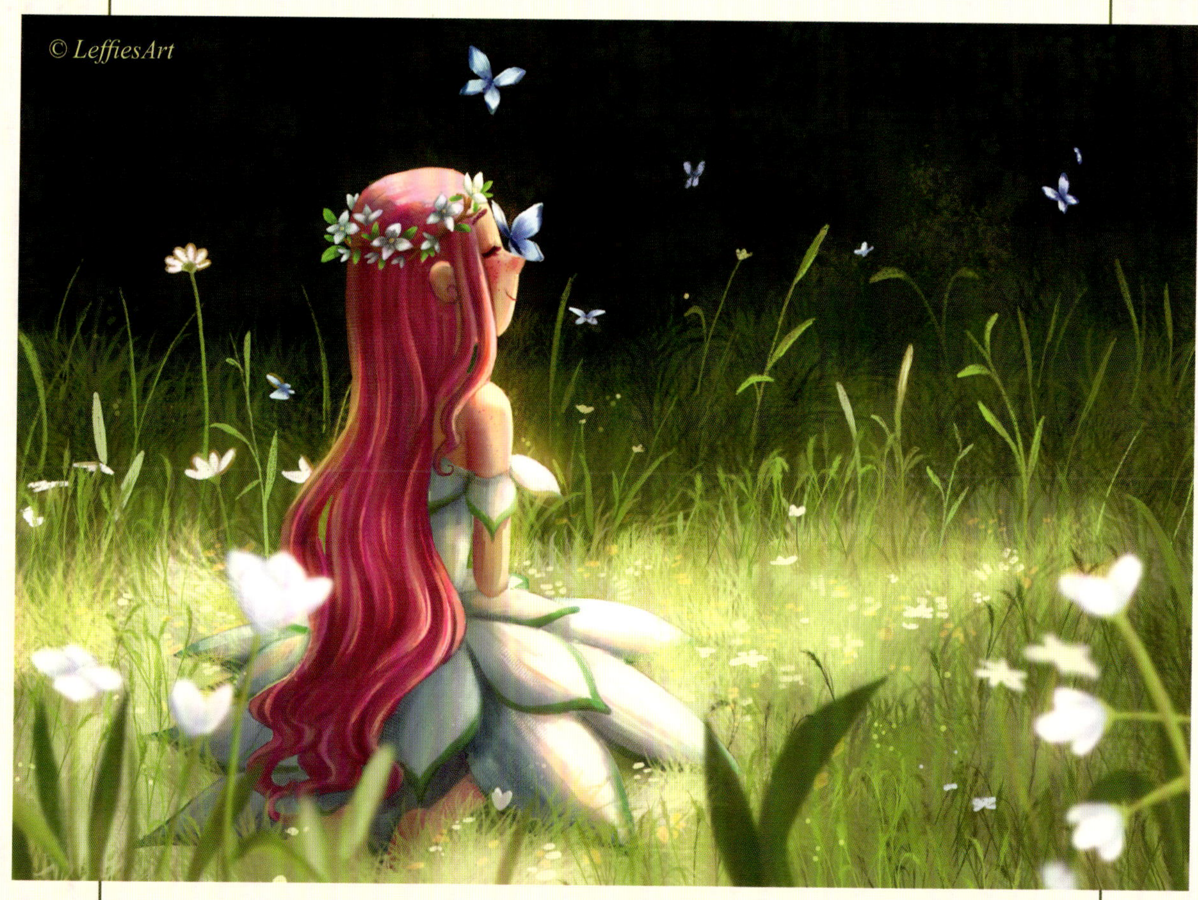
© LeffiesArt

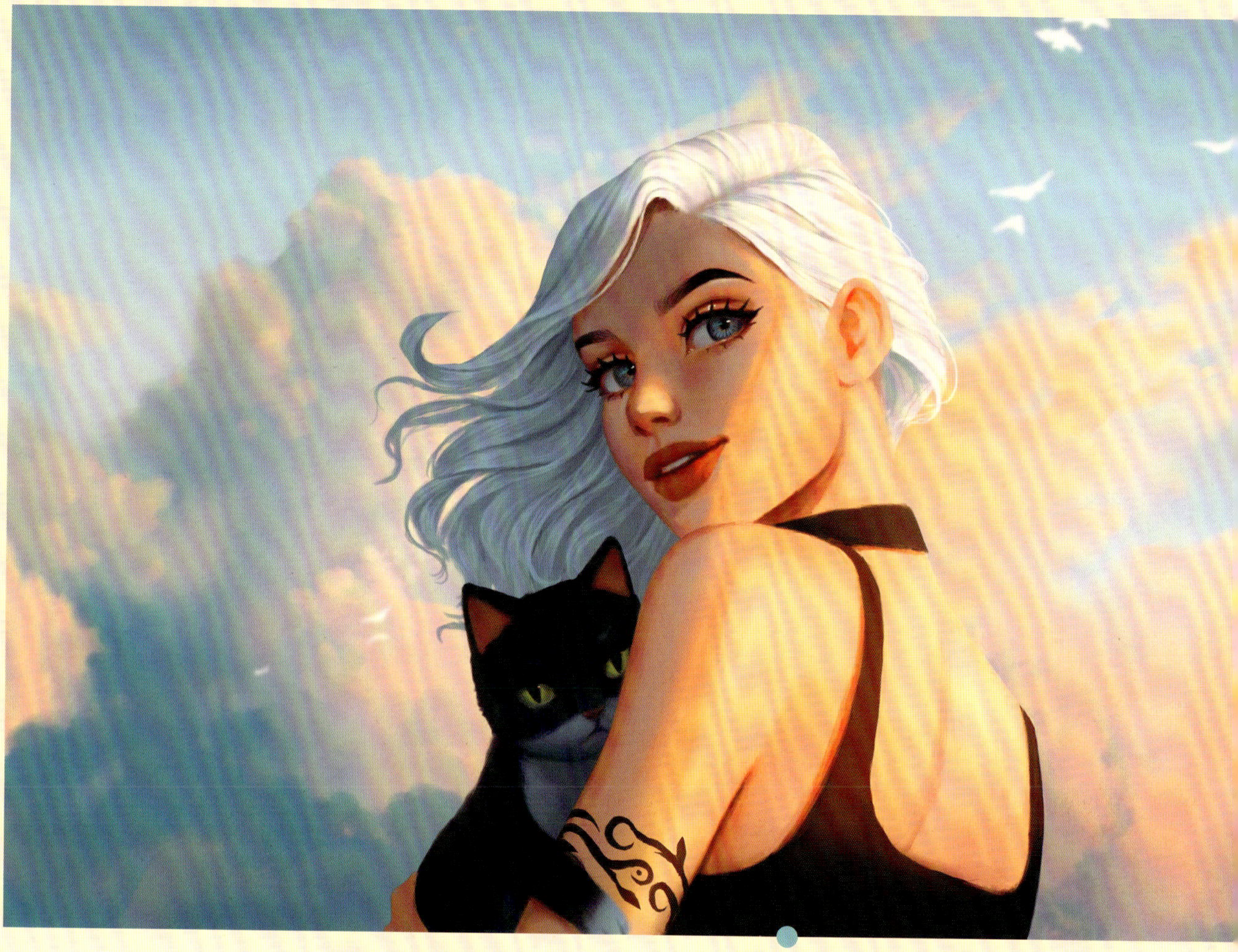

When Sam Yang hosted a drawing challenge back in 2020, I had to join! I matched the colours of the clouds with the colours on the character in order to blend everything together. I loved coming up with the soft palette for this entry

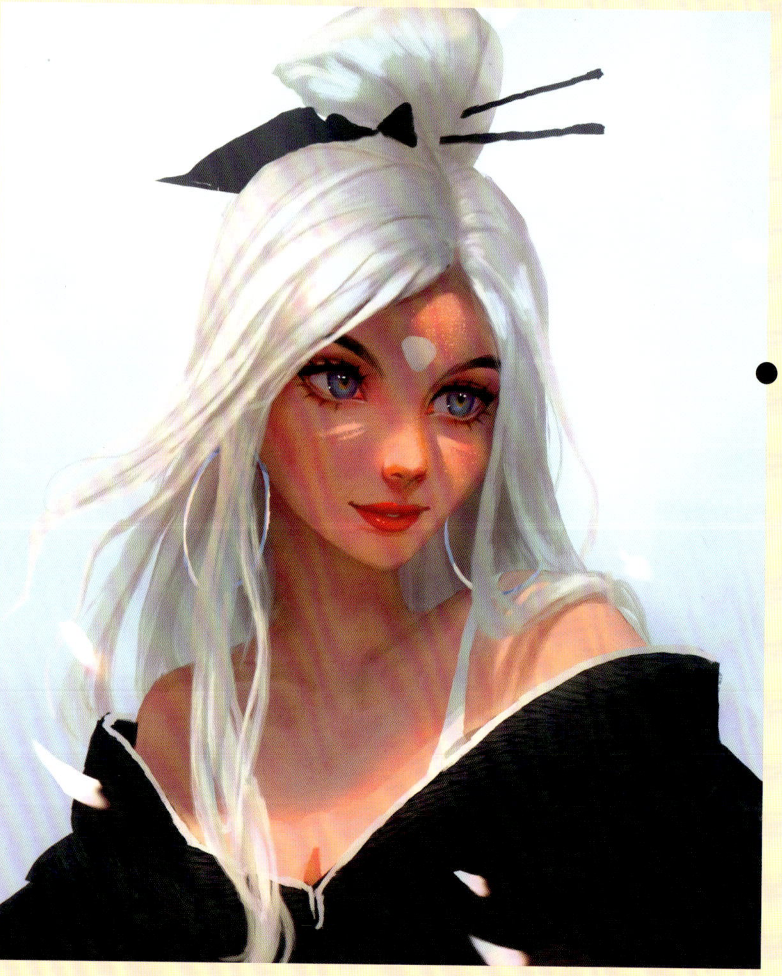

This is another entry I did for one of Ross Tran's challenges. I did my best to capture the features of his original character Nima, while still incorporating some of that organic lighting that is common in my style

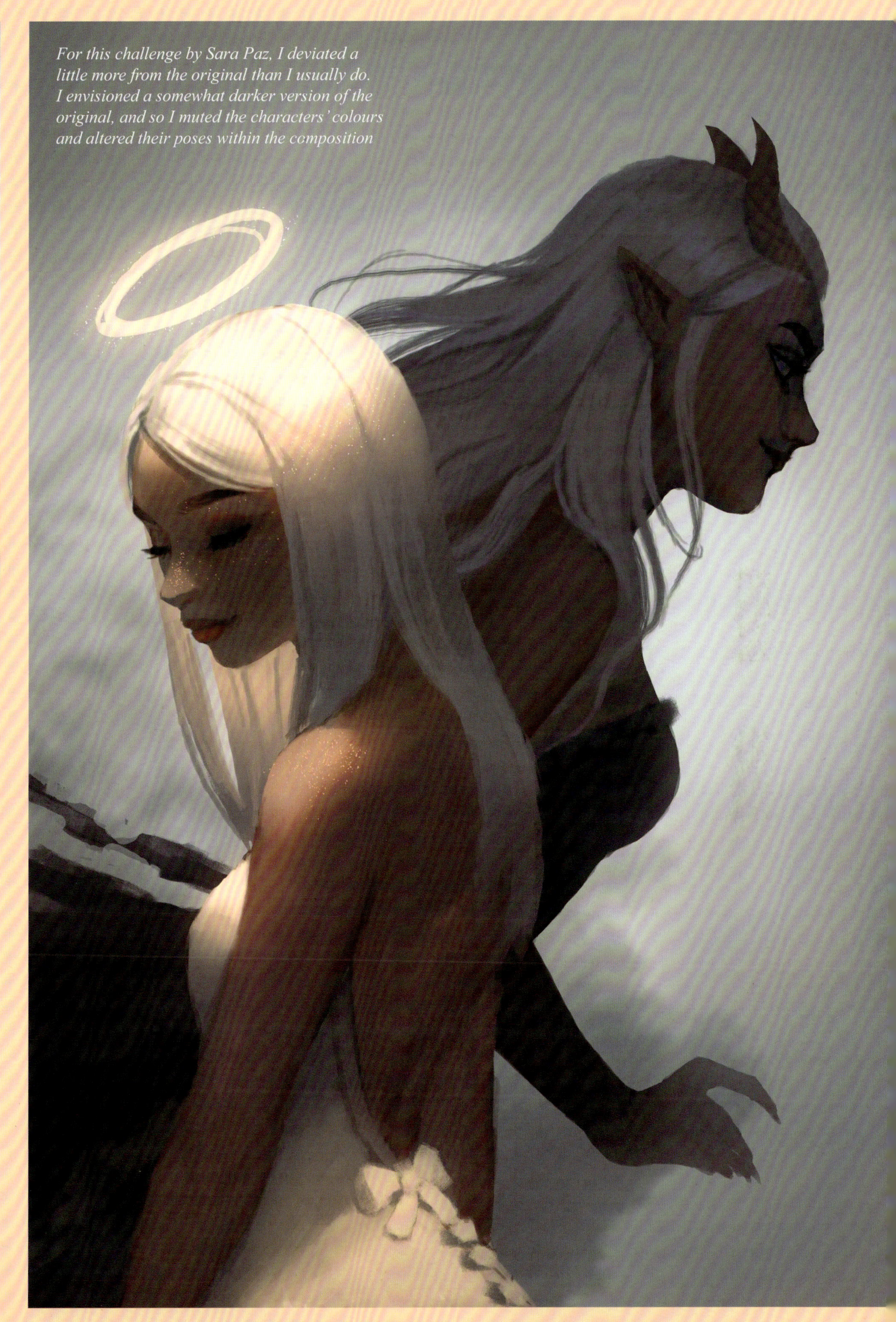

For this challenge by Sara Paz, I deviated a little more from the original than I usually do. I envisioned a somewhat darker version of the original, and so I muted the characters' colours and altered their poses within the composition

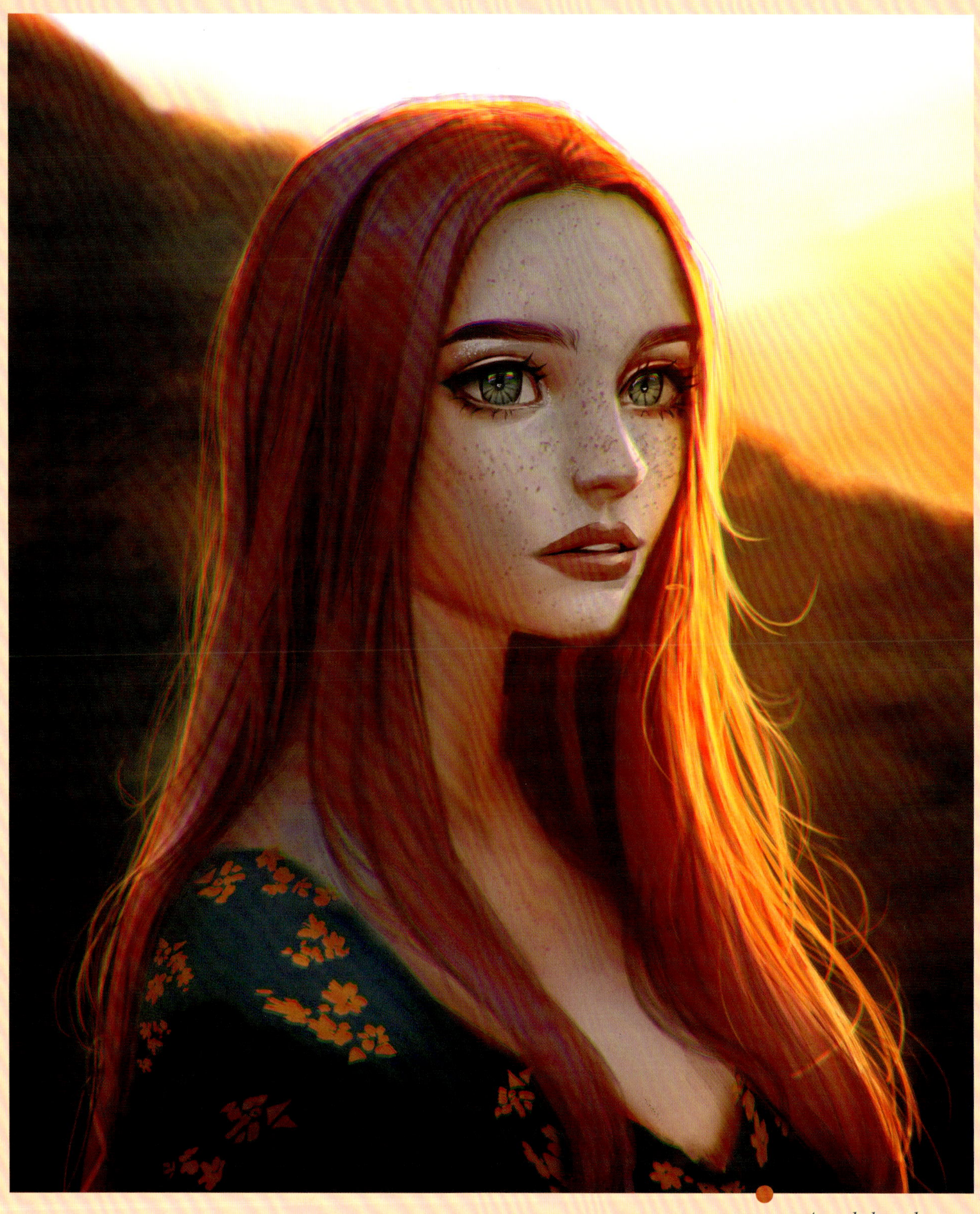

A study based on a gorgeous photograph of @kaitimackenzie by Abel Lares

LIGHTING STUDIES

An essential part of my art style is the inclusion of dramatic lighting. The way sunlight shimmers on the skin and reveals fine hairs along the edges has always captivated me. As a result of this, I looked into many references of interesting lighting patterns and tried to implement what I liked into my own works.

I find that the best way to learn lighting is to start with some studies. Understanding the relationship between the cool and warm undertones of light and dark areas is essential, and it took me some time to figure out. I studied dozens of photos over the years before I found an effective method for adding dramatic lighting.

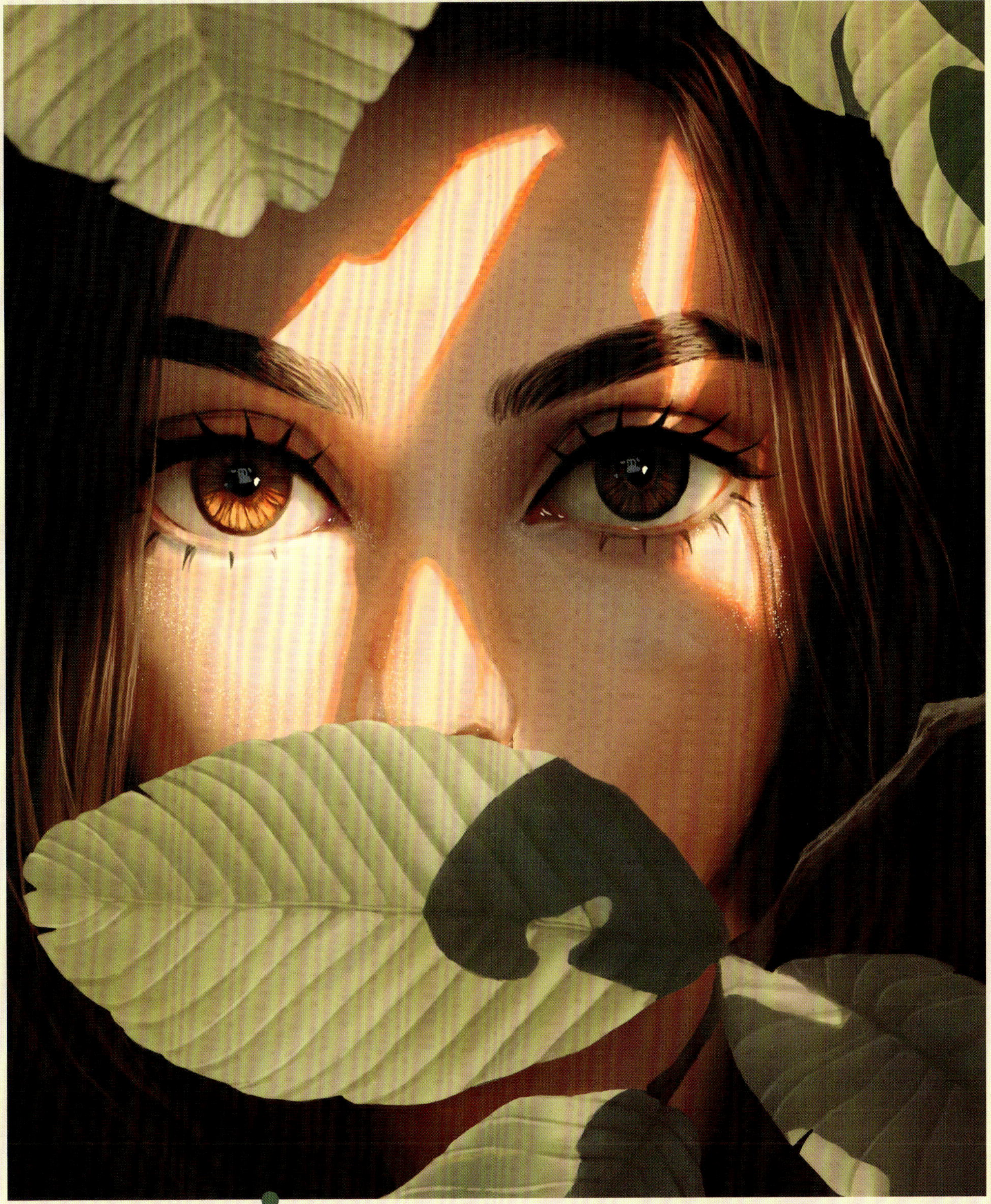

This is a study based on one of Vanderlei João Longo's photos on Instagram. The original image sparked my interest for adding striking lighting to portraits

My advice is to make a mood board. Save all the inspirational images you find, even if you don't plan on using them in the near future. Browsing through the references I've collected gives me so much inspiration – I always manage to find something that sparks an idea!

Over the years, I've developed a particular interest in combining strong dramatic lighting with elements from nature. I'm fond of images where the sunlight gleams on the skin through gaps in the foliage, creating a beautiful and almost ethereal effect. Around the time of the portrait shown above, I tried implementing organic natural lighting – especially warm sunlight – into my portraits to reveal the finer details of the face.

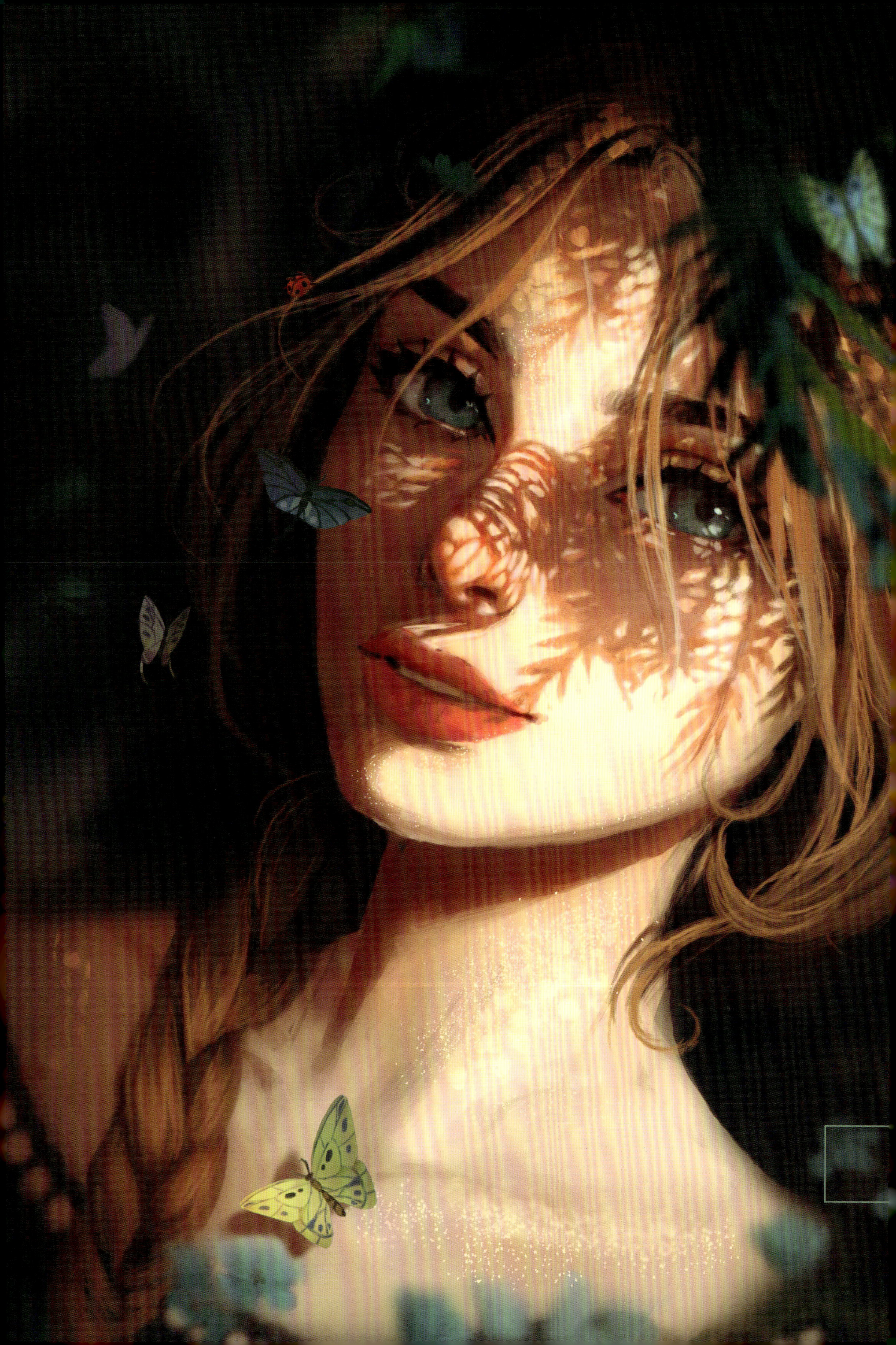

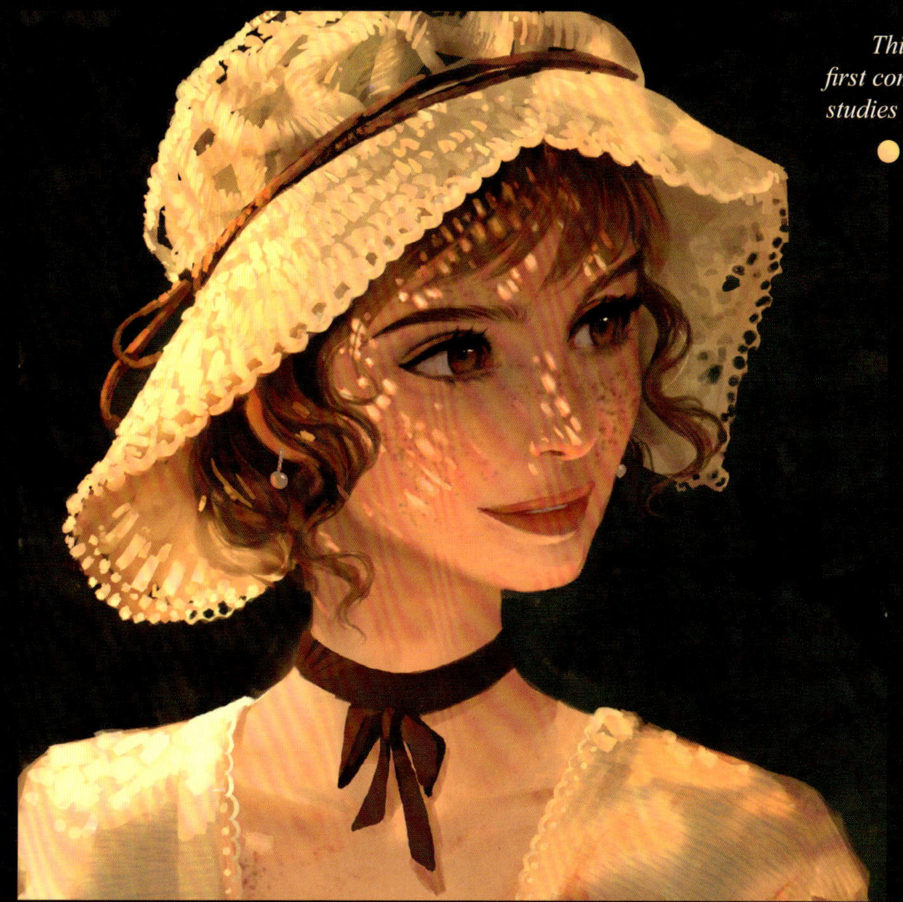

This is one of the first complex-lighting studies I ever created

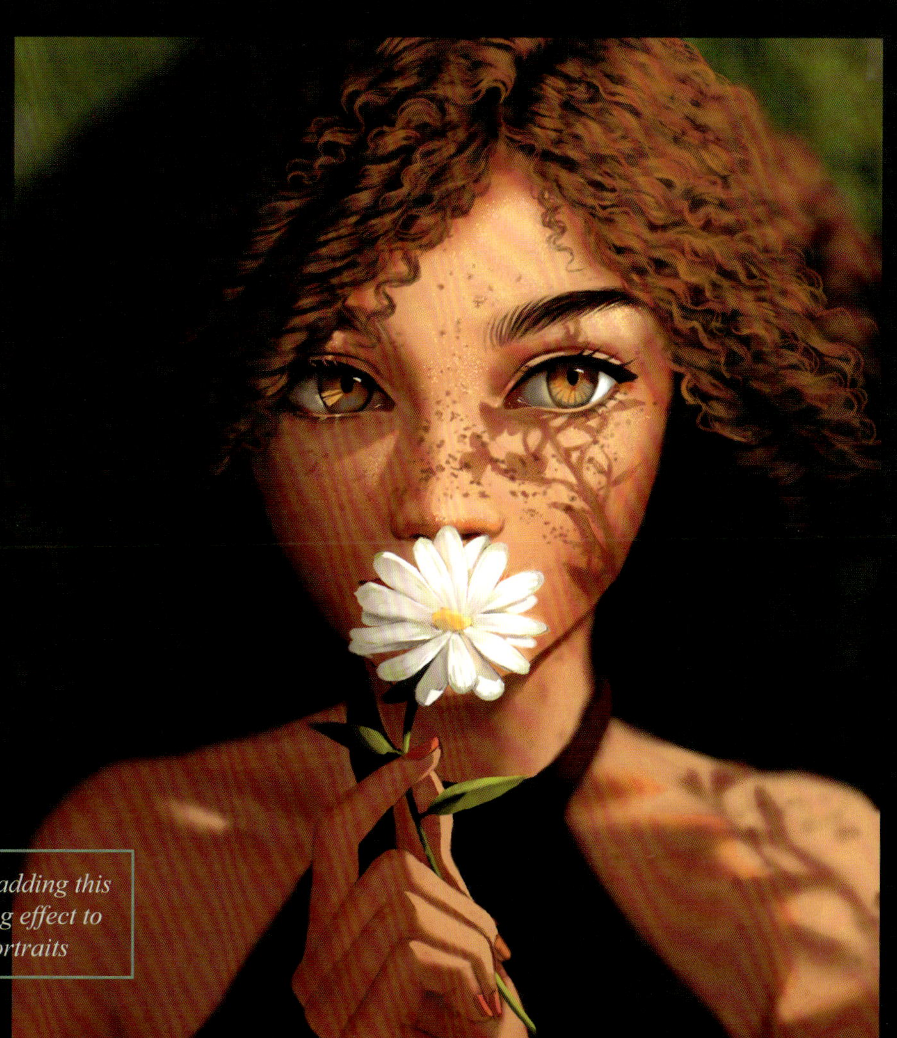

I really enjoy adding this foliage-lighting effect to many of my portraits

THE WORLD BELOW

I just adore underwater photography. It's so mesmerizing to watch how submerged hair and clothing create new and interesting organic forms. As part of my lighting studies, I've created multiple portraits of characters who are underwater. Through these images, I tried to convey a serene mood while capturing a frozen moment in time.

The movement and direction of the hair in this image adds a sense of weightlessness

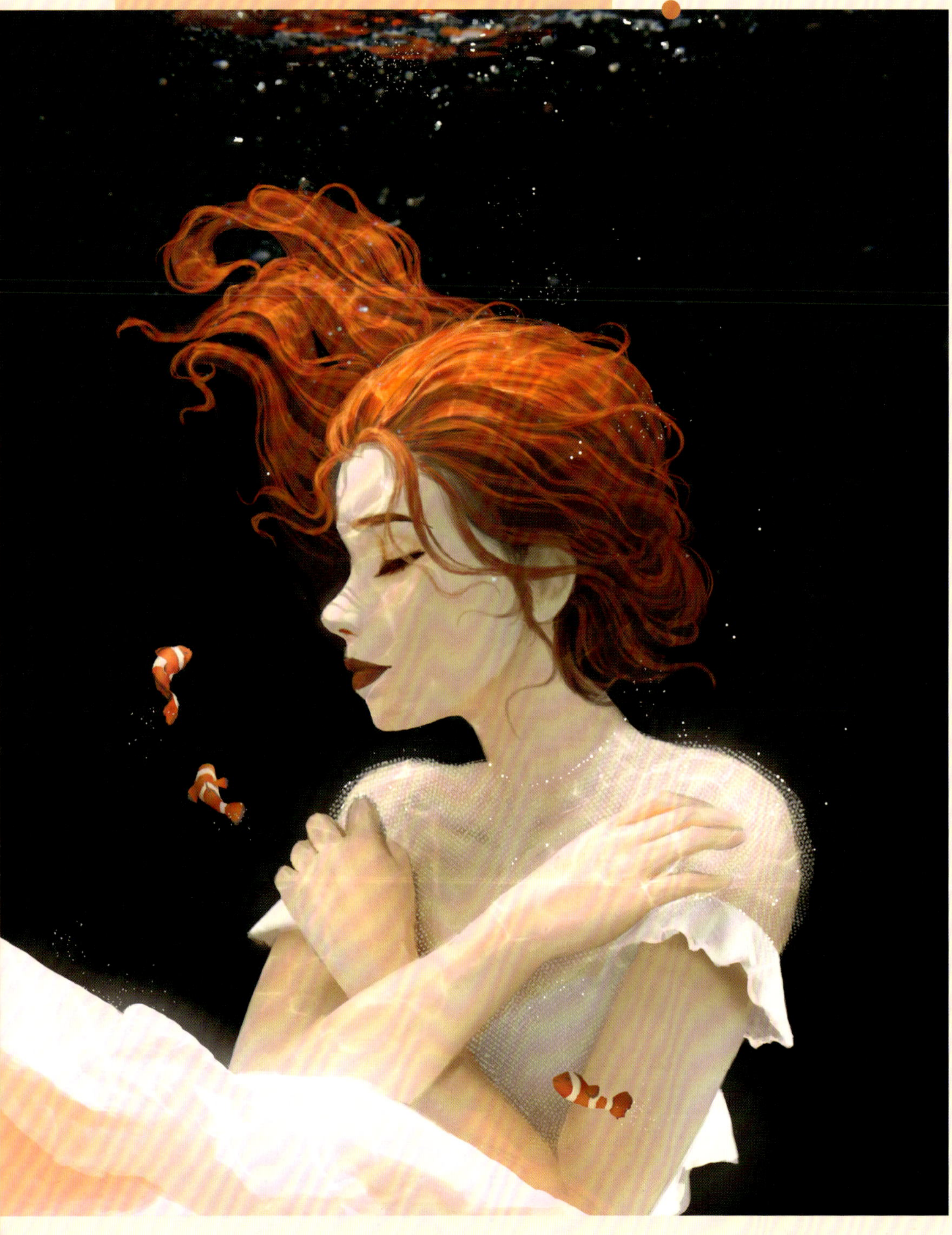

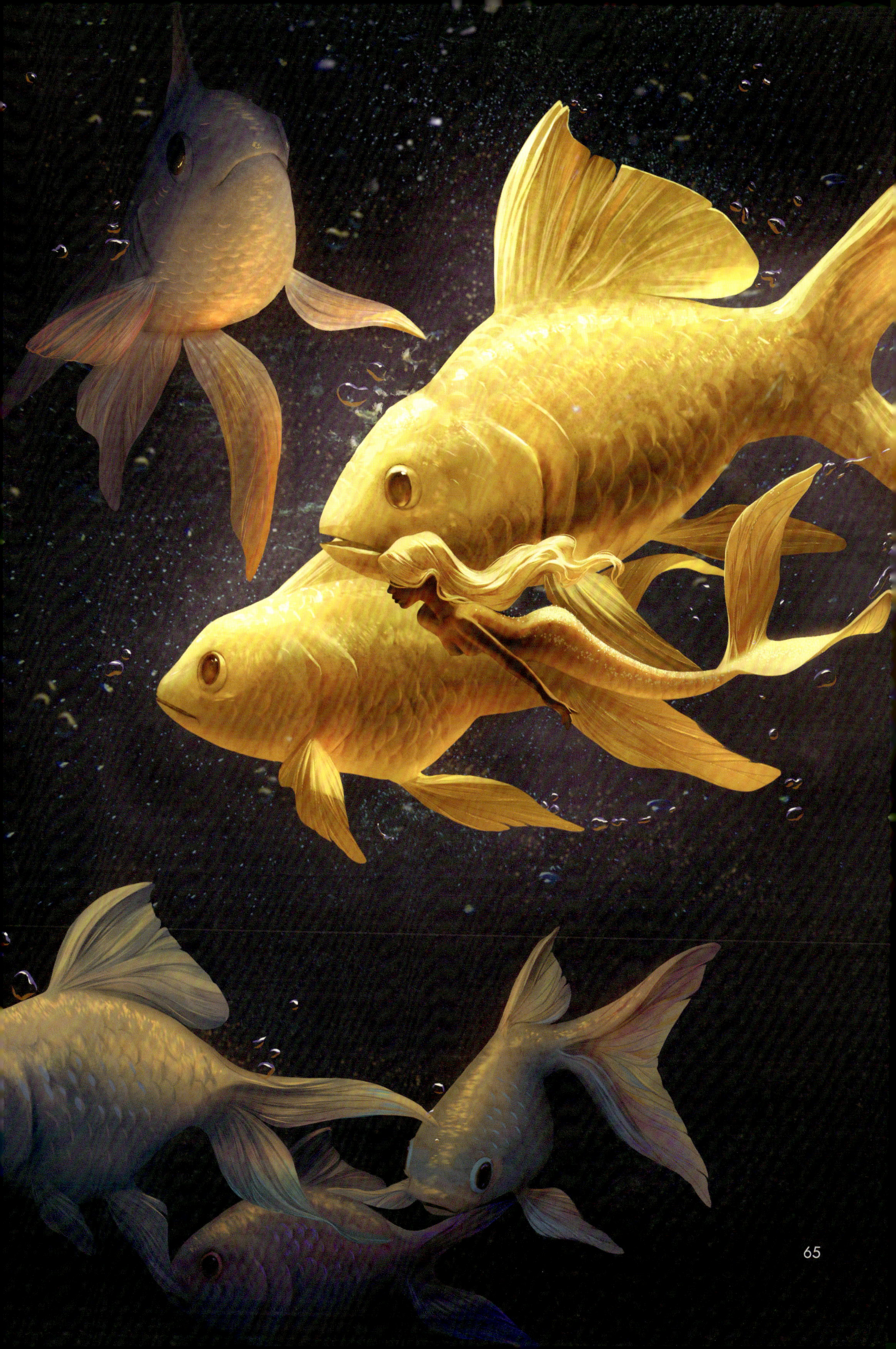

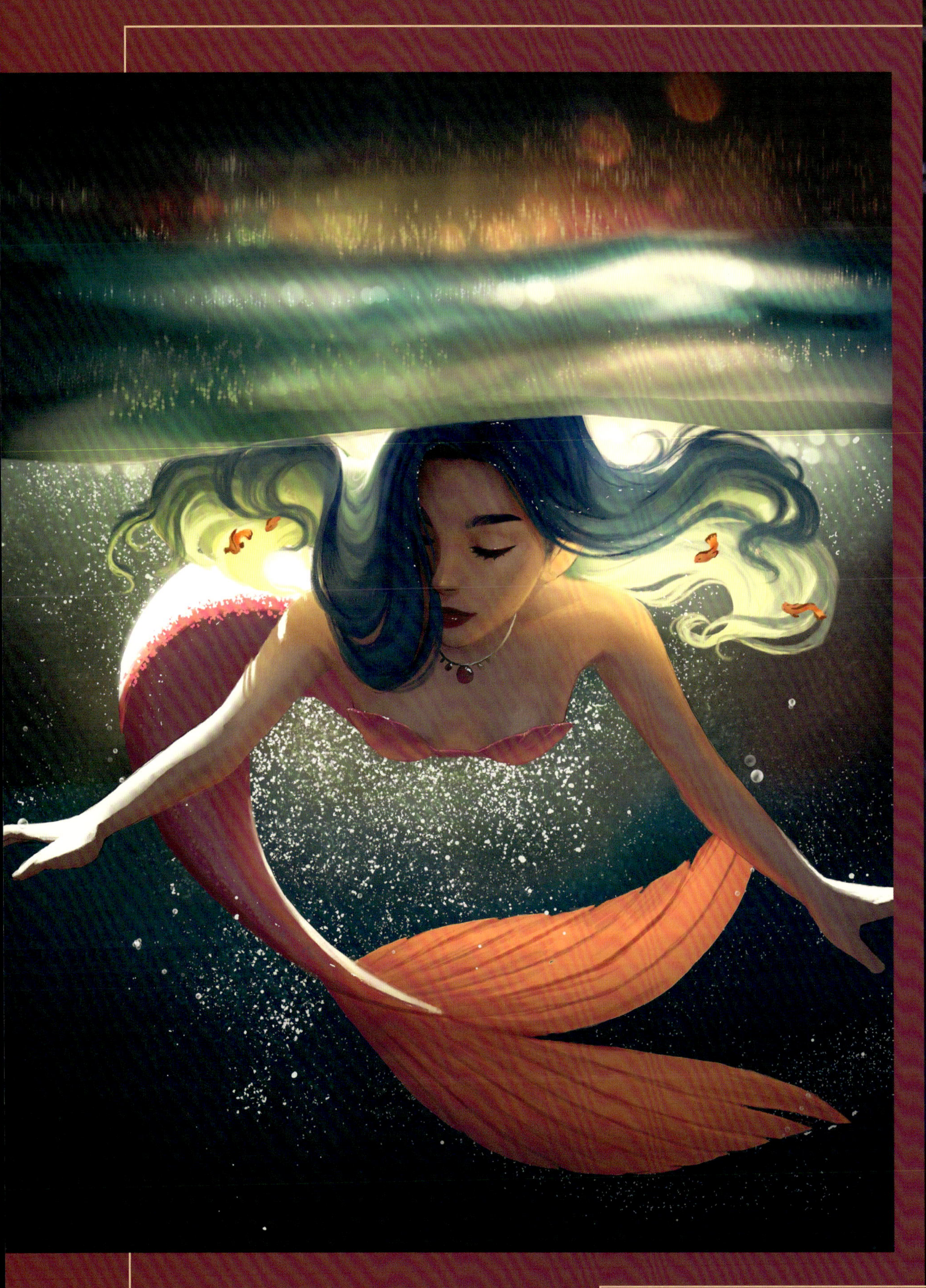

I've always been amazed by split underwater photography. I love studying the lighting patterns of waves that border the world above and below

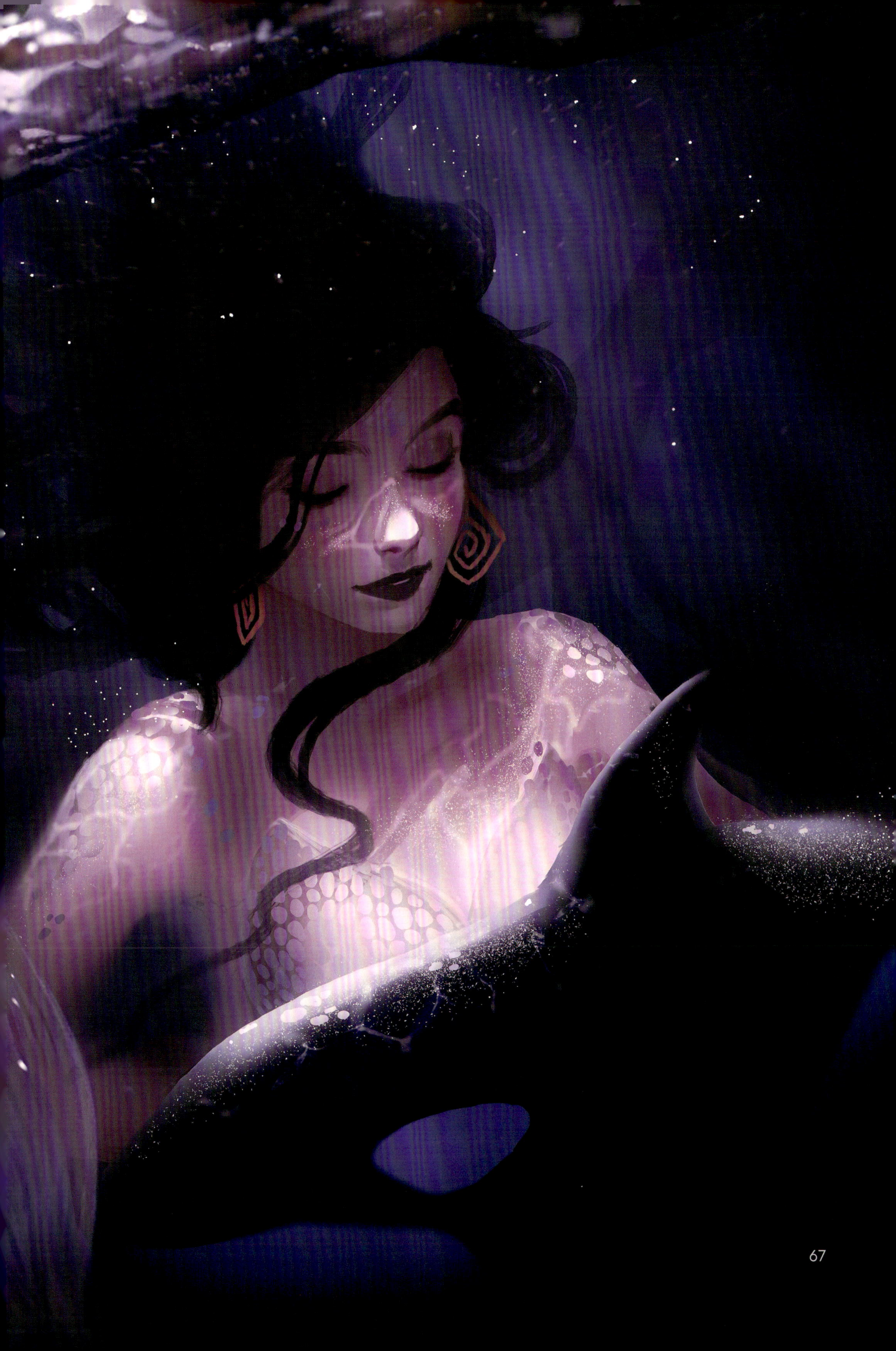

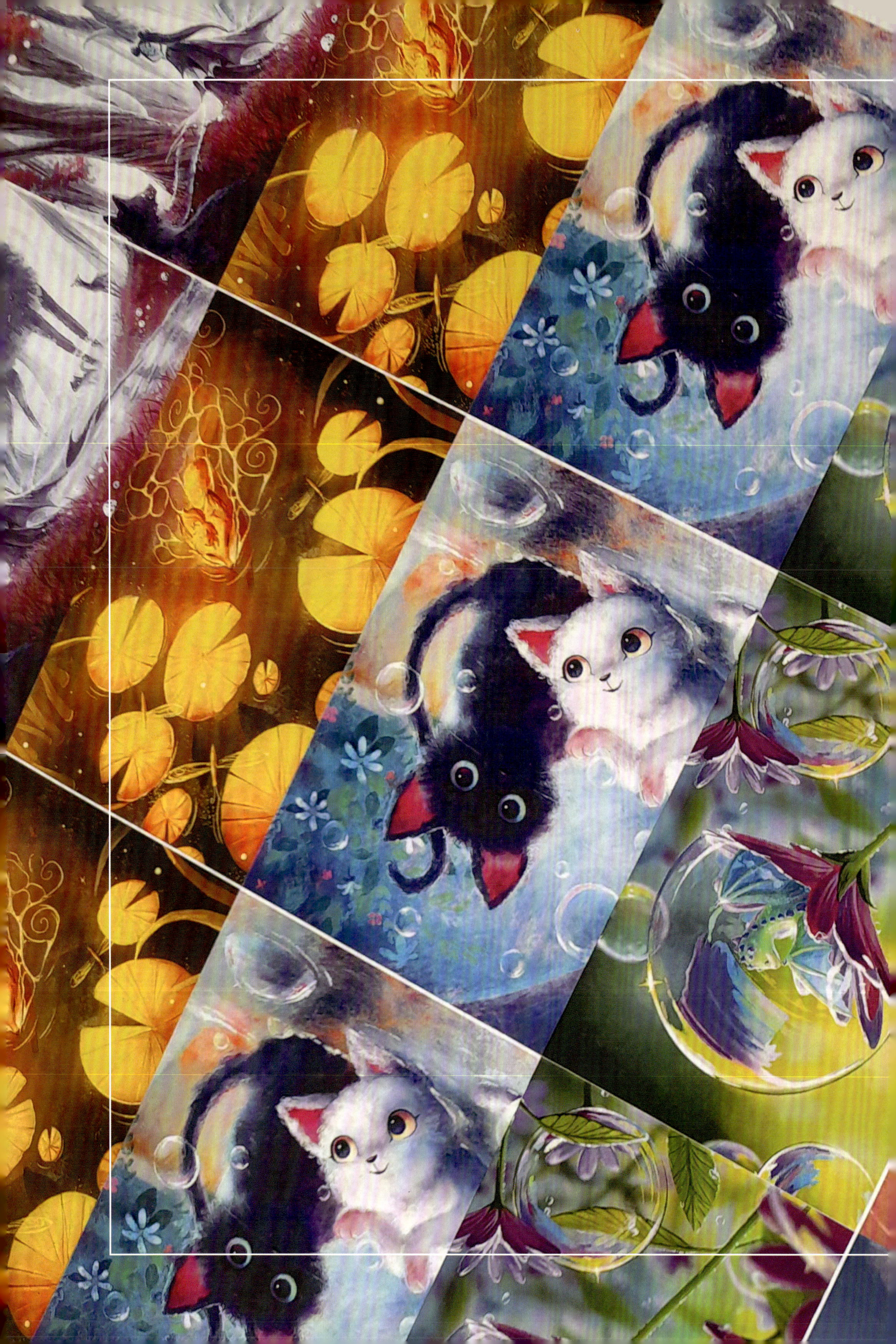

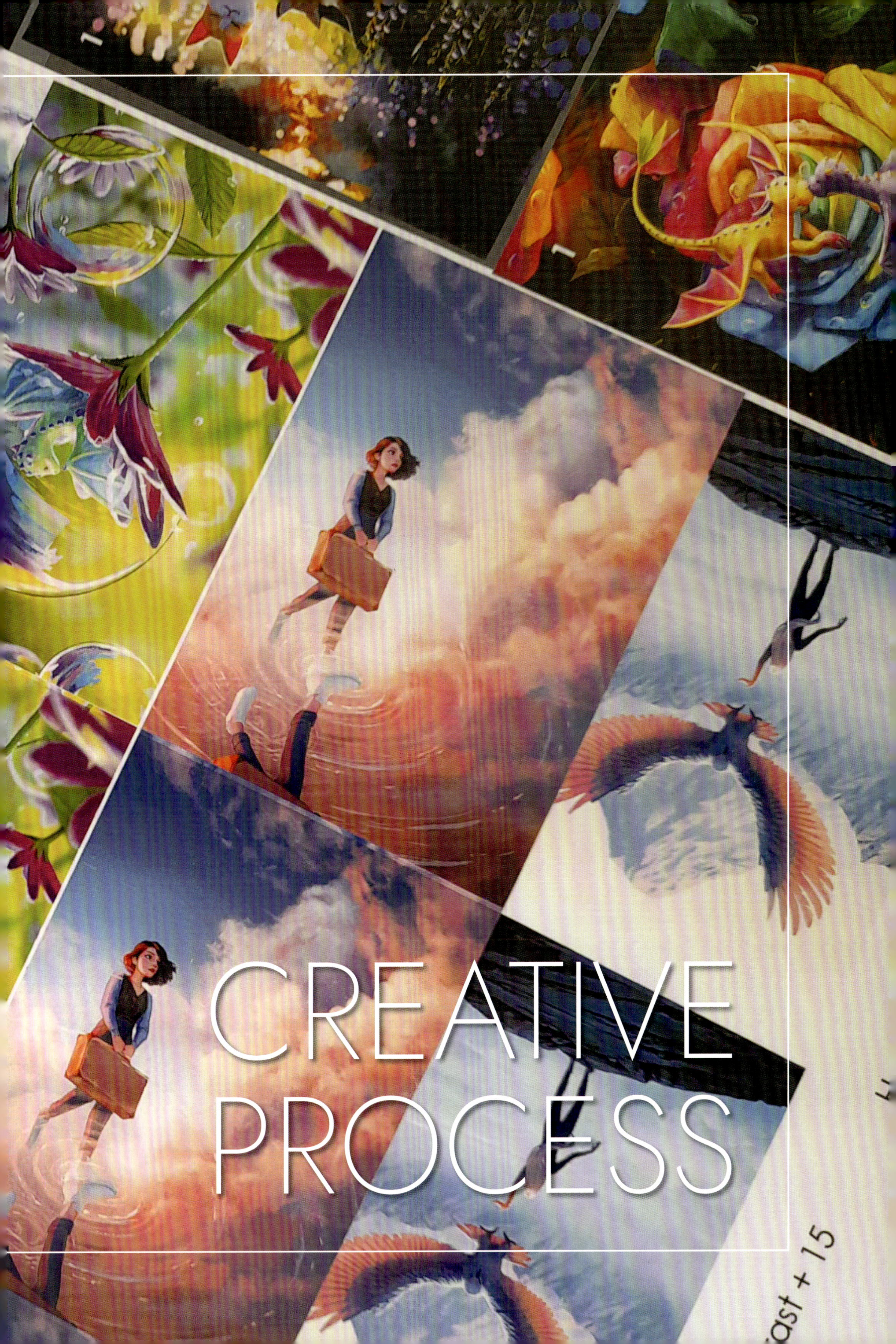

CREATIVE PROCESS

WORKSPACE

My workspace is always changing. Since enrolling in university, there's barely been a time where I've stayed in one fixed spot for more than a couple of weeks. I'm always on the go, both in my private life and for business-related reasons, and my workspace definitely reflects that. This is why it usually only consists of these five key elements:

1. My laptop (HP, running Windows 11)
2. My tablet (Huion Kamvas Pro 16)
3. An internet connection
4. My headphones
5. A simple table with whatever chair is at my disposal

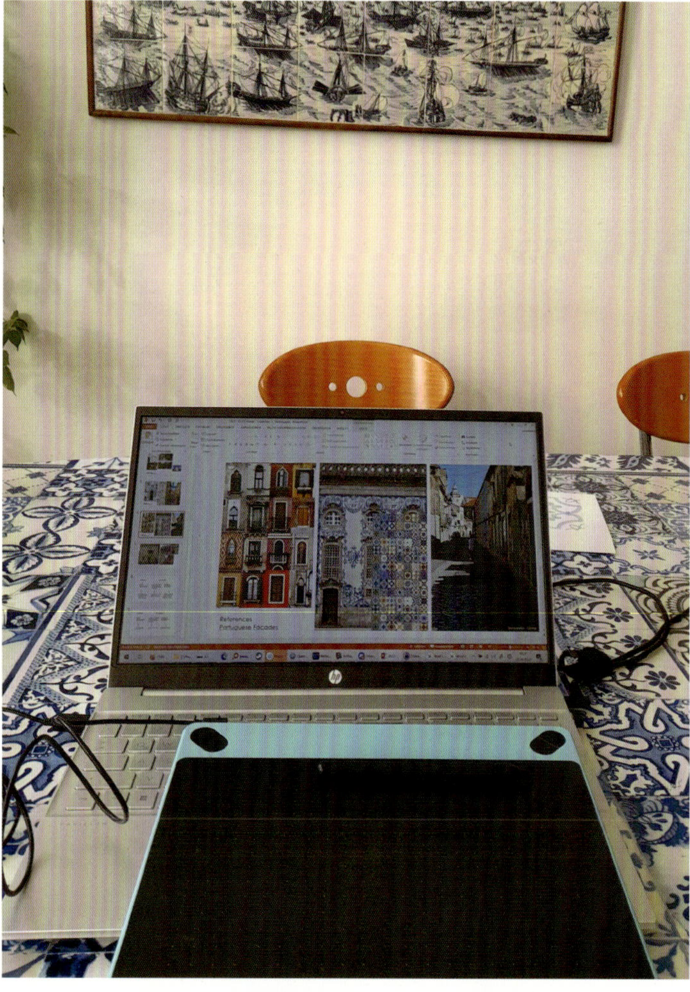

There tends to be no decorative items, artworks, or plants to accompany me on my long drawing sessions – just the essentials. My setup must be as simple as possible. Since I travel a lot, I need to be able to carry my entire workspace with me, and this is the reason why I prefer to work with smaller drawing tablets.

That all being said, I don't think my current workspace is ideal. It certainly works for me at the moment, but I hope that I'll eventually be able to find a permanent creative space to call my own. In that space, I would love to surround myself with art and books by other artists to create an environment that I find inspiring.

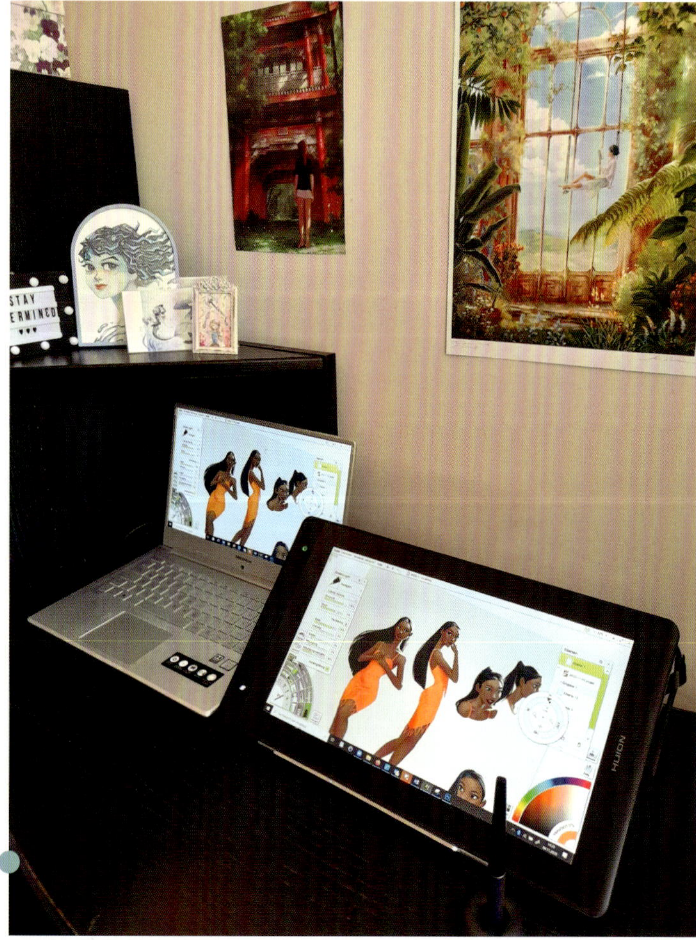

This little desk is one of my workspaces

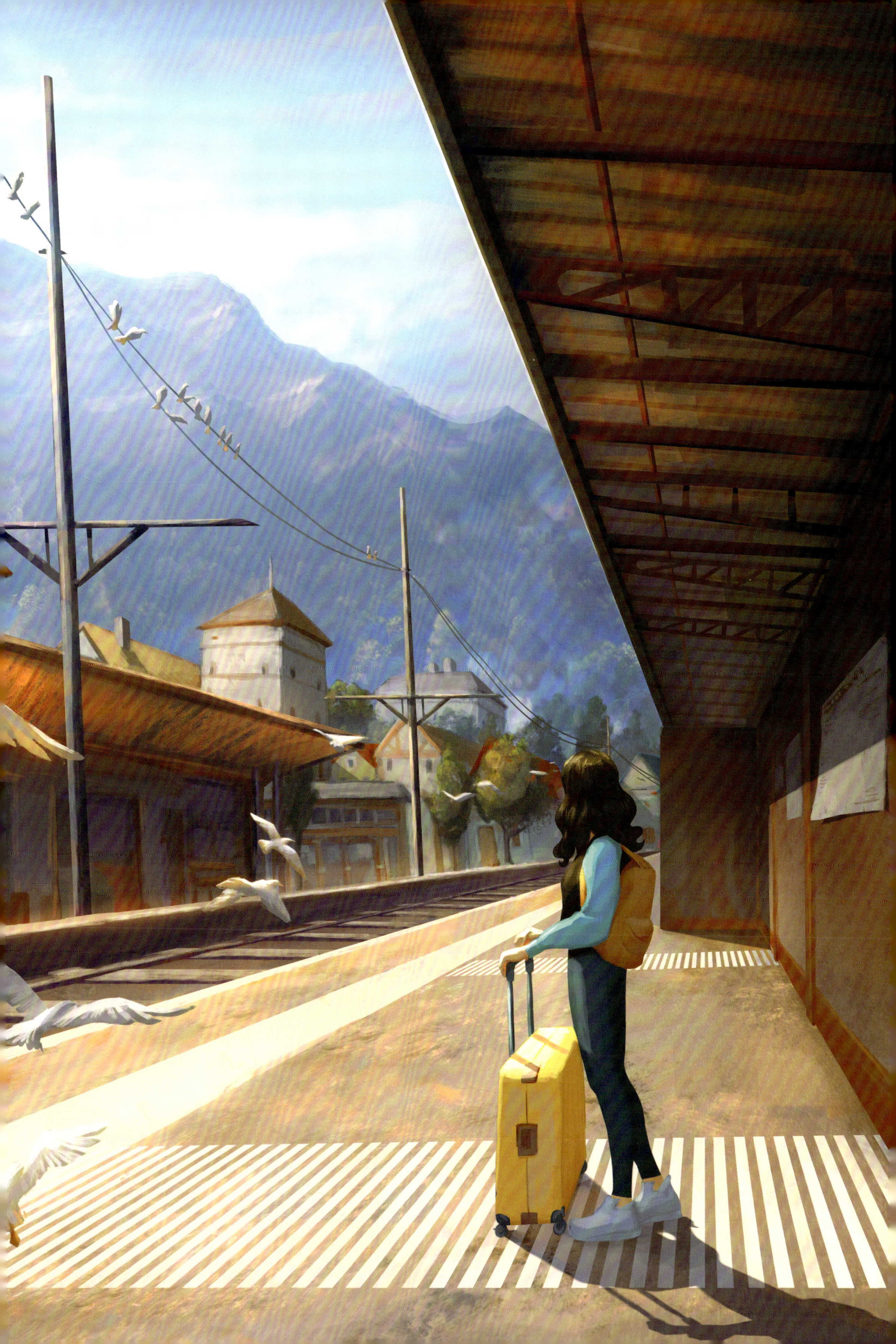

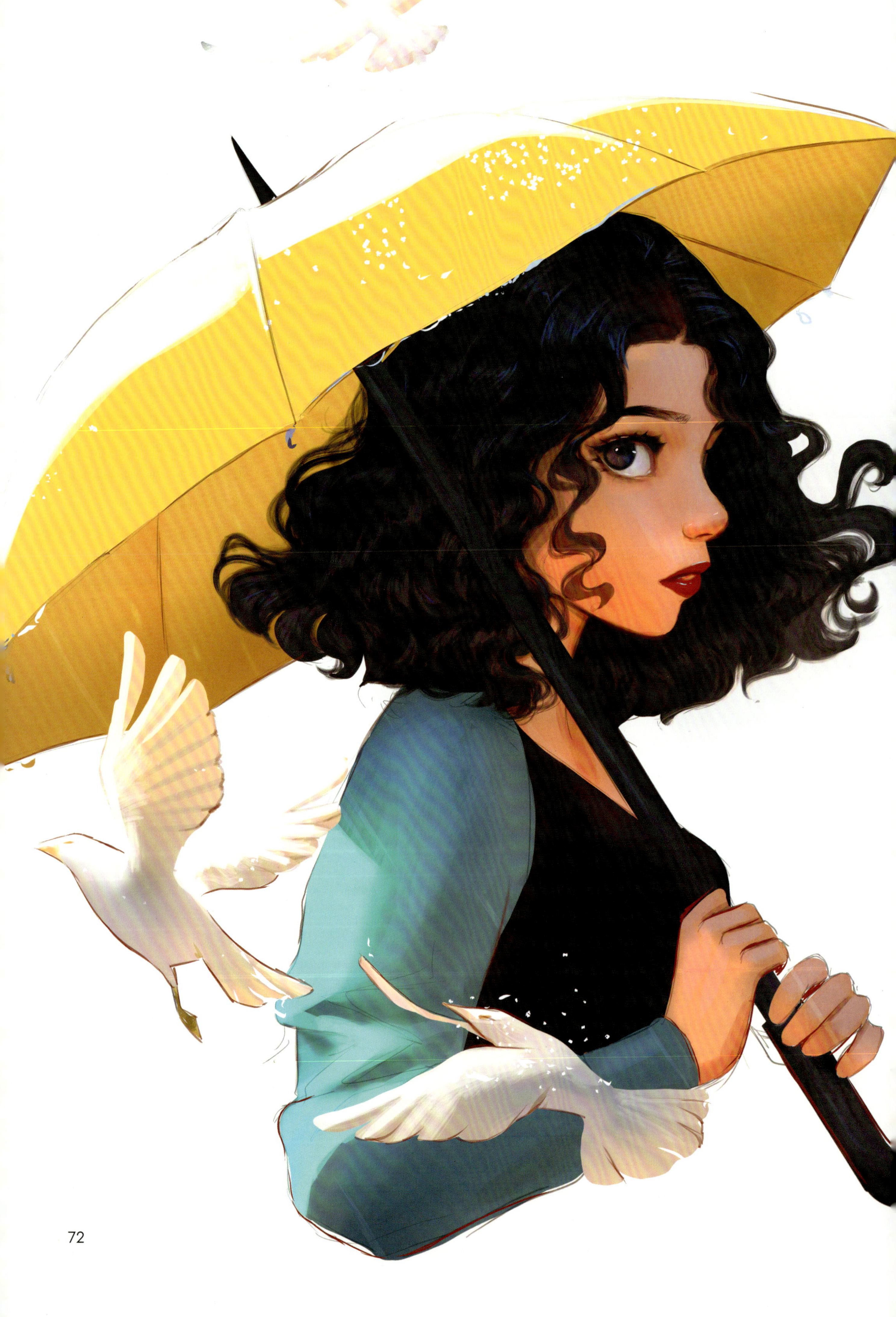

SOFTWARE

Ever since I was introduced to digital art at around ten or eleven years old, I've been using ArtRage and its various versions. Back in the day, I started with ArtRage 3, but I'm currently using the latest version for all my digital work.

ArtRage is a software that mimics traditional painting tools. When I first started using the program, I pretty much used all the brushes and tools that were available. Exploring the program and its possibilities aided me in developing my own personal workflow. I enjoy being able to paint freely without having to worry about technicalities concerning the program I use. This is why I still use ArtRage to this day.

As it's software that's intended for painting, there are no extensive colour-correction functions; the focus is purely on the available brushes and tools. However, I like enhancing the colours in my pieces, which is why I also love using Adobe Photoshop as part of my workflow. The colour-correction specifics I apply in Photoshop always depend on the piece, but there are certain settings that I often like to use to edit my illustrations. These include enhancing the darker tones by shifting them to a blue or purple hue and darkening them slightly. Likewise, I edit the lighter tones to make them warmer and slightly lighter, creating a nice contrast between the cool darker areas and the warm lighter areas using the Colour Balance setting.

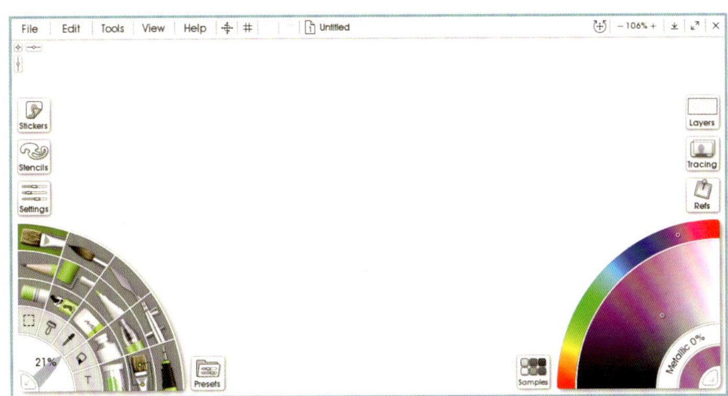

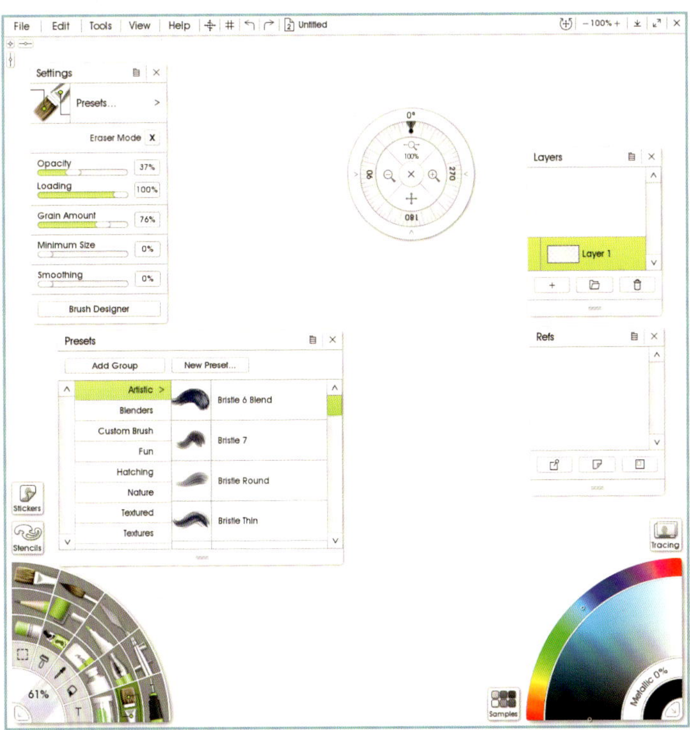

ALTERNATIVES

I'm always open to trying out other tools and workspaces. I have had the opportunity to work with Clip Studio Paint in the past, as well as tablets from different companies, such as XP-Pen, Huion, and Wacom. I don't find myself leaning towards certain brands as they all offer different products for different needs. As long as I have some time to prepare and familiarize myself with them, I can work with pretty much any program or tablet at my disposal.

MUSIC

My workspace would be incomplete without a pair of headphones and an inspiring playlist. I simply can't imagine working without music. Not only is it a way for me to maintain concentration, but it's also very inspirational. Listening to a certain song sometimes sparks an idea in me and I'll create artwork that reflects the song's mood. On the other hand, if I already have an idea in mind, I'll search for music that fits the atmosphere of the piece I want to create. This helps me immerse into my artworks. It also makes my drawing process incredibly meditative and fun!

BRUSHES

I don't find myself regularly using all of the brushes in ArtRage. There are some that fit more with my workflow and art style than others, and I like being experimental when trying different brushes and techniques. However, there are certain sets of brushes and settings that I default to.

Ink Pen & Pencil

These tools are great for sketching! While the Pencil tool shows the present texture of the paper/canvas, the Ink Pen tool is a smooth brush that can also be used to block areas without any texture. For sketching, I use the Ink Pen more often than the Pencil, but I enjoy using them both equally.

Oil Brush

I often use this brush when it comes to painting plants and portraits. Like the title suggests, this tool mimics the behaviour of oil paint. The oil paint's dryness level can greatly alter the look of the painting. Wet Oil brushstrokes will mix with each other to create new and interesting colours if the strokes are on the same layer, but I like to use the Dry Oil brush more in order to have more control.

Airbrush

This brush is simple and soft, which is ideal for adding glowiness. I use it when I need to add soft lighting to backgrounds, such as a bokeh effect.

Paint roller

This one is ideal for filling in large areas with a general colour. It also mixes colours well and adds in richer tones.

Glitter Tube

The Glitter Tube comes with various head options. I regularly use the Grit option to add a little texture and sparkly effects to my illustrations.

Custom Brush

As the name suggests, the Custom Brush tool can be used to create new brushes. There are settings in the Brush Designer that are exclusive to this tool and allow me to tweak the dab spacing, texture, size, direction, and so much more. These brushes can also be inverted and used as an eraser.

Regular brushes (found on the left side of the interface)

Ink pen

Pencil

Oil brush

Airbrush (soft)

Airbrush (hard)

Paint roller

Glitter tube

There are dozens of different custom brushes available, but the ones I mainly use are:

Custom Brush presets
(each of these are organized in their respective groups)

BRISTLE THIN

I use this brush when adding textured strands to my characters' hair.

BRISTLE 6 BLEND & BRISTLE WORN

These two brushes have a rough, almost rocky texture, and are ideal for adding texture to background elements such as tree trunks, buildings, and mountains.

SQUARE CANVAS (1–5)

I like to use a mix of these for blocking colours and textures. They are all slightly different but they mix nicely with each other and can be used to add variation to base colours for buildings and other background elements.

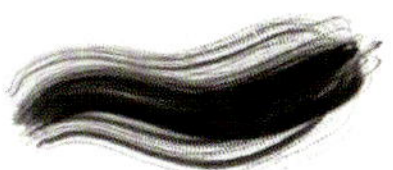

Bristle Thin

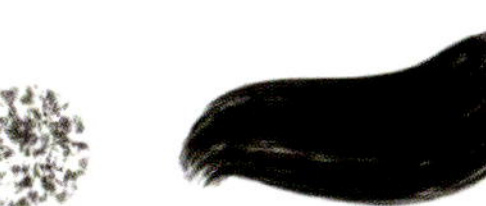

Bristle 6 Blend

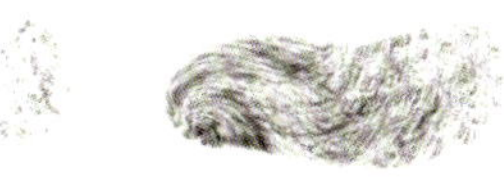

Bristle Worn

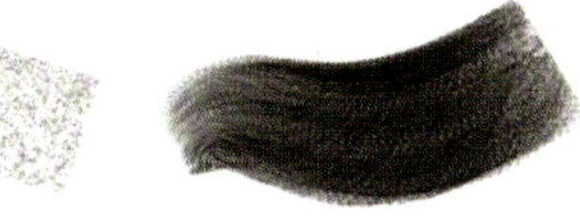

Square 6

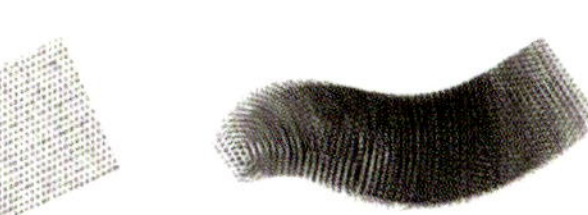

Square Canvas 1

Square Canvas 4

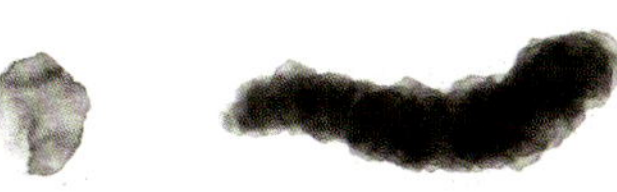

Watery 1

Watery 2

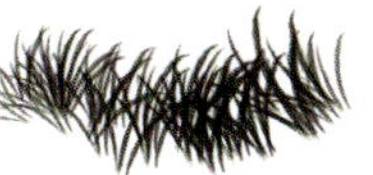

Fur Grass 5

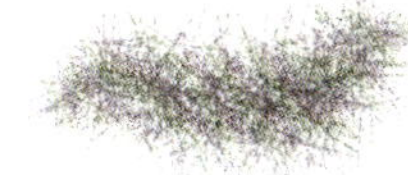

Faint Crackle

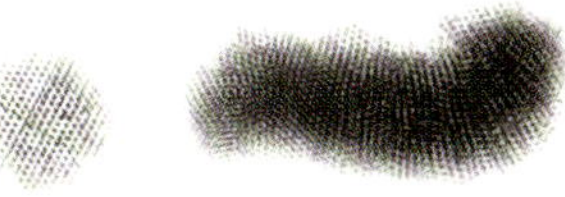

Round Canvas

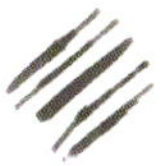

Lines V2

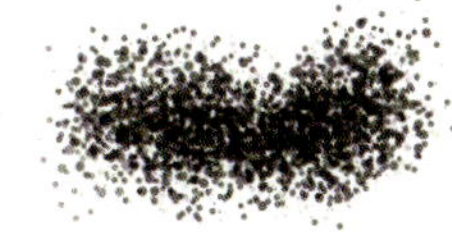

Dots

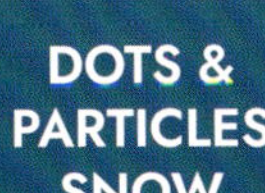

Particles Snow

Particles Snow 2

FUR GRASS 5

This brush is nice for adding basic textures to meadows.

FAINT CRACKLE

While I don't find myself using this brush often, I love using it to create icy textures in some of my colder illustrations.

ROUND CANVAS & LINES V2

I like to use a mix of these to add a rough texture to clothing.

DOTS & PARTICLES SNOW

Mixing these with Glitter Tube can add some interesting texture and freckles to the skin.

WATERY (1–5)

As the name suggests, these brushes have a soft, clear texture. I use them for painting clouds, watery textures, and smoky effects.

PREPARING & PRINTING

A big part of my work as a freelance artist is printing and selling my illustrations at conventions or in my online shop. Seeing my art displayed in someone's home makes me feel so fulfilled! Over the years, I've gathered many positive and negative experiences with printing companies, but I ultimately decided to buy a printer to print my work at home. Having complete quality control without the need to wait for proofs is what made me invest.

I currently use the Epson ET-8550 A3+ printer and Canon Premium Matte Photo paper. The combination of the six Epson inks and the fine paper quality results in beautifully warm, saturated colours – perfect for my art! I print my artworks through the print settings in Photoshop. Since I was so used to seeing my illustrations glow on the backlit screen of my laptop, I found that my artwork didn't have the same pop of colour when printed on paper. Of course, this is to be expected, so when I bought my printer, I spent a lot of time and money completing various test pages with different types of paper. After much trial and error, and testing multiple matte and glossy options, I discovered that my printer (when combined with the Canon paper) was the best option for me.

Since there is always a bit of colour tweaking involved when it comes to printing, I like to create a few small thumbnails with different colour settings on the test page. It's important to directly compare the printed results. It took many tests to get to the printing settings I use now, but it was definitely worth it!

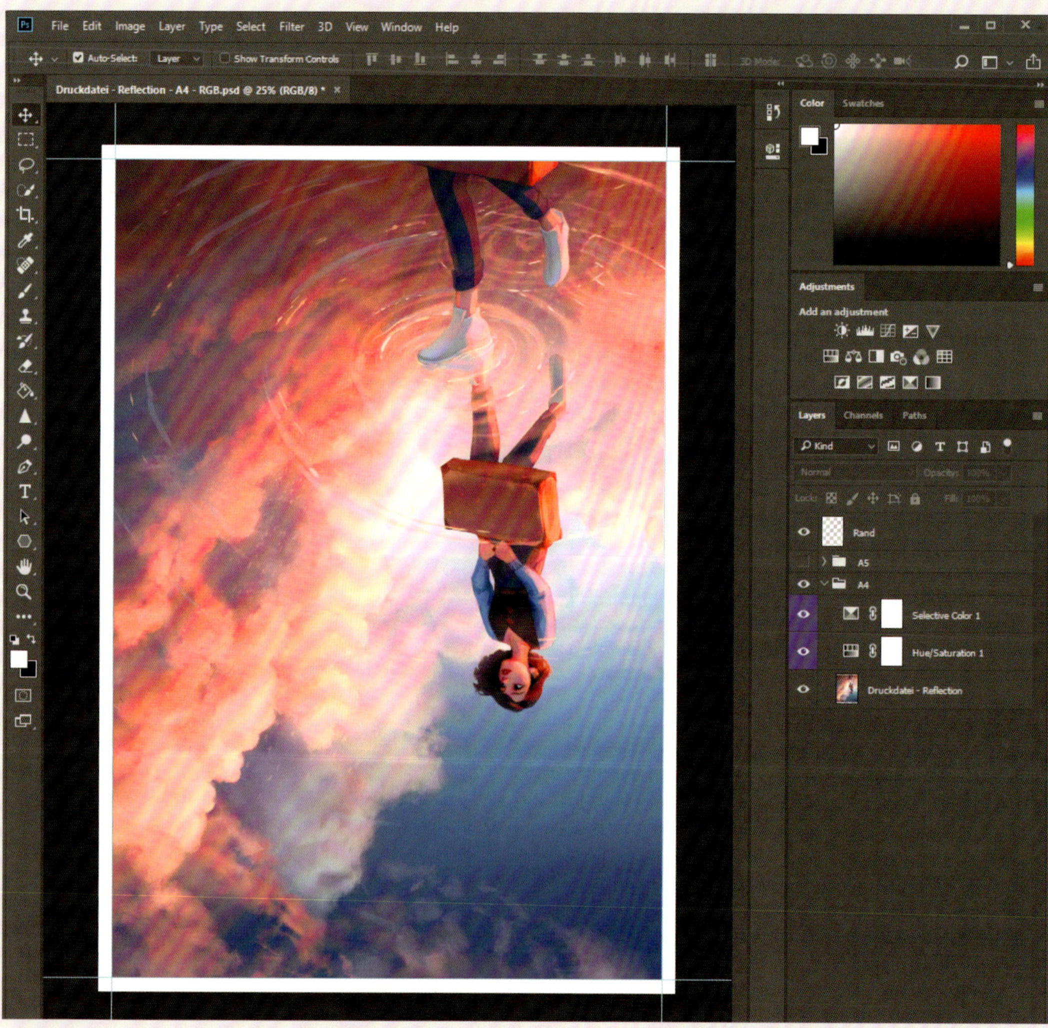

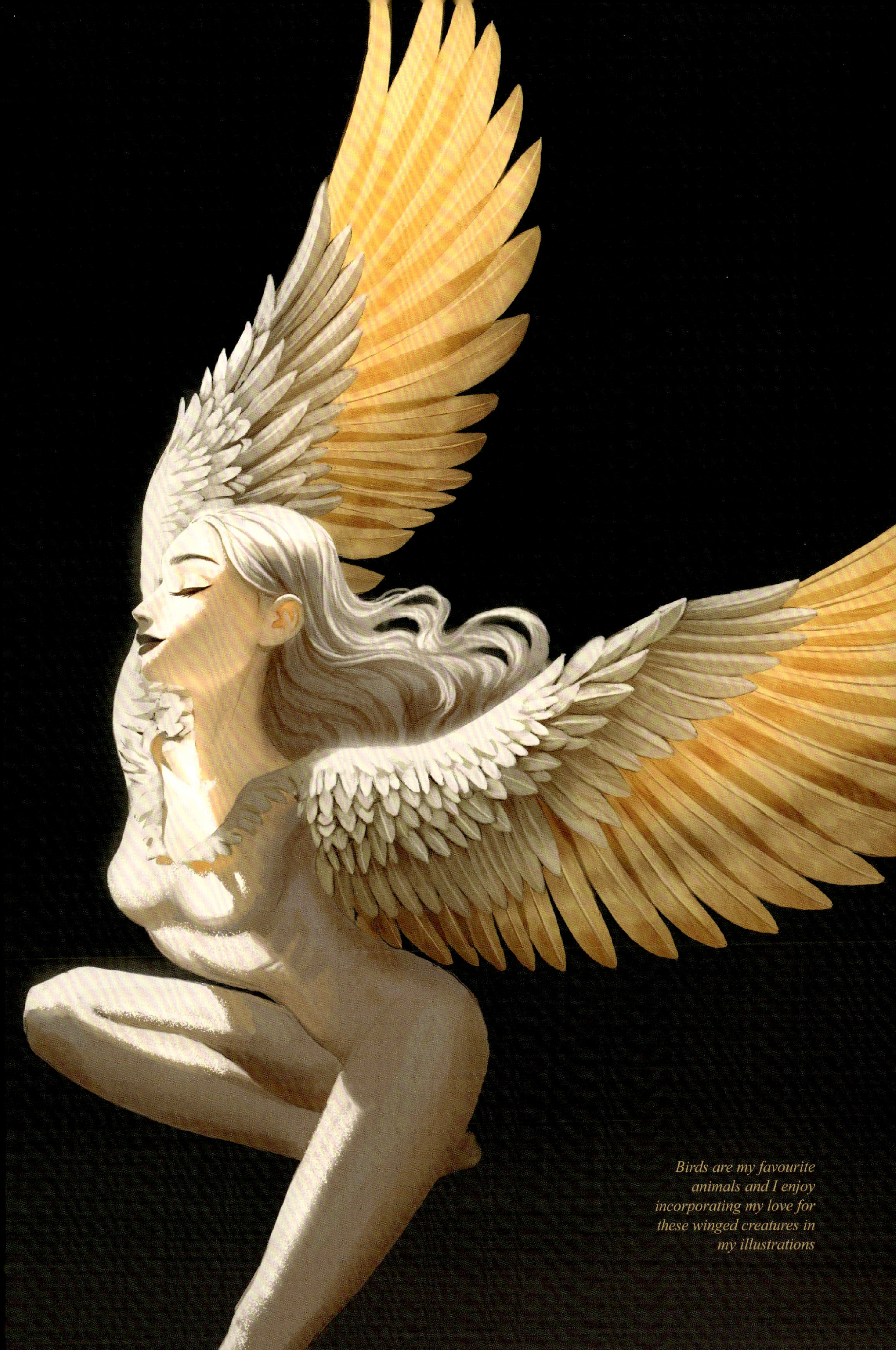

Birds are my favourite animals and I enjoy incorporating my love for these winged creatures in my illustrations

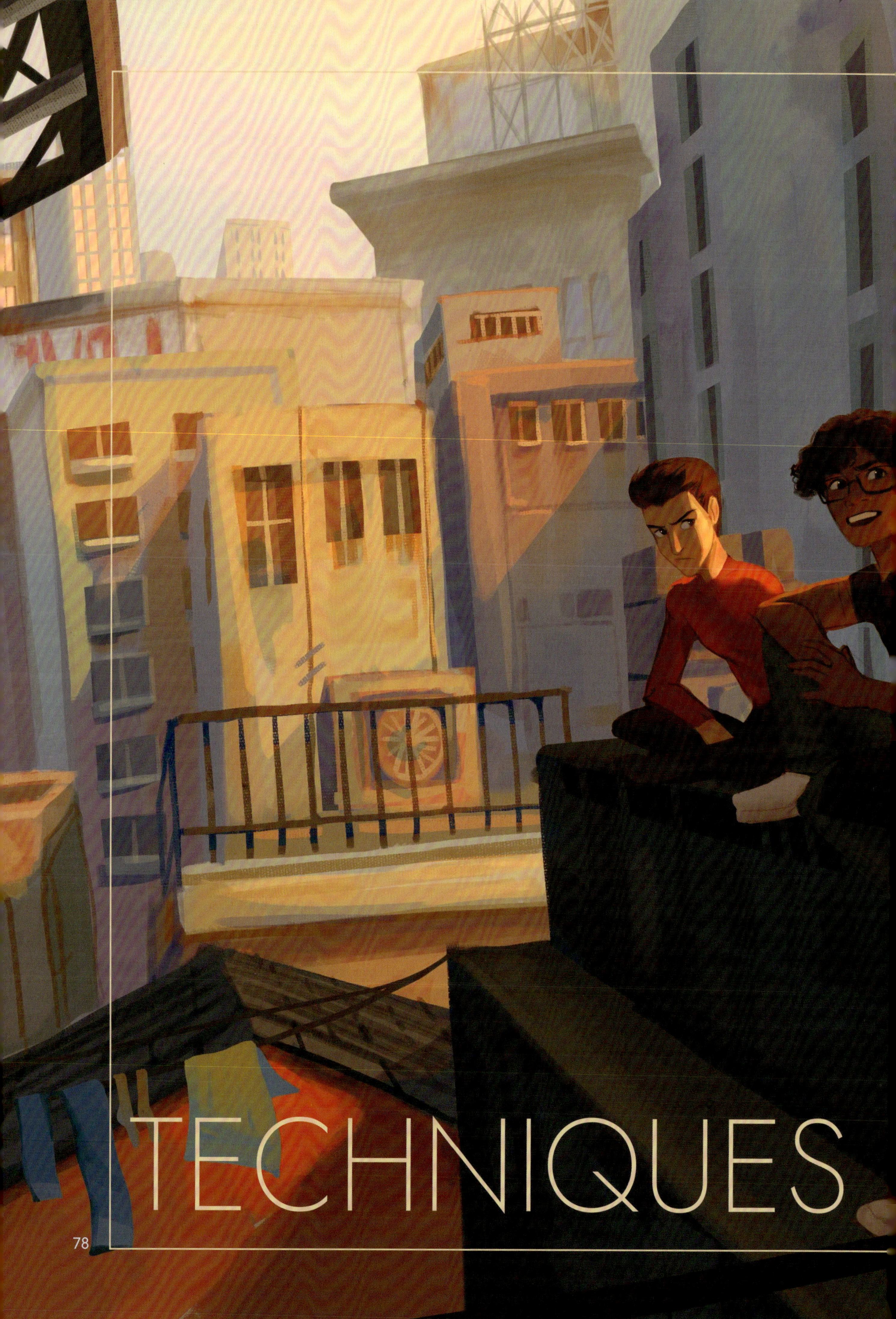

TECHNIQUES

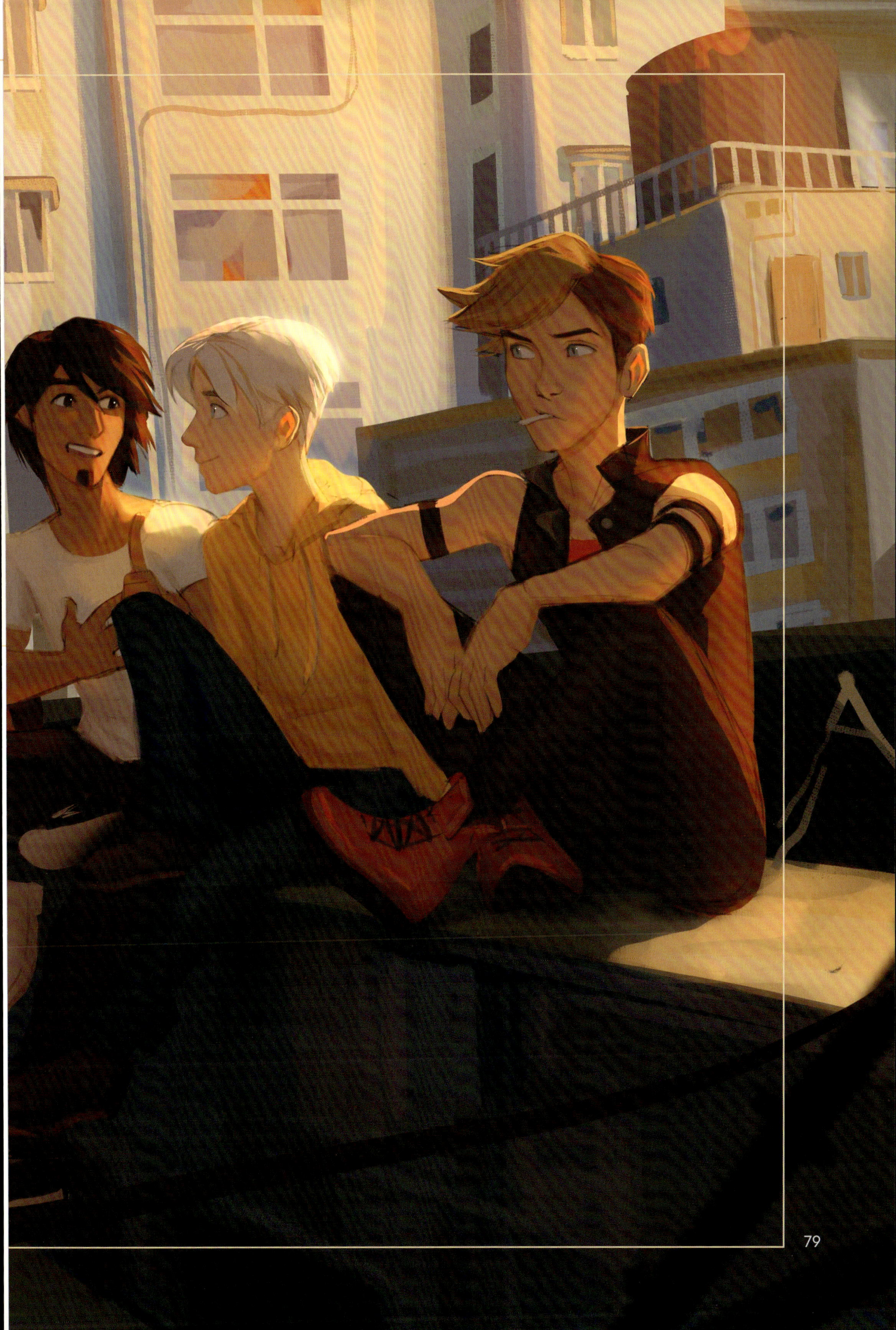

Striking lighting

Good lighting can turn any portrait into an eye-catcher! I like to use a mix of Soft Light and Overlay blend modes in order to achieve an appealing look. The colours and brushes I use always depend on the look and intensity of the lighting scenario I'm aiming for.

It's a great idea to gather some reference images with interesting lighting patterns. A brilliant way to learn from them is by applying the same lighting scenarios to a basic portrait. This exercise allows me to refine my technique and explore the possibilities of other blend modes.

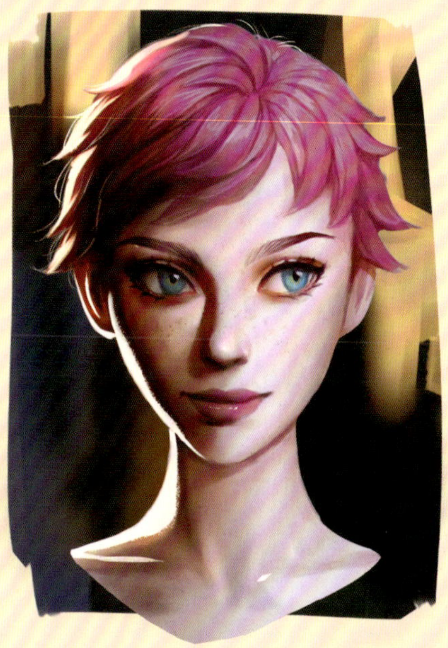

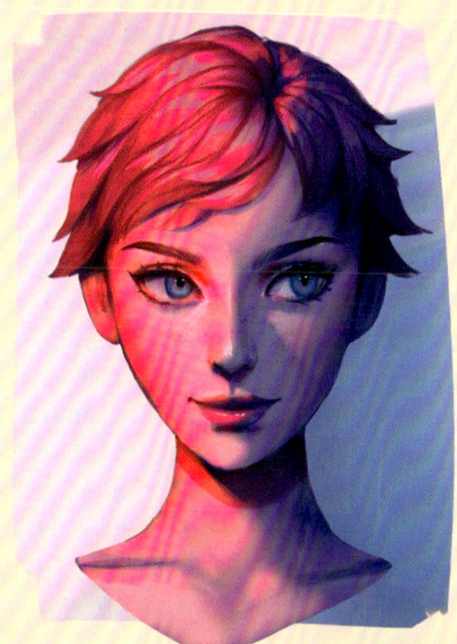

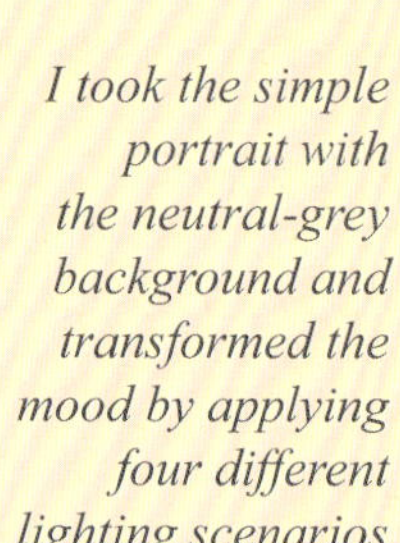

I took the simple portrait with the neutral-grey background and transformed the mood by applying four different lighting scenarios

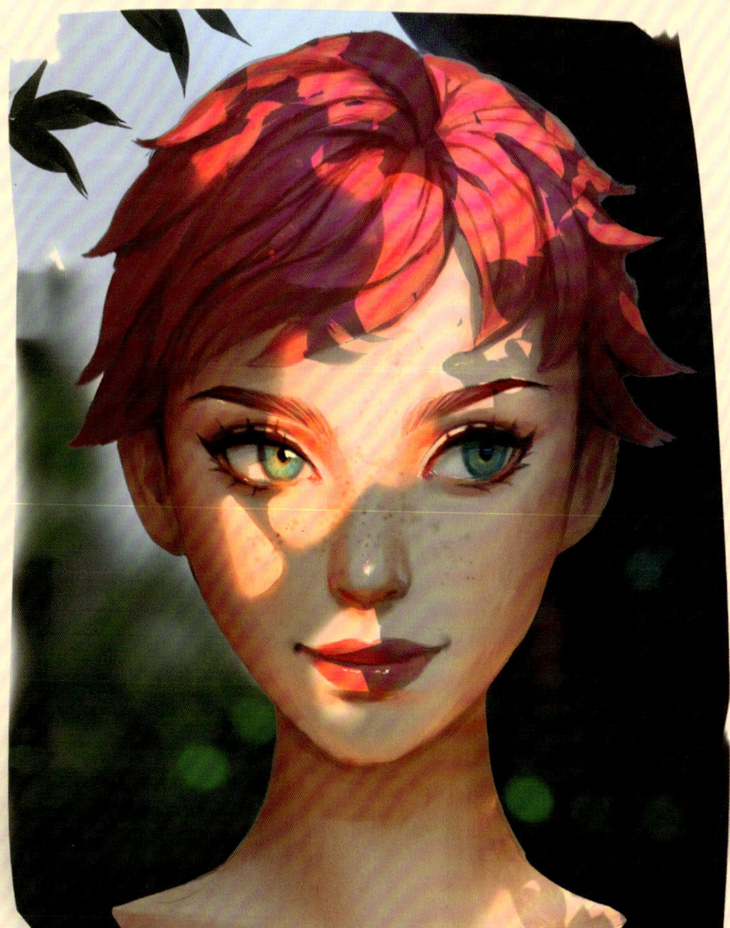

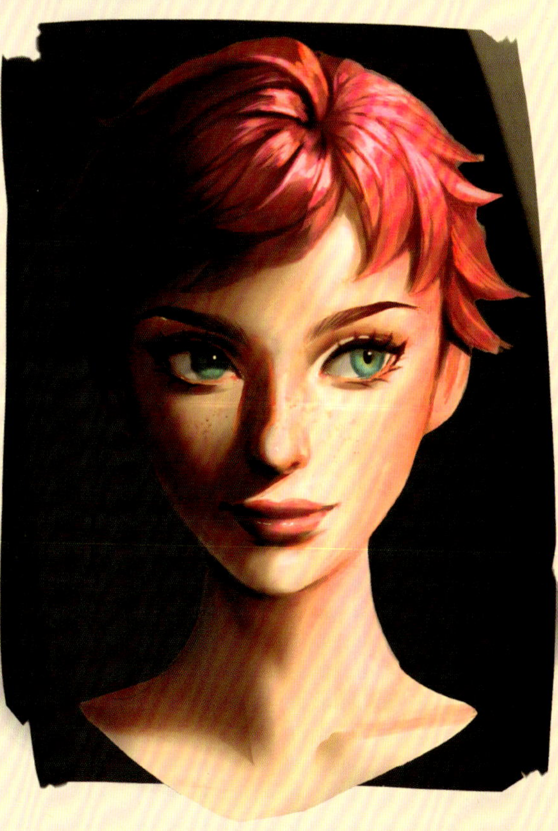

Detailing: skin texture & hair strands

This part is the most fun for me! Adding small details to a face can really elevate a portrait and make it feel alive. I particularly love adding details to skin and hair.

I like to add single strands along the edges of the hair, giving it more dimension. The Bristle Thin custom brush in ArtRage is great for this, since it has a nice hair-like texture to it. I also enjoy adding single hair strands with the Oil brush.

When it comes to skin details, I like using the Glitter Tube brush and Dots or Snow Particles custom brushes. I love applying a sparkly texture along the edges of brightly lit skin with Glitter Tube in particular. Adding this gives the impression that fine, light hairs are illuminated by sunlight. It's small details like these that really draw me in!

Since this portrait is zoomed in quite close, I decided to add a lot of skin and hair details

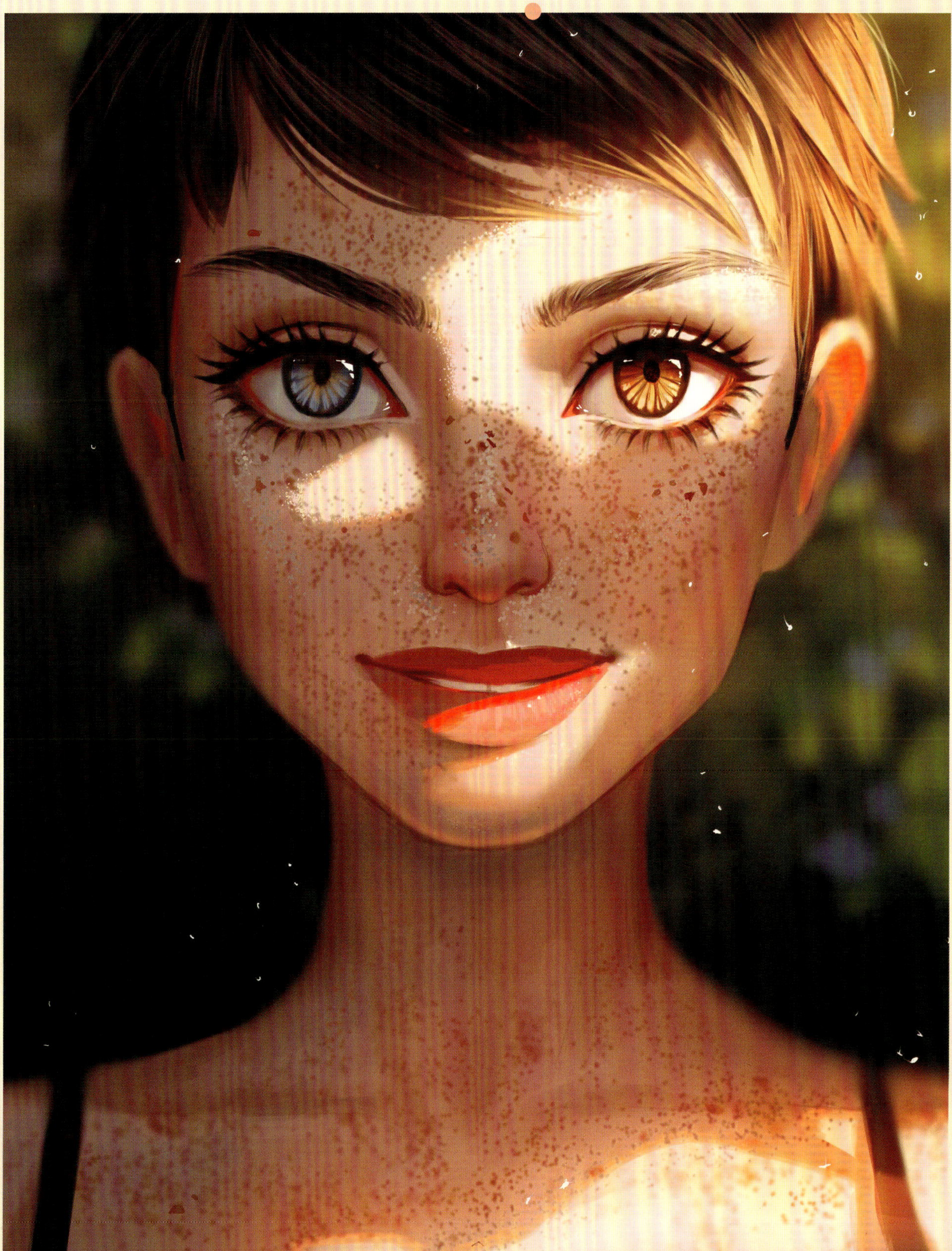

Storytelling: Creating cinematic illustrations

Telling stories is a fundamental part of human nature. Whether we reminisce about the past, tell a joke, or simply explain how our day went, humans are storytellers by default. Mastering visual storytelling is no easy task though. There are so many elements that carry weight and importance, from composition to colour to contrast. All of these elements of design are incredibly significant. When combined effectively, they can create some powerful stories.

I wouldn't call myself a visual storytelling master – I still have so much more to learn! But I recently started improving my skills by creating various illustrations for my original story called *The Yellow Umbrella*. In short, it's about two childhood friends reconnecting years after they last saw each other, crossing paths again one rainy day. With this story, I wanted to evoke a strong sense of nostalgia and atmosphere.

Since I love to create atmospheric pieces, I took the characters from this story and created various cinematic illustrations that featured them. Throughout the painting process, I have learned some helpful techniques that I would love to share with you. Most of them came naturally to me as I was painting the scenes and exploring methods on how to improve. I also enhanced my knowledge by watching helpful tutorials and time-lapse videos of other artists' creative processes.

This is one of the first illustrations I made of my original characters. I really wanted to capture their mixed emotions, so I focused on their body language and expressions

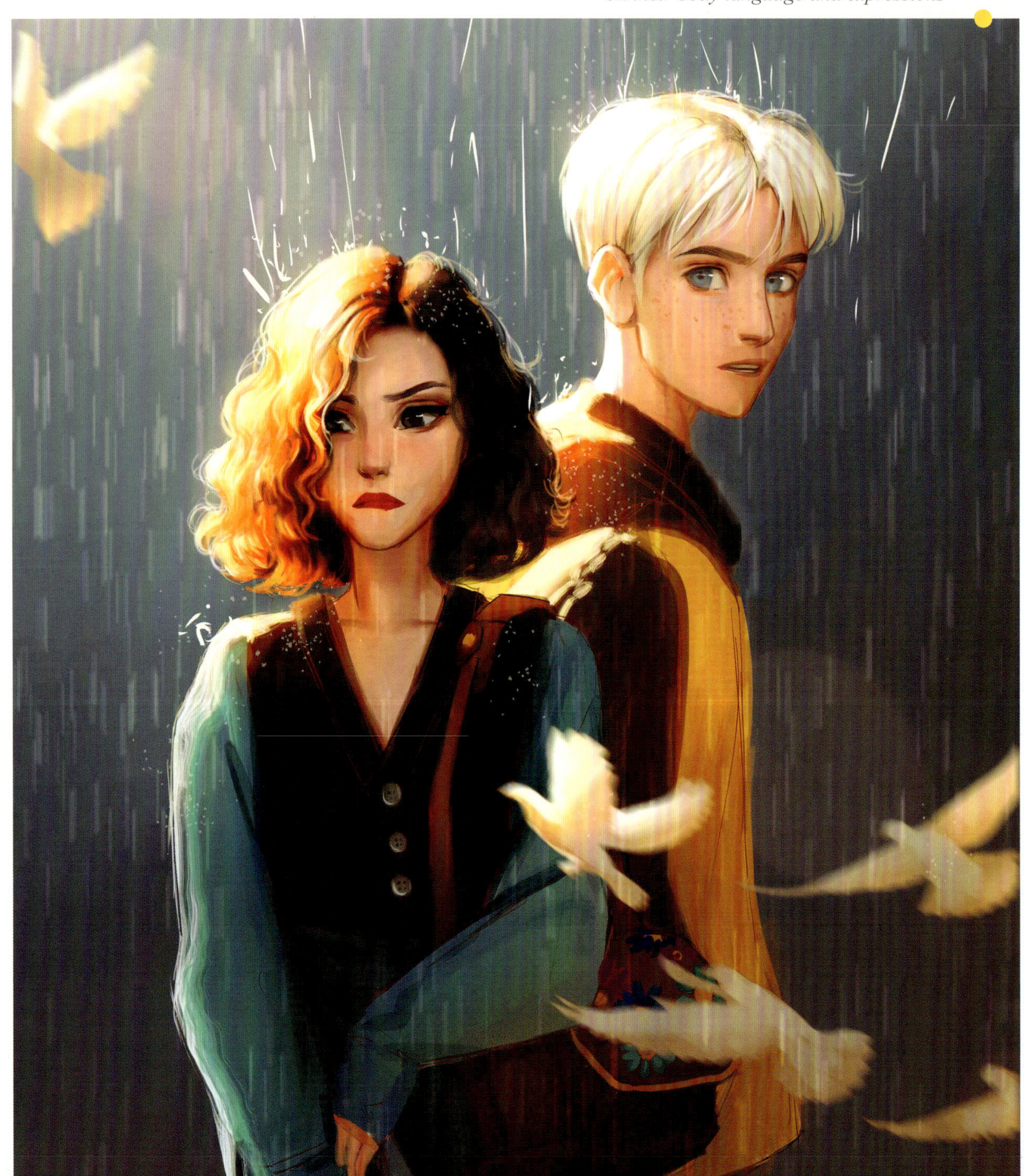

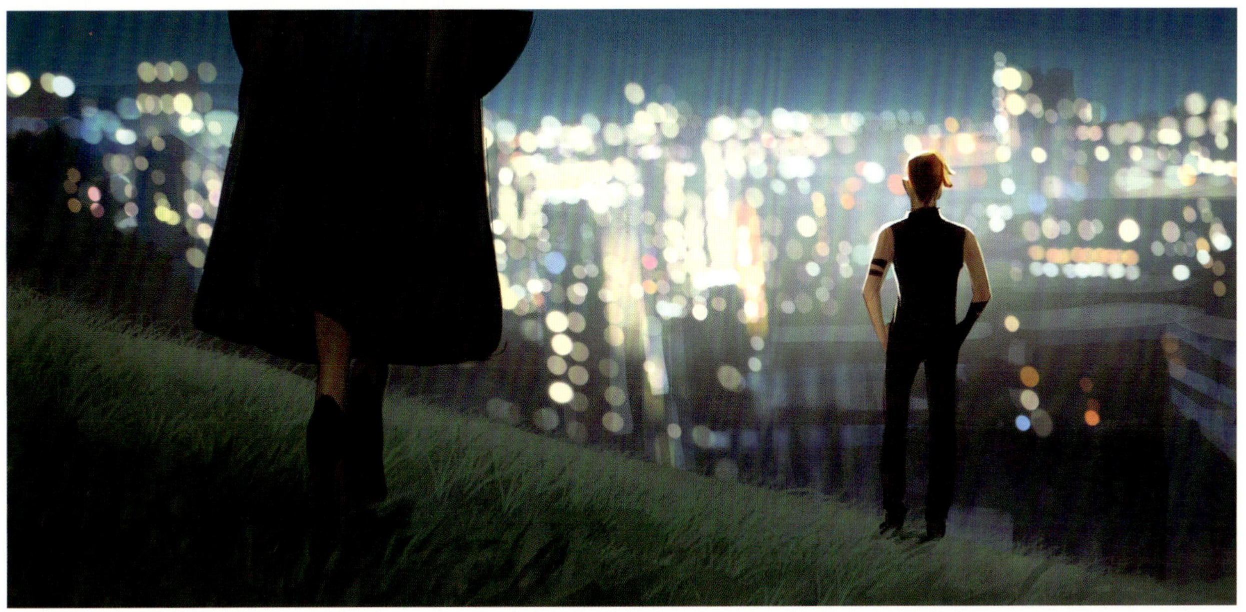

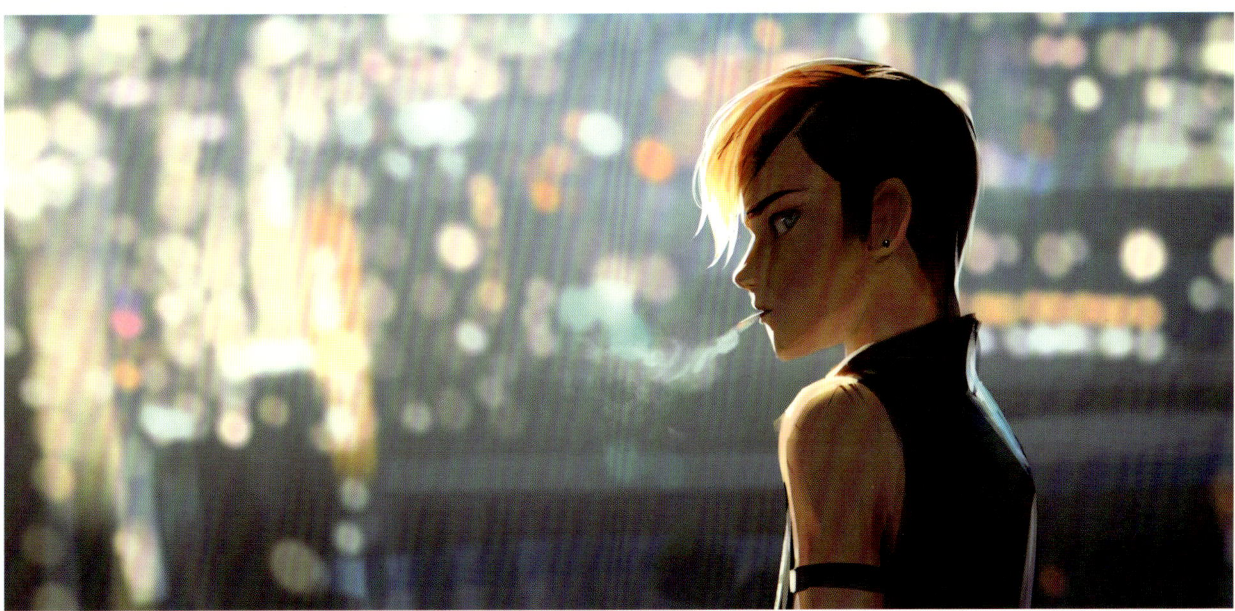

While I never expanded on this cinematic series, I still enjoyed painting it. I looked at several references of bokeh light effects and tried to implement this beautiful phenomenon in the background. This created a dramatic base for the characters

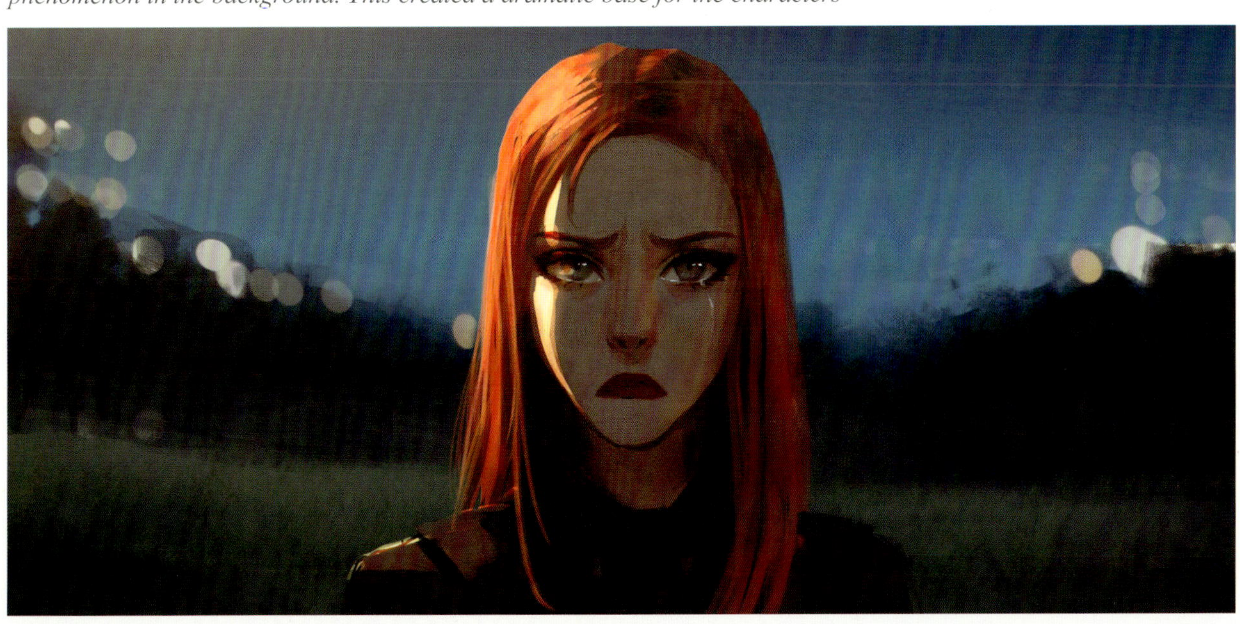

Composition & thumbnail sketches

Thumbnail sketches are quick drawings that explore the contrast, composition, and other elements of a project. I create them to plan my illustrations and use them throughout the painting process as a guide. Having a clear vision and an interesting composition makes any artwork more effective, especially when it comes to cinematic illustrations.

Many artists like to create black-and-white thumbnail sketches, where they can define the contrast between the lightest and darkest values within a piece. It guides the viewer's eye and establishes which areas are more important than others. I prefer to create coloured thumbnails, as colour is such an important part of my work.

I usually load the thumbnail sketches into my artwork files as references. In my experience, using them as a guide makes the painting process much more effective. I definitely feel like I can work faster when I have a blueprint of the illustration by my side.

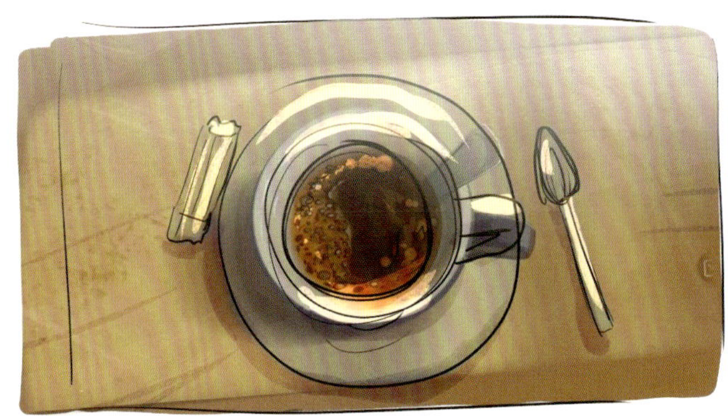

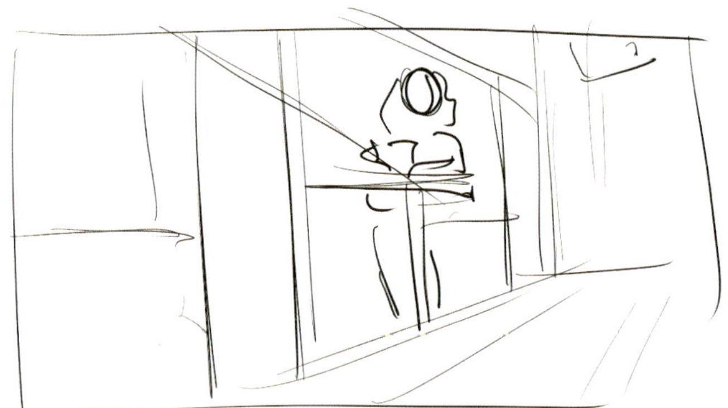

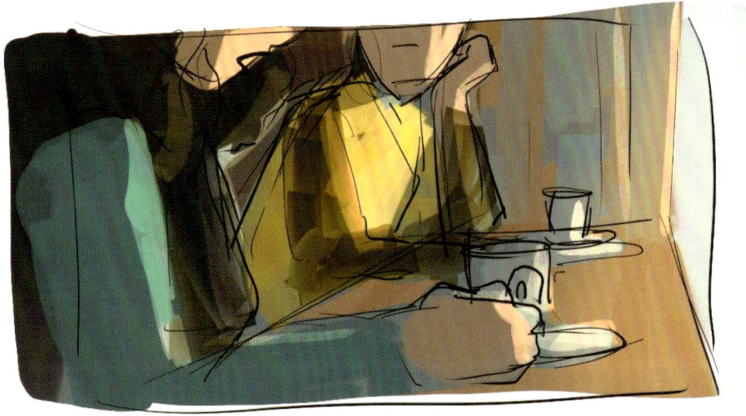

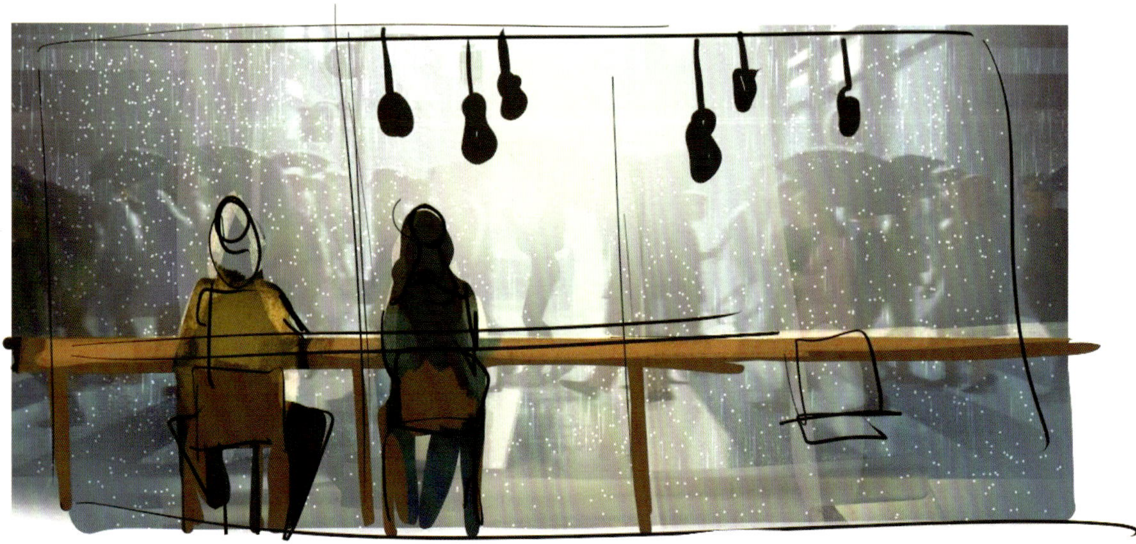

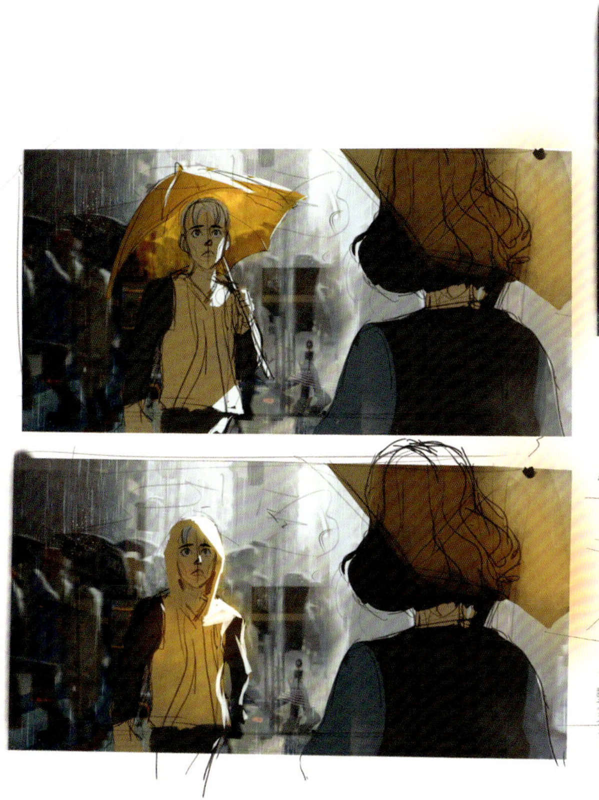

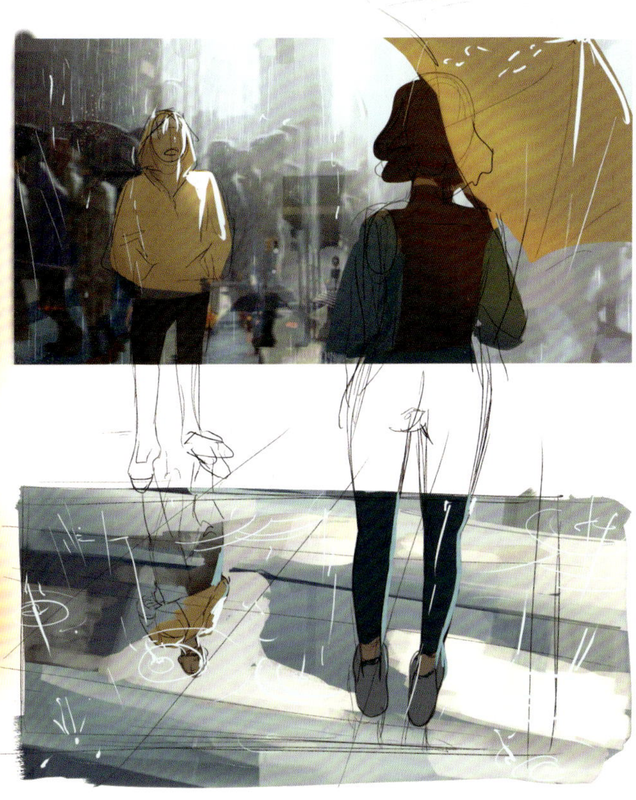

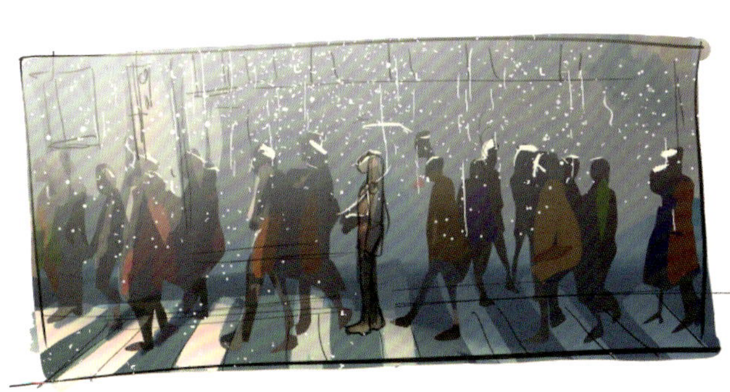

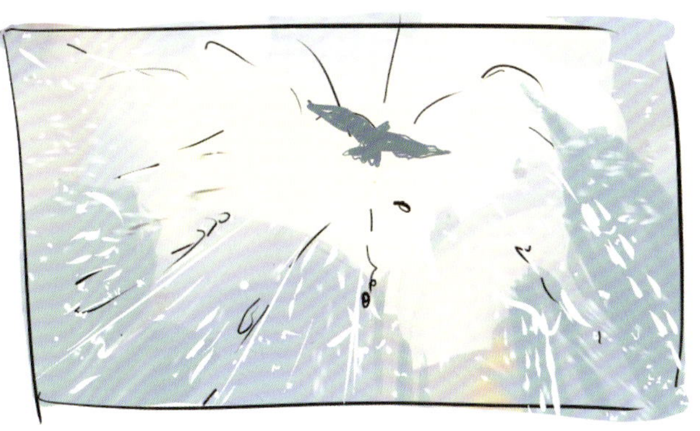

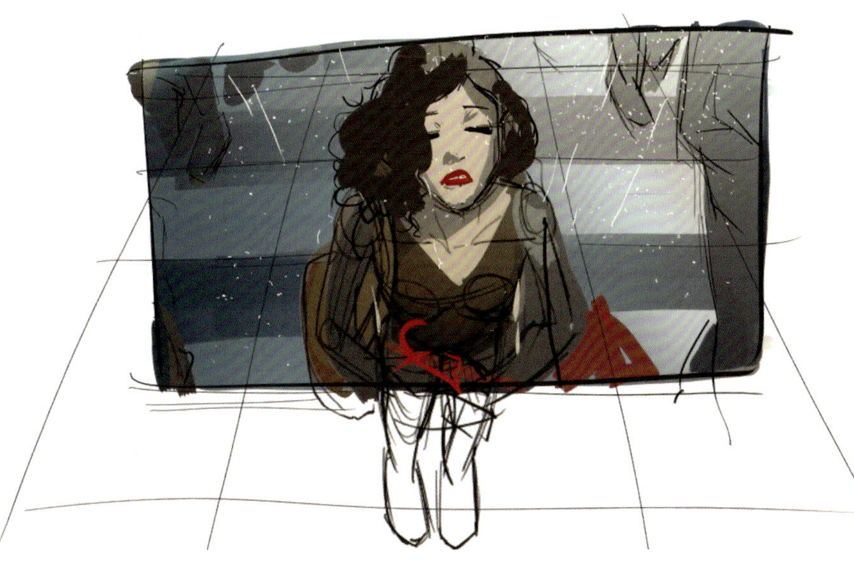

This is a collection of a few coloured thumbnail sketches I made for The Yellow Umbrella *series. I don't often go for the first sketch that comes to mind – I like exploring other compositions in order to find a shot that portrays the story in the most effective way*

Perspective

Understanding perspective is so important when it comes to creating illustrations for storytelling purposes. From whose perspective do we see the characters? Is the perspective high or low for a reason? How much of the scene are you showing, and why? These are questions I asked myself while planning *The Yellow Umbrella* series.

Painting faces is my greatest forte – I honed that skill by participating in many portrait-focused art challenges. However, by doing so, I neglected drawing full characters in perspective. This became increasingly apparent during the making of this series, but I wanted to learn, so I forced myself out of my comfort zone and started giving my characters their own background scenery.

Since this series included a couple of buildings, the thought of forgoing a perspective grid was almost unthinkable for an inexperienced artist like I was at the time. I looked up perspective tutorials and found that a good way to create a one-point-perspective grid is by using the Polygon tool in Photoshop. Once selected, it changes the property of a shape with 'no fill' and a one-point stroke. If you click the gear icon, you'll be able to make it a star with one hundred points. I indented the points by 99%.

I love this method of creating perspective grids in Photoshop, but since it's not the software I prefer to use for my painting process, I have explored different methods for adding these grids in ArtRage as well. For a simple, one-point-perspective grid, I use two methods regularly:

1. Creating perspective grids from scratch using the Ink Pen tool. While pressing Control on the keyboard, I can draw straight lines protruding from a certain vanishing point. With this method, I draw as many lines as I please in order to give me a general guide. Additionally, holding Control and Shift at the same time allows me to draw straight lines at 15-degree inclines. I normally use this method when I need a quick and general guide for a one-point perspective.

2. Using the Transform tool to stretch things into perspective. By adjusting the corners of the content when selected, I can transform and distort the shapes to fit any perspective I need.

There is also an extensive perspective tool in ArtRage, which, admittedly, I haven't used on a regular basis. However, I definitely want to explore this helpful tool in the future because it offers some handy settings for one-point and two-point-perspective grids!

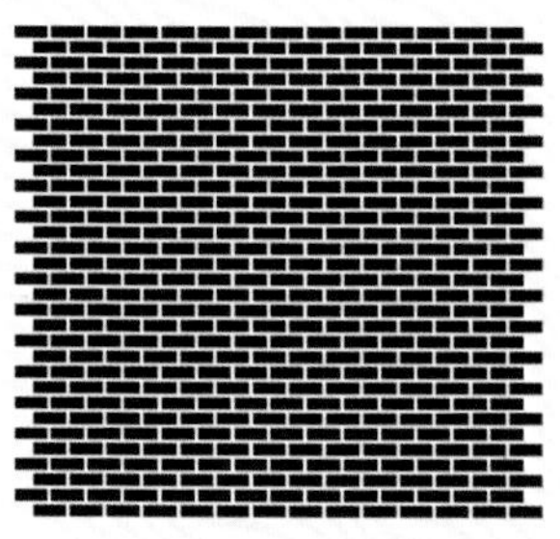

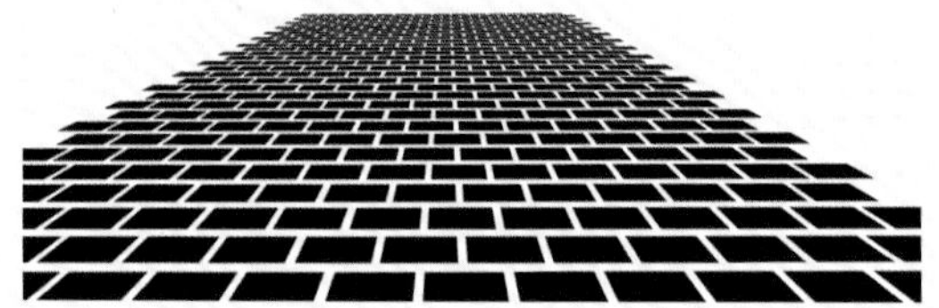

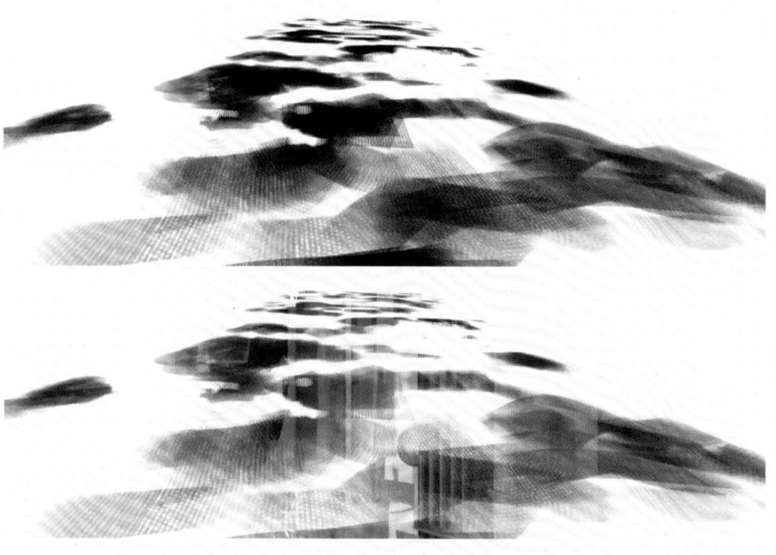

This lower-perspective illustration was tricky, but I like the result. It was largely inspired by the gorgeous art of Devin Elle Kurtz. I tried applying some of her helpful techniques in the piece too

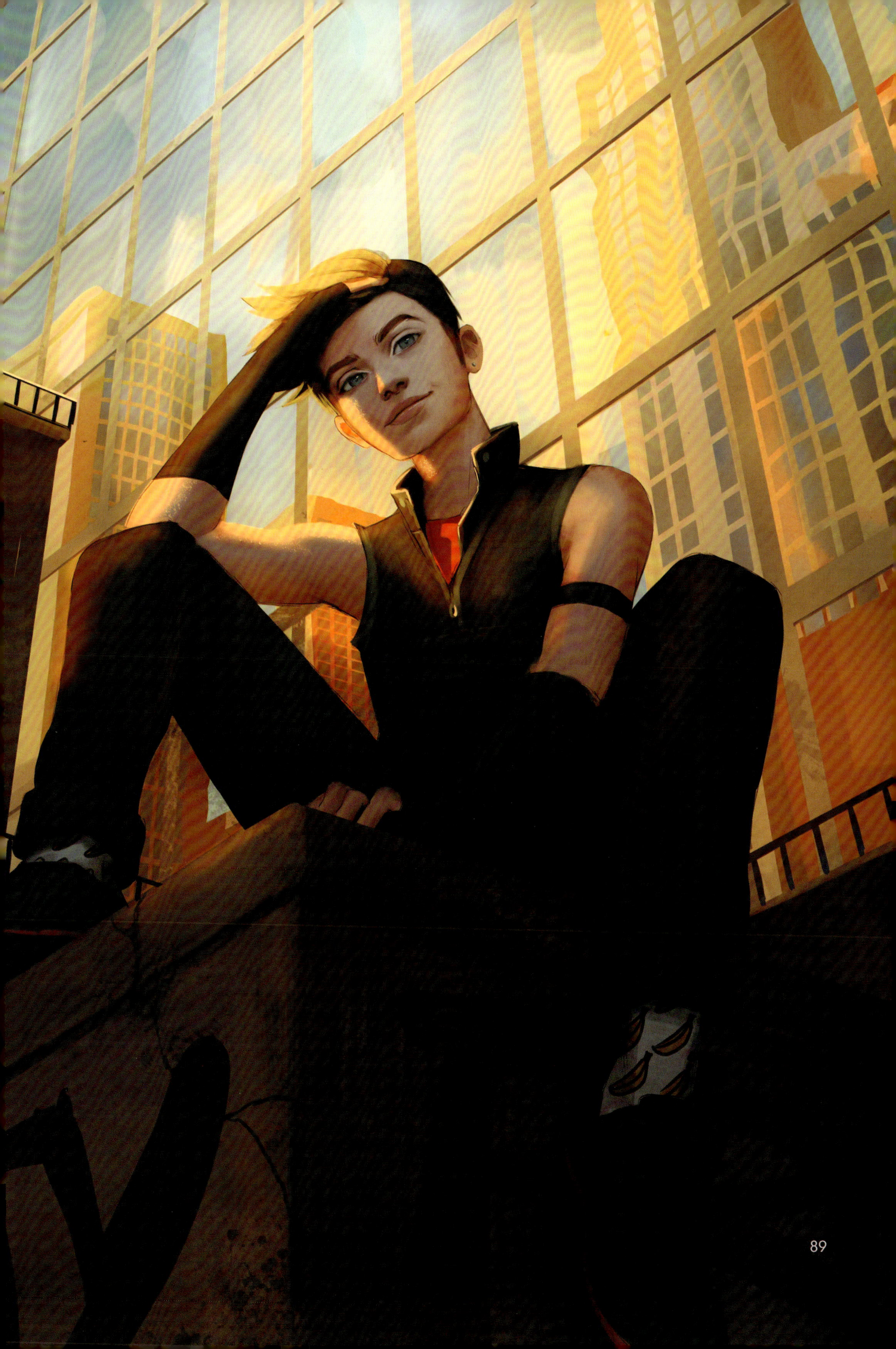

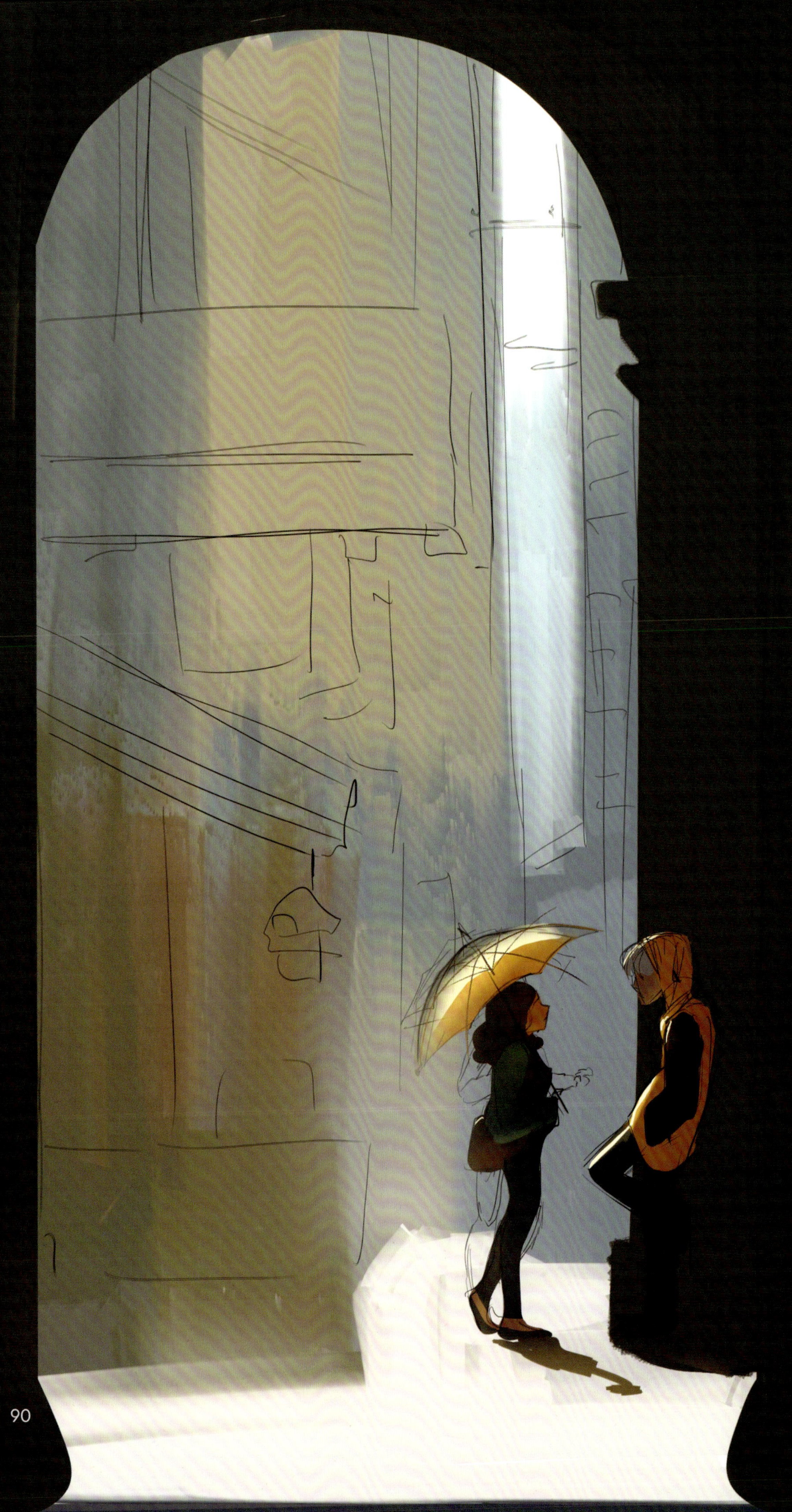

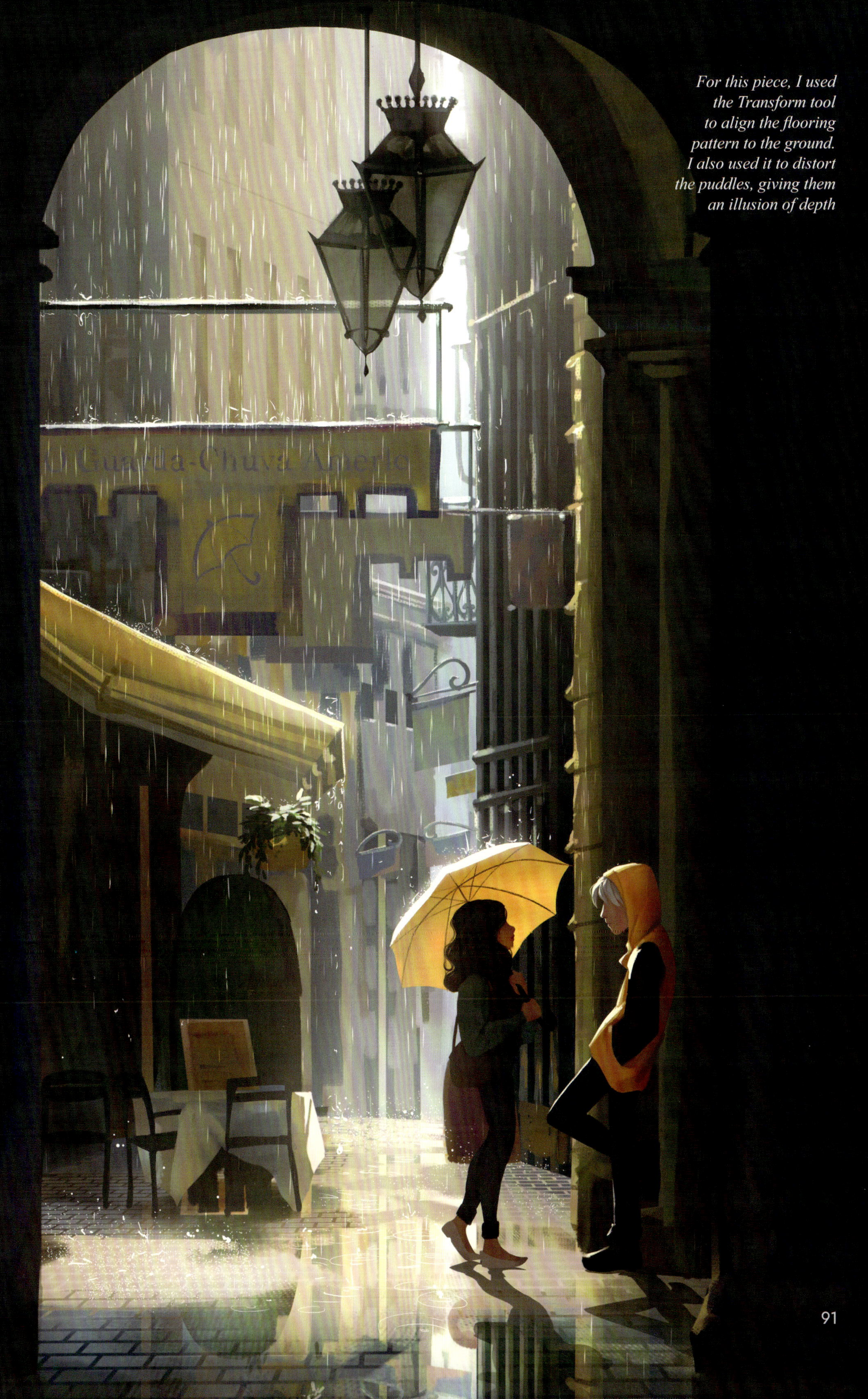

For this piece, I used the Transform tool to align the flooring pattern to the ground. I also used it to distort the puddles, giving them an illusion of depth

COLOUR & LIGHT

Understanding colour theory is an essential part of creating aesthetically pleasing cinematic illustrations. I warmly recommend the colour-theory videos of Marco Bucci. Since I never had a formal education in art and illustration, going back to the basics helped me improve my painting skills.

In my art, colour and light take the centre stage; both are equally important to me. I always make sure they have a significance in regards to the meaning and emotion of my artworks.

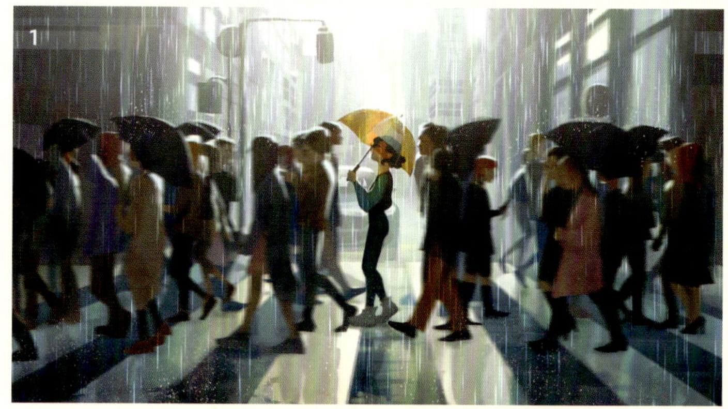

1

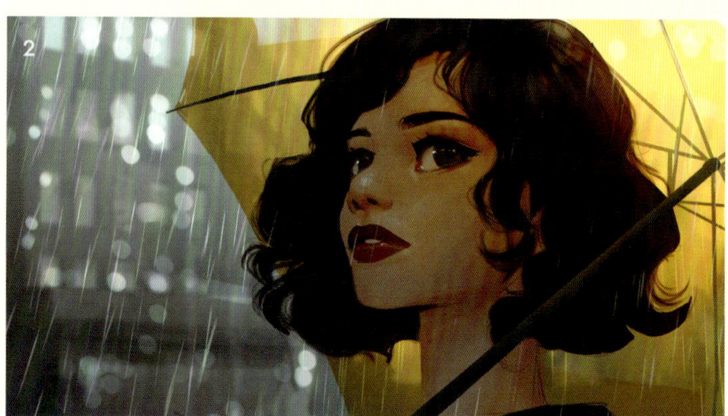

2

Accent colours

When it comes to *The Yellow Umbrella* series, blues and greys dominate the colour palette. Yellow is an important accent colour because its warmth contrasts nicely with the cooler tones of the scenery, and thus draws the viewer's attention to those specific areas. Additionally, both main characters, Susie and David, have yellow elements in their design. This makes them stand out from the crowd, despite their relatively ordinary looks.

I would always advise artists not to overuse overly saturated colours unless it's for a good reason. I prefer to use relatively dull base colours, as this allows me to add saturated colour accents later. I find that this mix of duller bases and saturated highlights results in an aesthetically pleasing colour scheme.

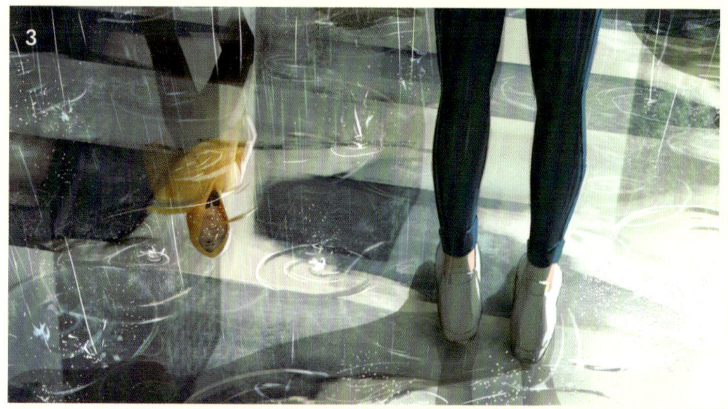

3

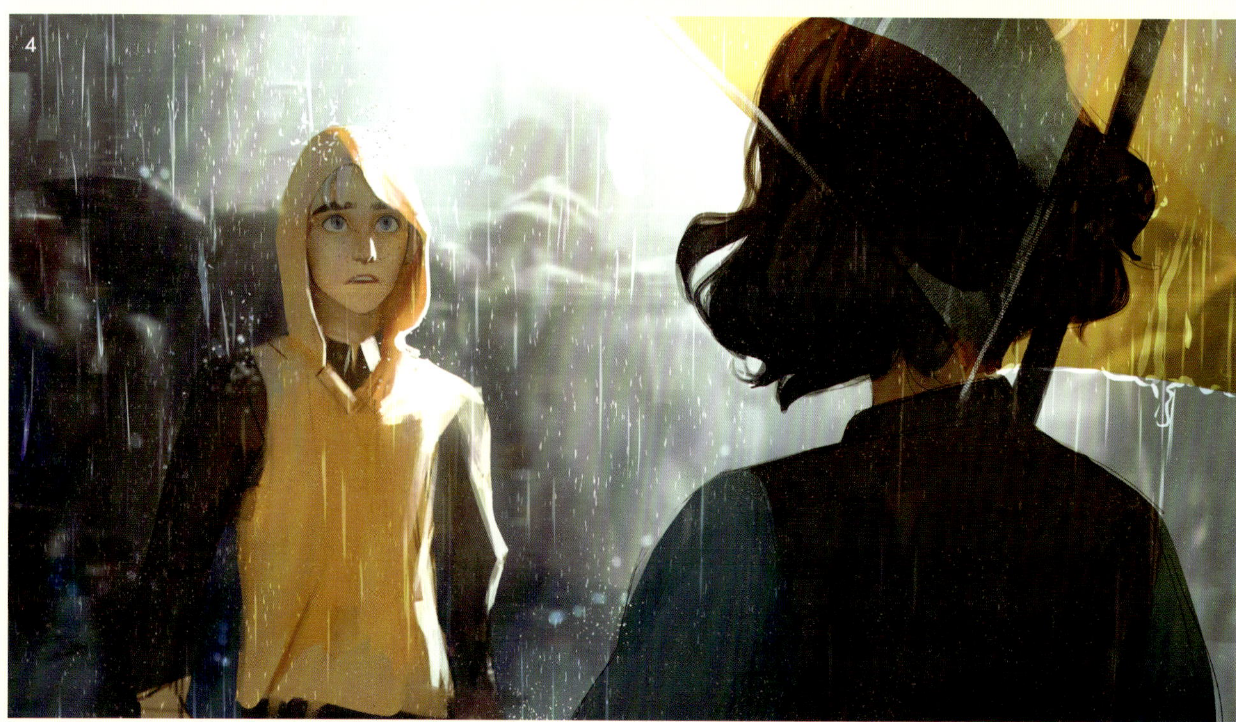

4

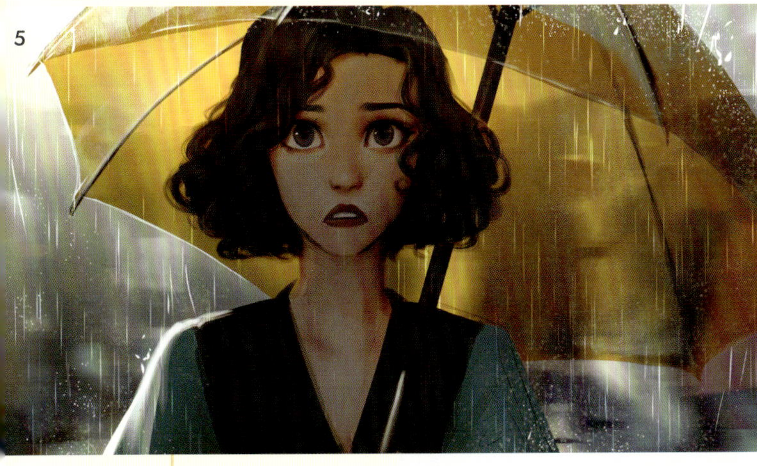

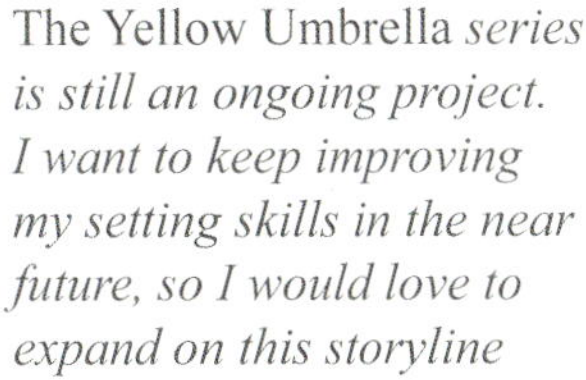

The Yellow Umbrella *series is still an ongoing project. I want to keep improving my setting skills in the near future, so I would love to expand on this storyline*

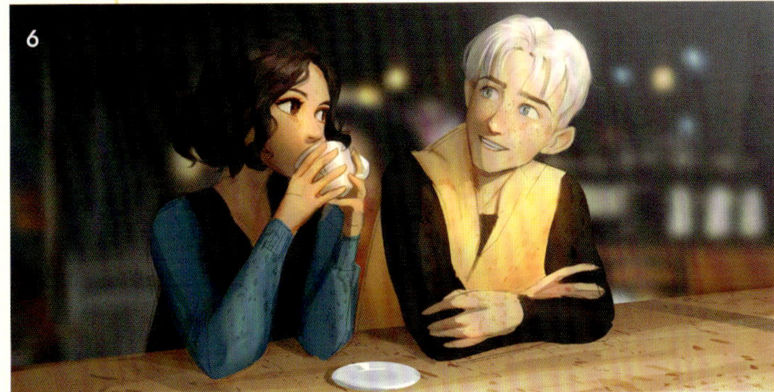

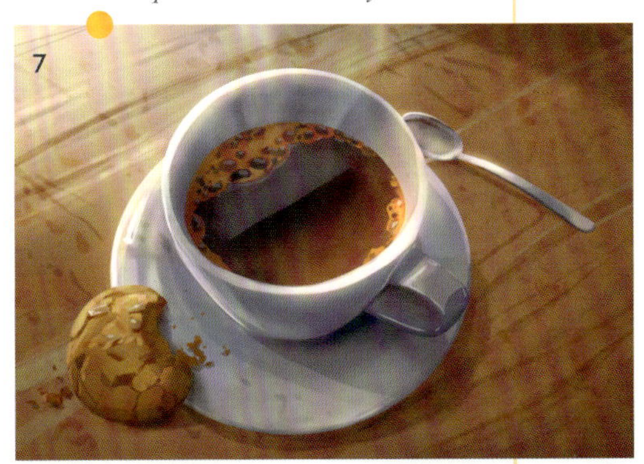

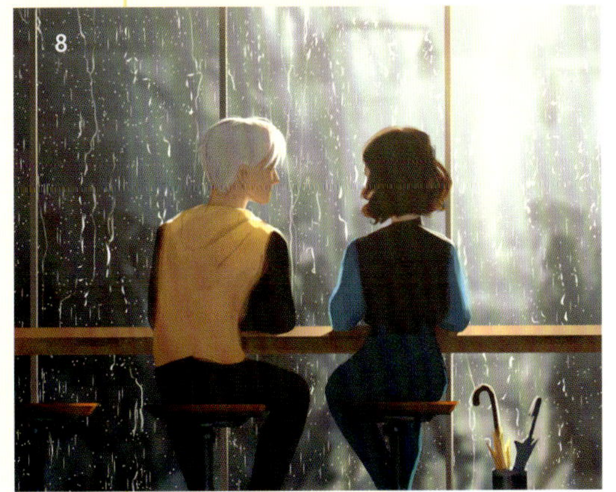

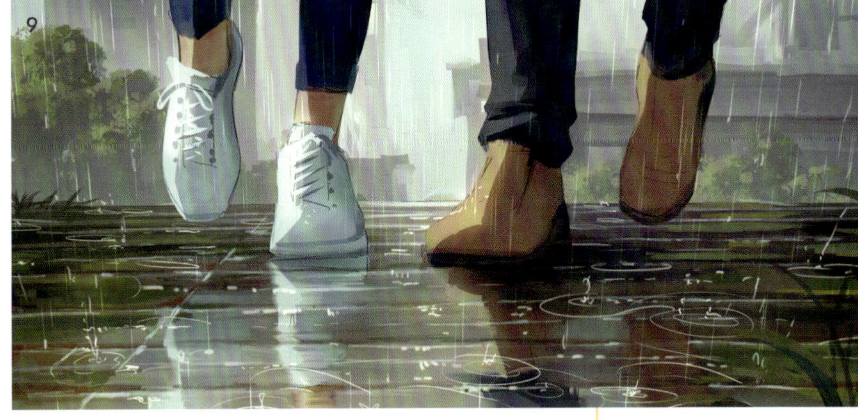

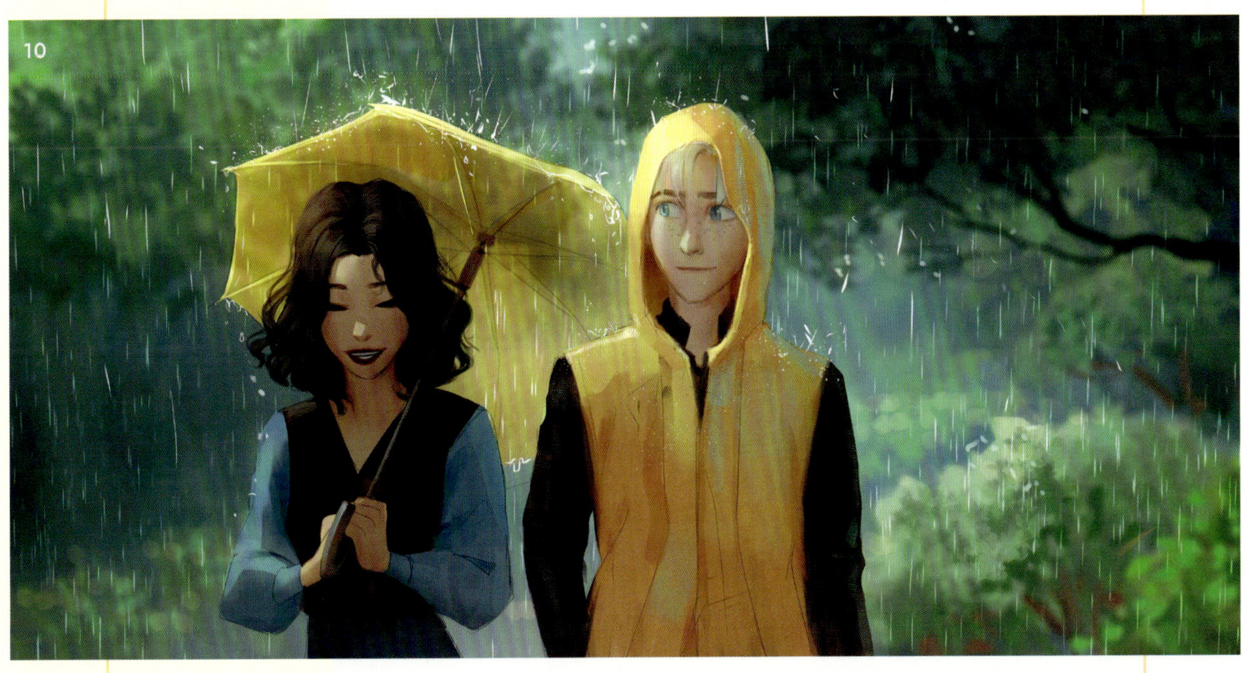

Referencing & colour picking

I often use references to understand the relationship between light and colour in real life. As I am not the most experienced painter of backgrounds, it was important for me to use references for buildings, streets, and rain when it came to *The Yellow Umbrella*. I also like to use references for colour palettes belonging to other projects. I just love studying photos and the relationship between colour and light in real life – it's a great way to increase my visual library.

It's important to mention that when I use references, I am careful about not directly copying the colours with the Pipette tool. However, from time to time, I think it's good practice for beginner artists to pick the colours straight from the reference in order to get a feeling for how different colours appear in different contexts. Placing those reference colours on a neutral grey or white background is always fascinating, since colours in real life are often darker and greyer than one might expect.

Although colour-picking is a good method for learning more about colour theory, I wouldn't recommend relying on it completely. It won't help if you don't check the values or try to understand the relationships between the colours. It's only an effective technique when it's used properly.

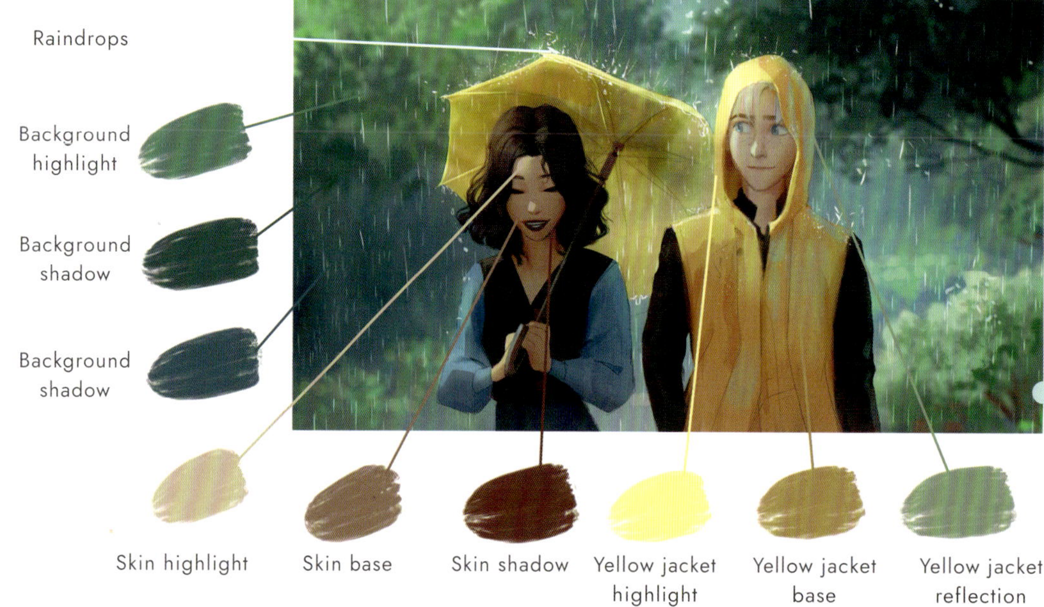

The overall palette and tones of the skin, clothing, and so on greatly depend on the environment in the illustration

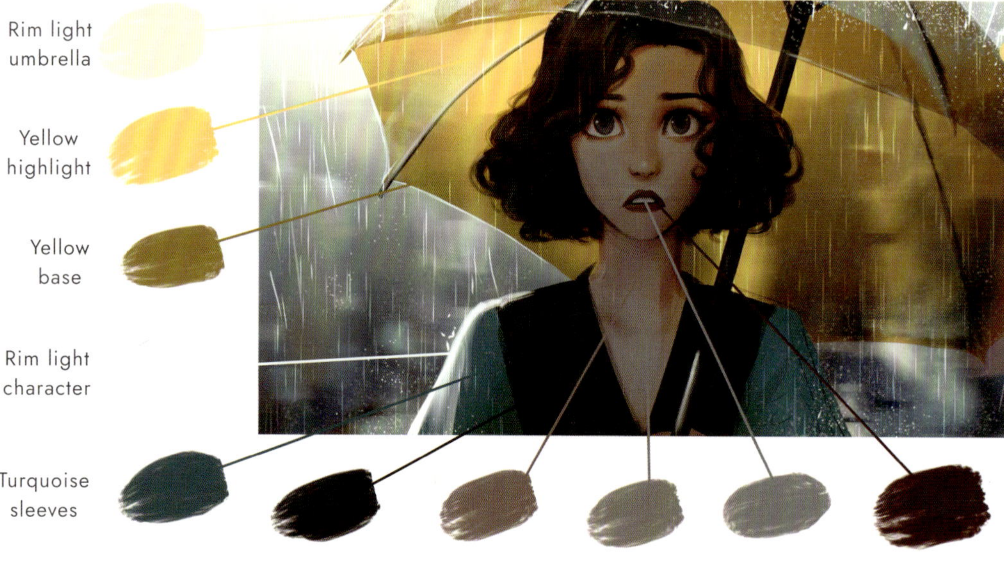

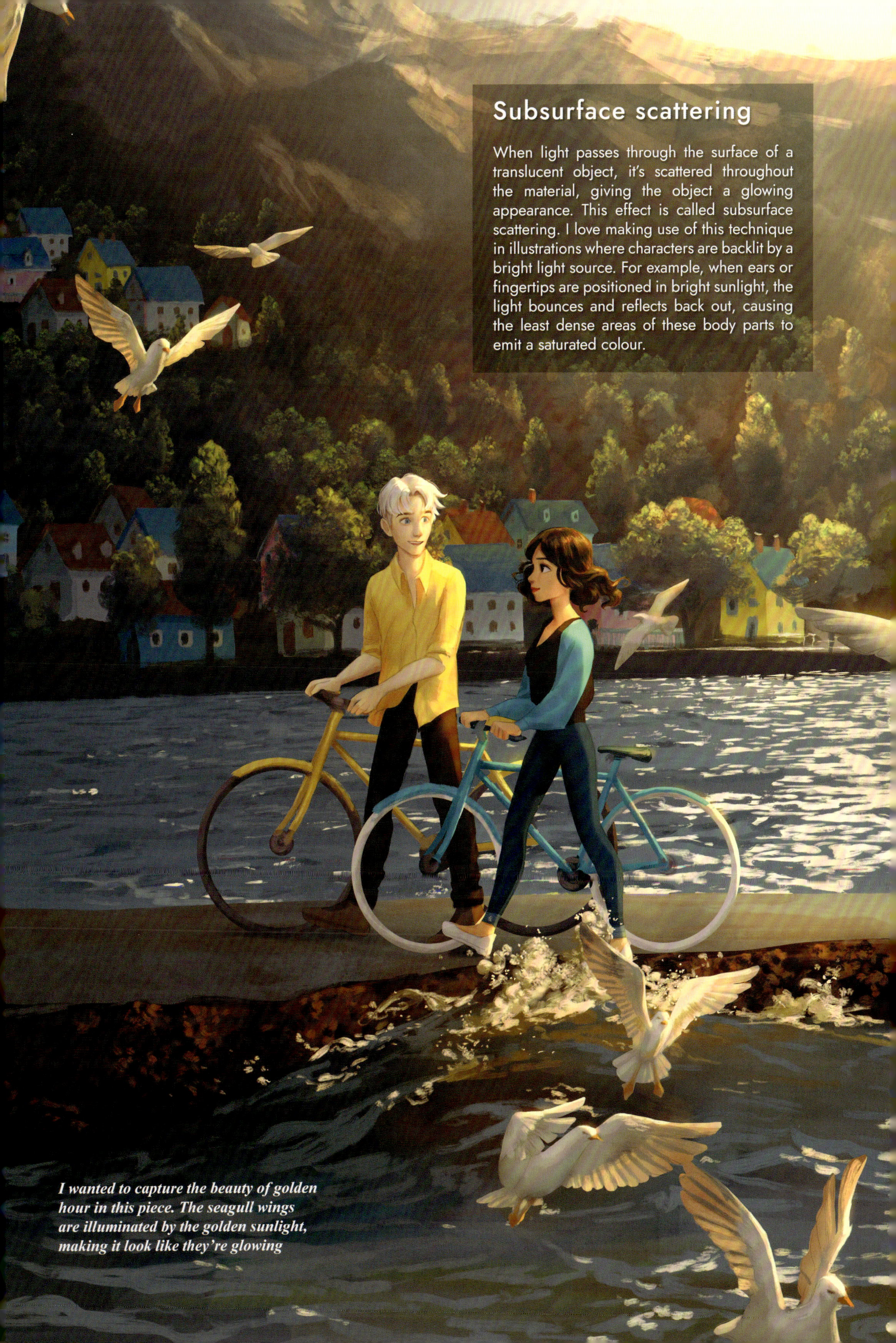

Subsurface scattering

When light passes through the surface of a translucent object, it's scattered throughout the material, giving the object a glowing appearance. This effect is called subsurface scattering. I love making use of this technique in illustrations where characters are backlit by a bright light source. For example, when ears or fingertips are positioned in bright sunlight, the light bounces and reflects back out, causing the least dense areas of these body parts to emit a saturated colour.

I wanted to capture the beauty of golden hour in this piece. The seagull wings are illuminated by the golden sunlight, making it look like they're glowing

Bounce/reflective light

During my yearly travels to Portugal, my family and I would often go to the beach. I used to carry my sketchbook with me and doodle whatever came to mind. I often noticed that my legs would appear lighter at the bottom when I was standing in the sand. This is due to bounce light – light that reflects off the surface and back onto the subject. It creates a soft lighting effect where the surfaces that are close to a strongly lit object appear lighter.

Adding bounce light to my illustrations not only adds to the semi-realistic look, but I also find it to be super fun and relaxing! I add this effect by using the Soft Airbrush, set to either Soft Light or Overlay blend mode. Using a light colour, I apply this brush in areas that are close to a highly reflective surface.

I usually add bounce light to the faces of characters who are outside on a sunny day

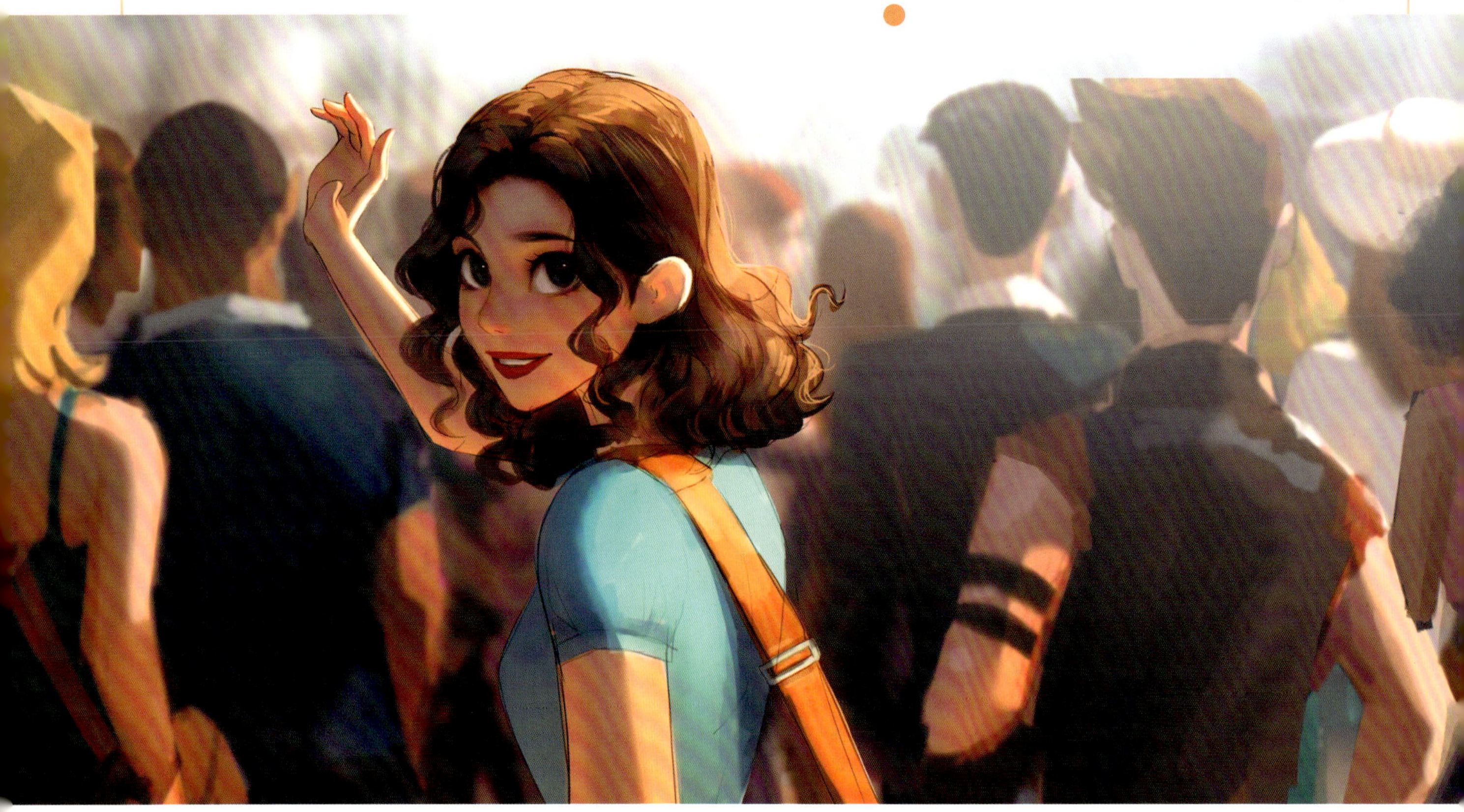

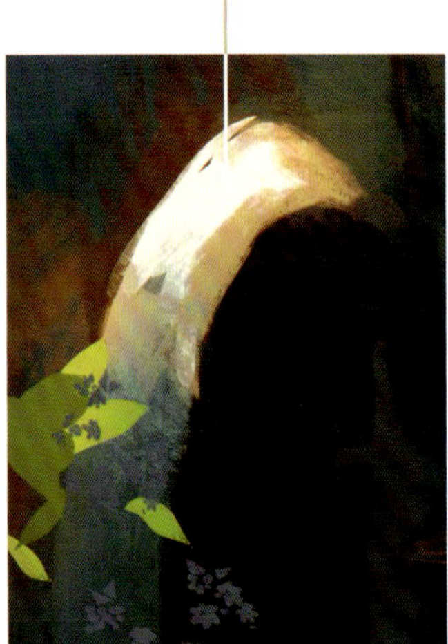

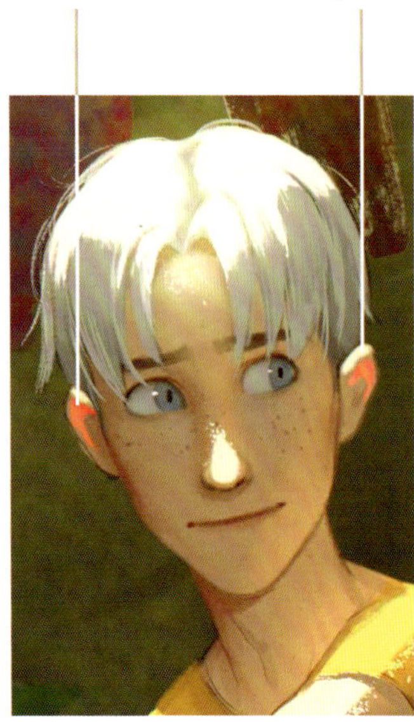

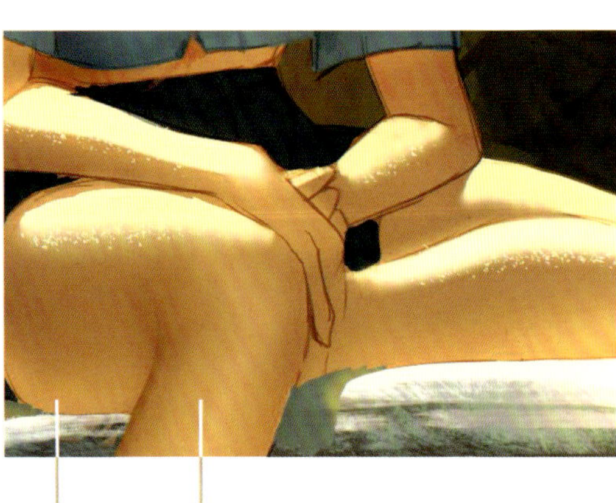

I used subsurface scattering and bounce light to add realism to the painting. The intense lighting from above reflects off the car and onto the characters

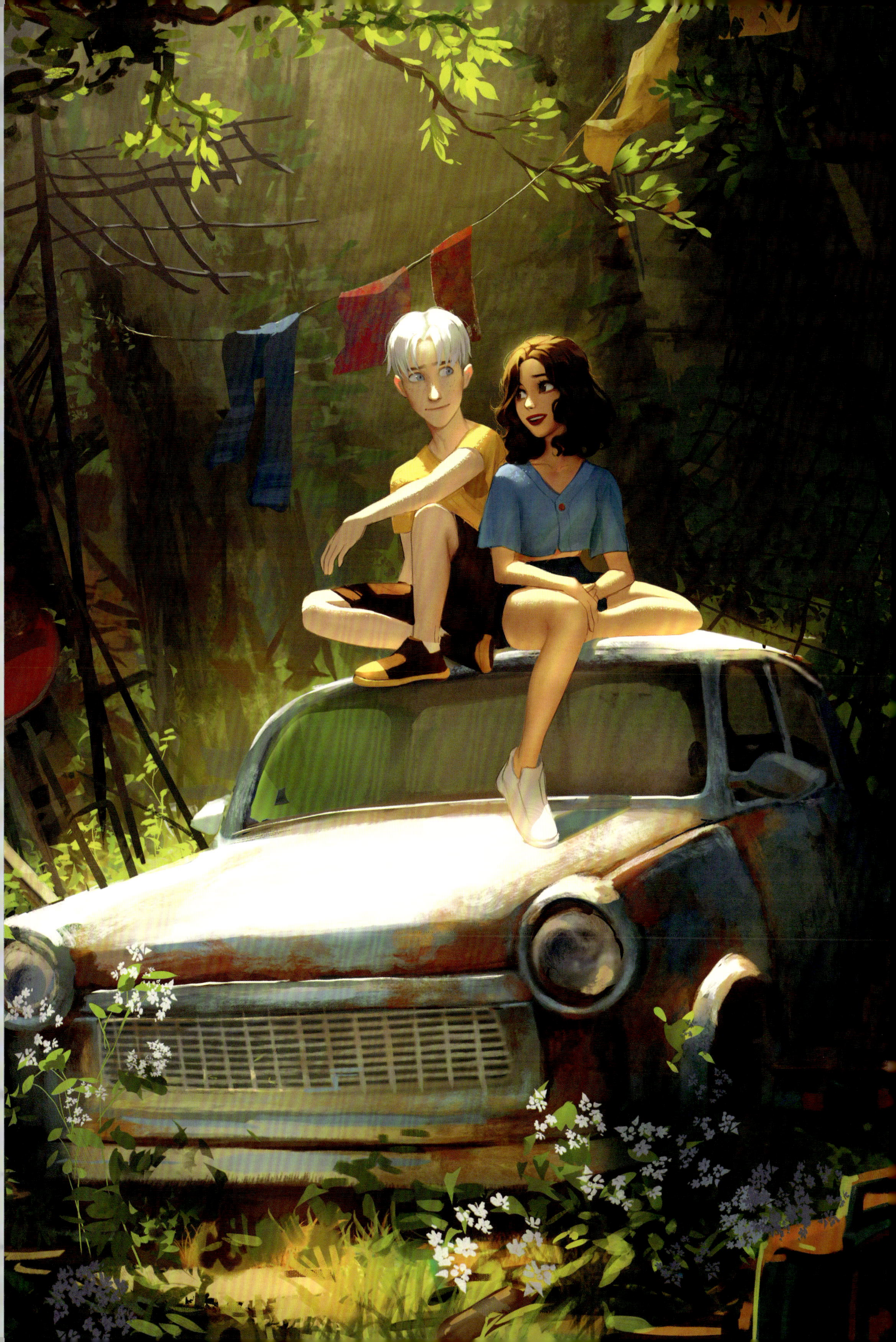

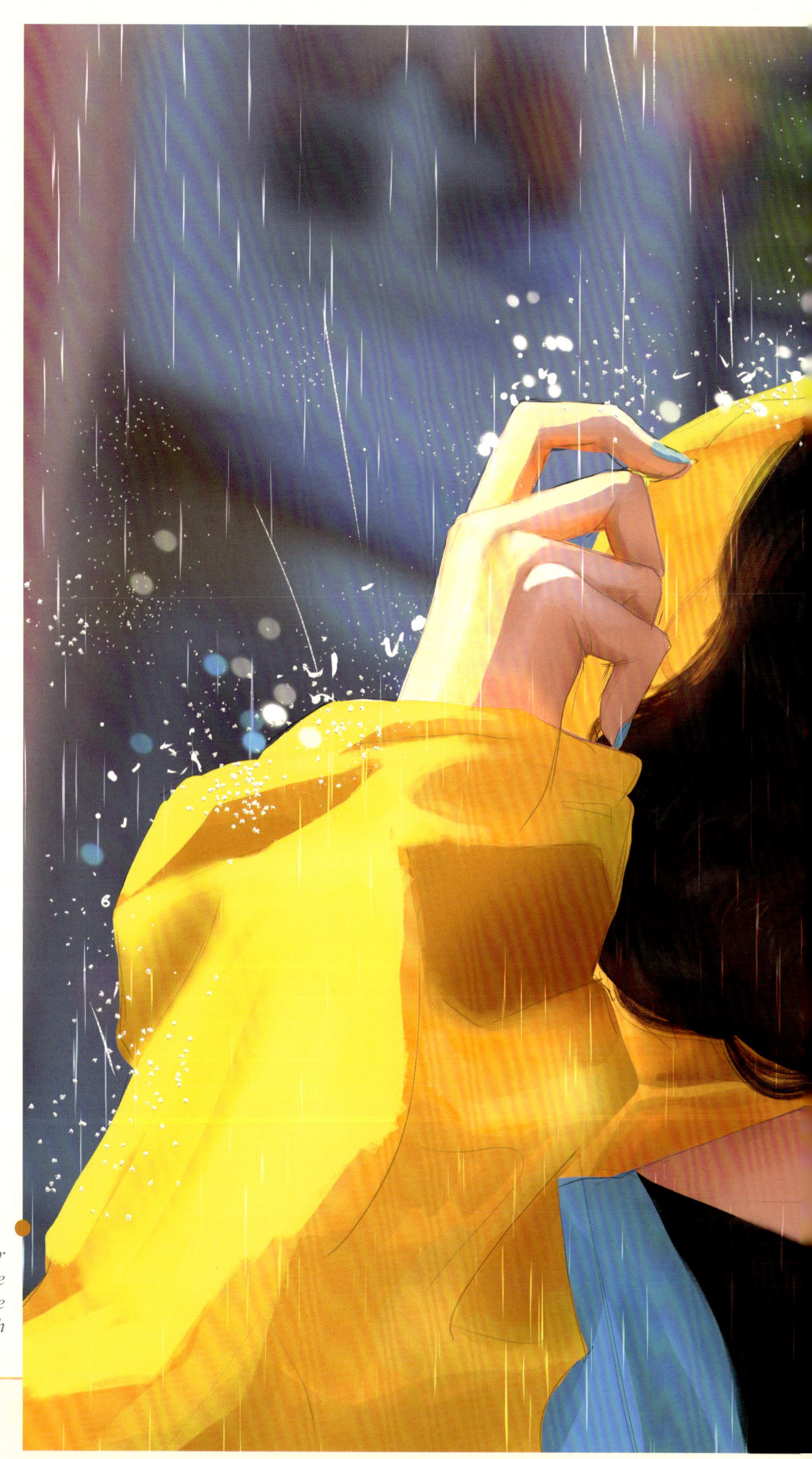

The larger raindrops were made with the Hard Airbrush

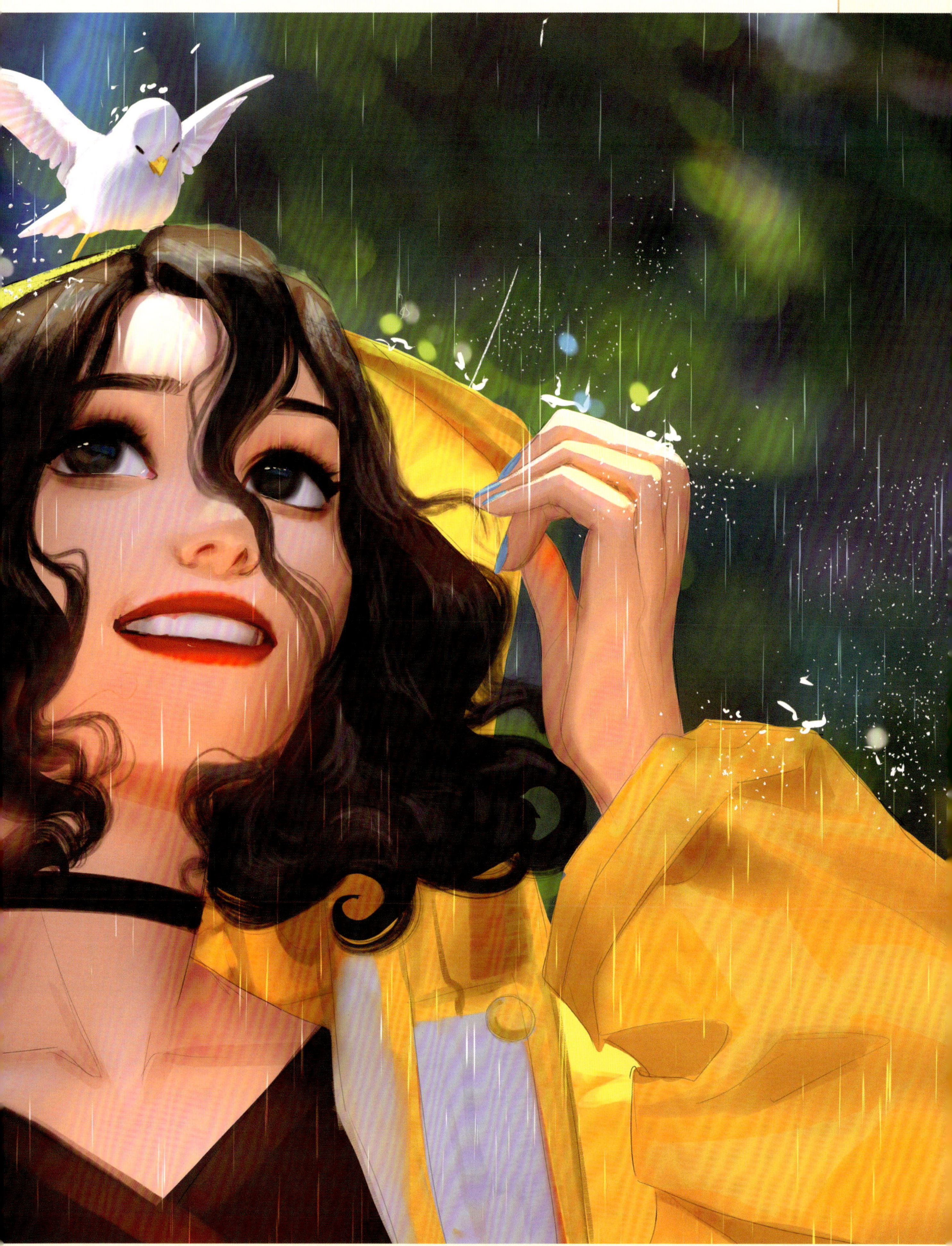

EXPLORING NATURE

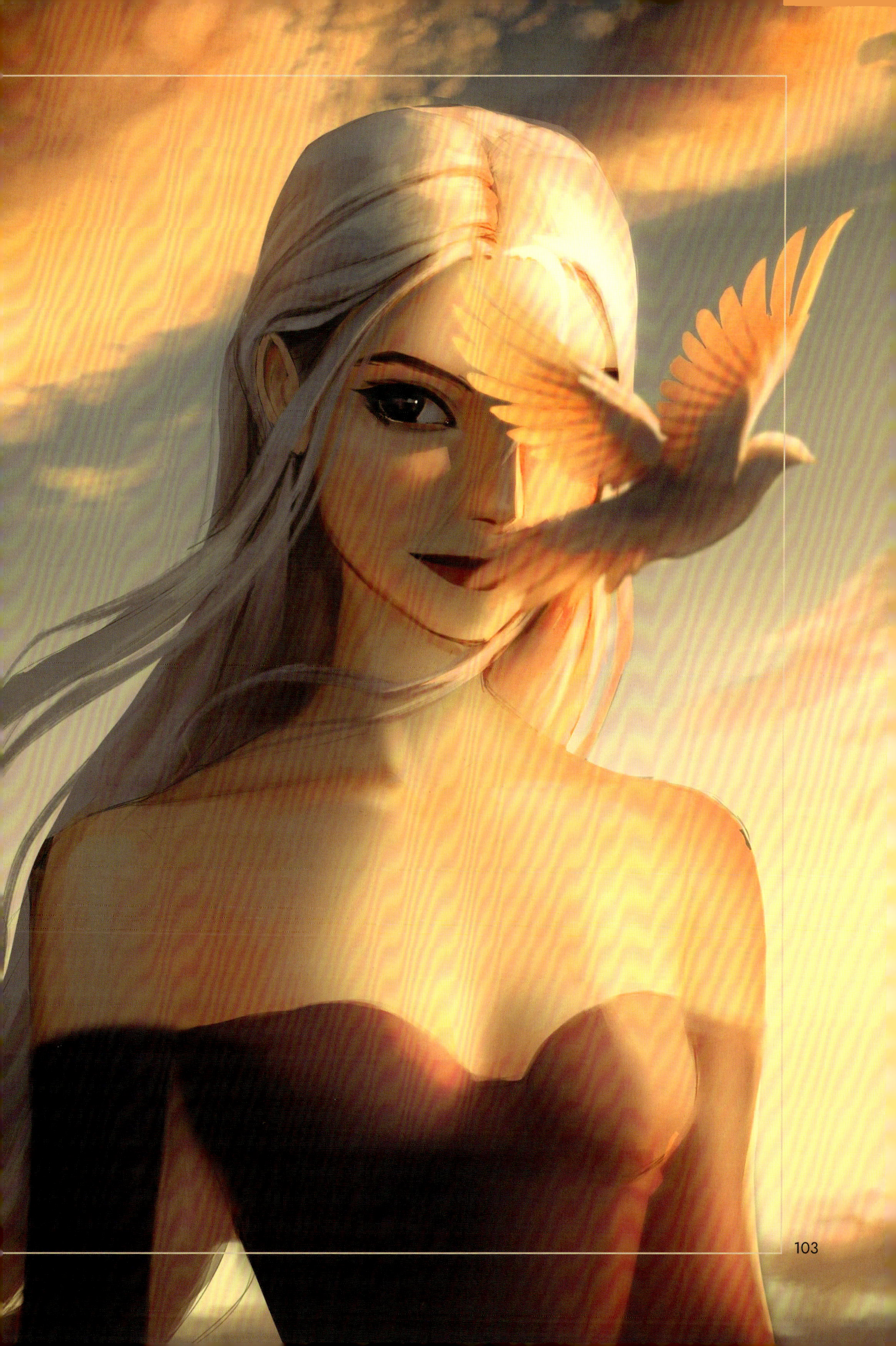

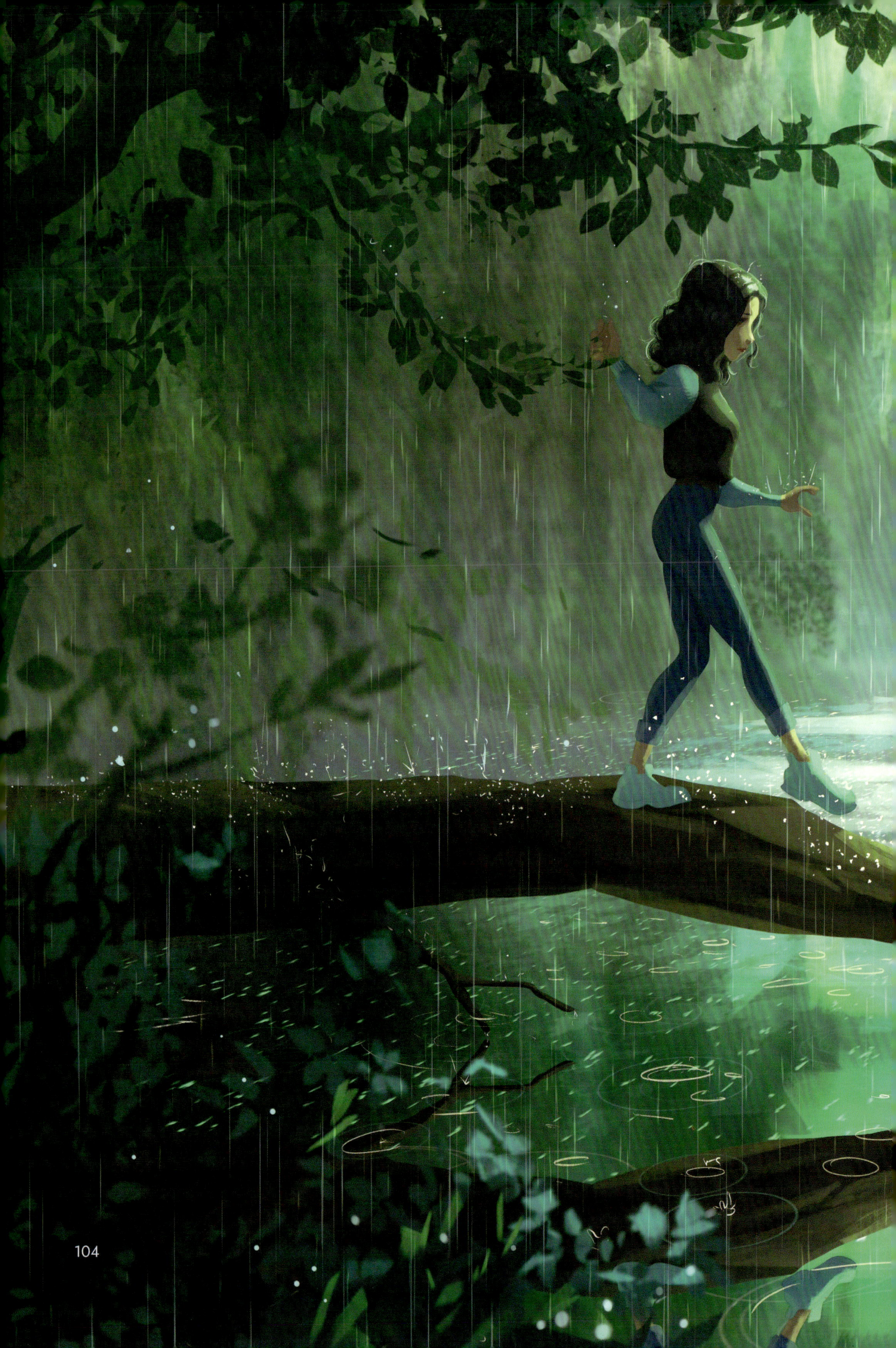

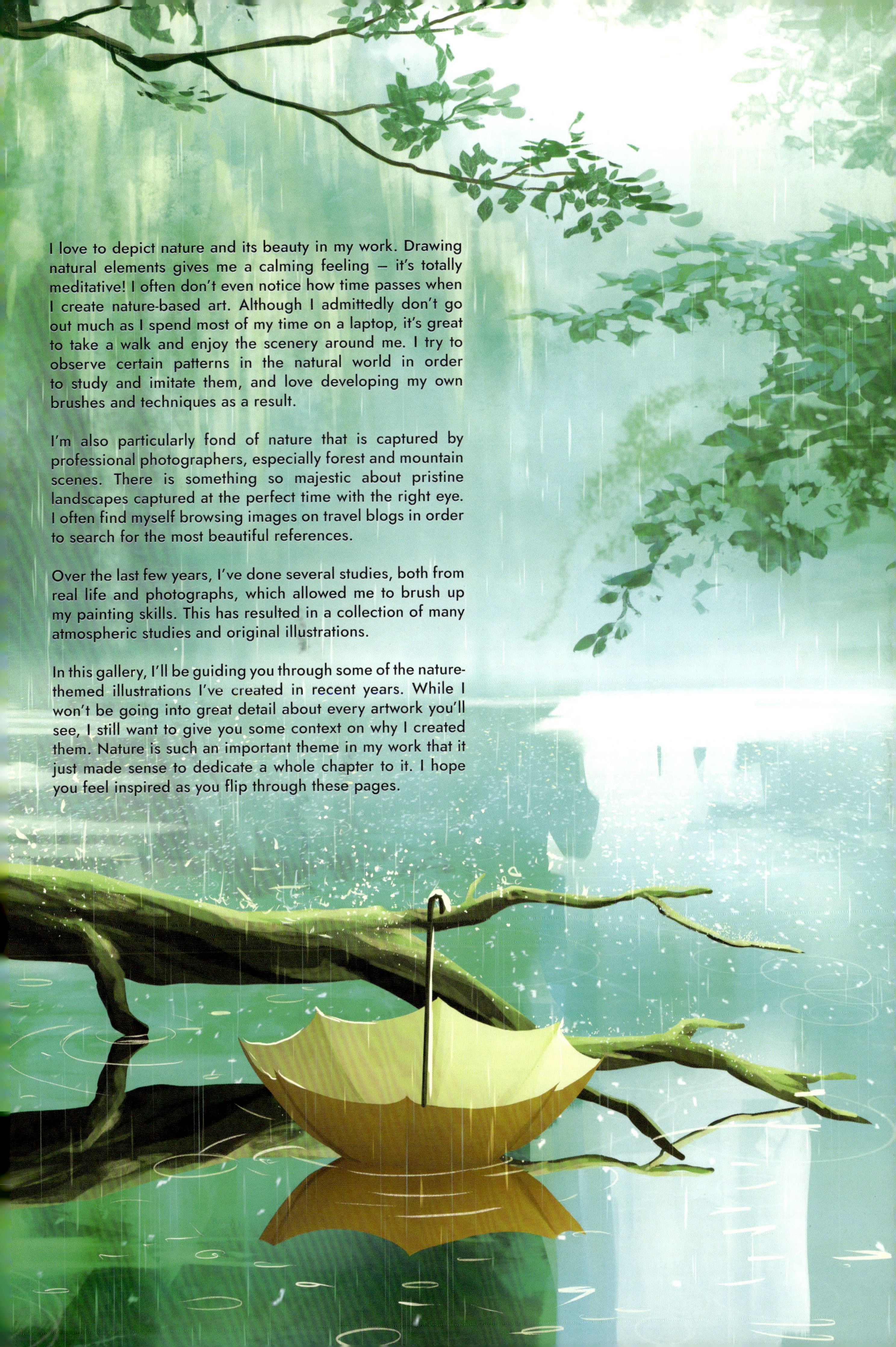

I love to depict nature and its beauty in my work. Drawing natural elements gives me a calming feeling – it's totally meditative! I often don't even notice how time passes when I create nature-based art. Although I admittedly don't go out much as I spend most of my time on a laptop, it's great to take a walk and enjoy the scenery around me. I try to observe certain patterns in the natural world in order to study and imitate them, and love developing my own brushes and techniques as a result.

I'm also particularly fond of nature that is captured by professional photographers, especially forest and mountain scenes. There is something so majestic about pristine landscapes captured at the perfect time with the right eye. I often find myself browsing images on travel blogs in order to search for the most beautiful references.

Over the last few years, I've done several studies, both from real life and photographs, which allowed me to brush up my painting skills. This has resulted in a collection of many atmospheric studies and original illustrations.

In this gallery, I'll be guiding you through some of the nature-themed illustrations I've created in recent years. While I won't be going into great detail about every artwork you'll see, I still want to give you some context on why I created them. Nature is such an important theme in my work that it just made sense to dedicate a whole chapter to it. I hope you feel inspired as you flip through these pages.

EIRA SERIES

I'd like to start off this section by introducing my original character, Eira. I first started drawing her in 2020, and gradually developed numerous nature-themed illustrations featuring her in them. I chose the name Eira as it means 'snow' in Welsh. I felt like the name suited her, given her light hair and sparkly design. I enjoy portraying her in cooler lighting, in order to reflect the icy nature of her name.

To me, Eira represents the beauty and elegance of nature. I like to draw her in graceful poses with calm facial expressions, while capturing the beautiful imagery the natural world has to offer.

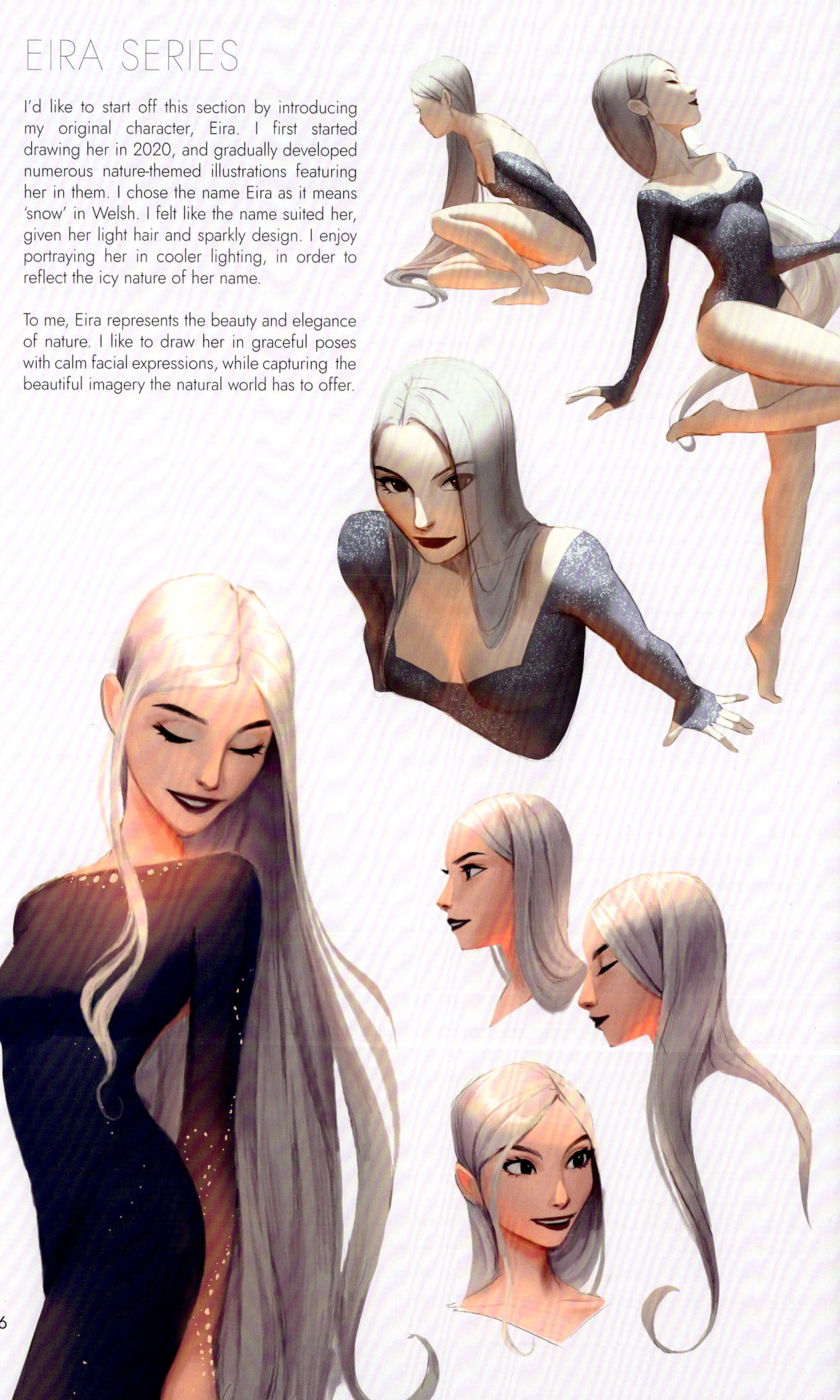

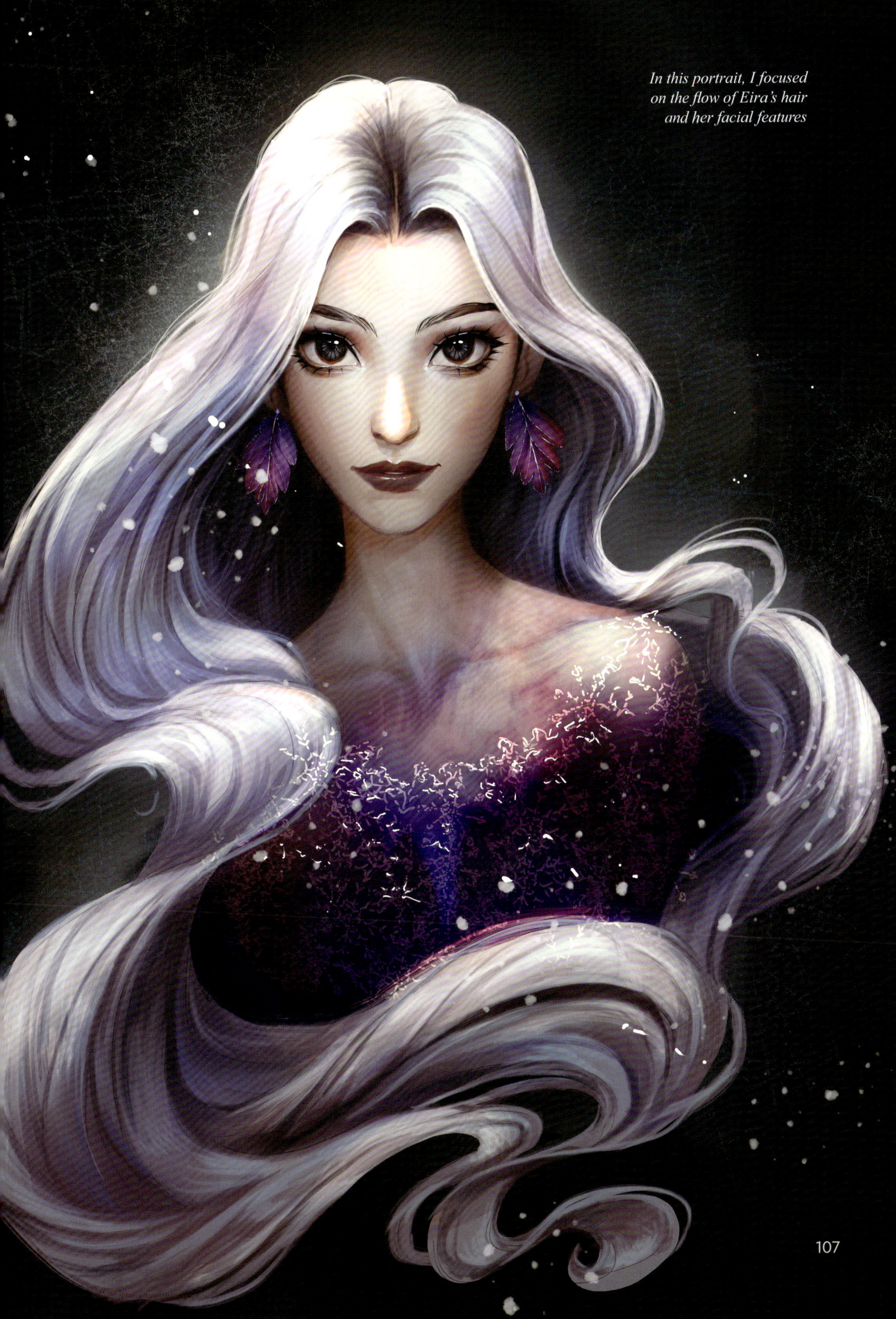

In this portrait, I focused on the flow of Eira's hair and her facial features

The images on the right are some unrendered concept drawings of Eira. I enjoyed exploring the long, curving shapes of her silhouette. The drawing below was going to be a sticker design, but I never followed through with that idea

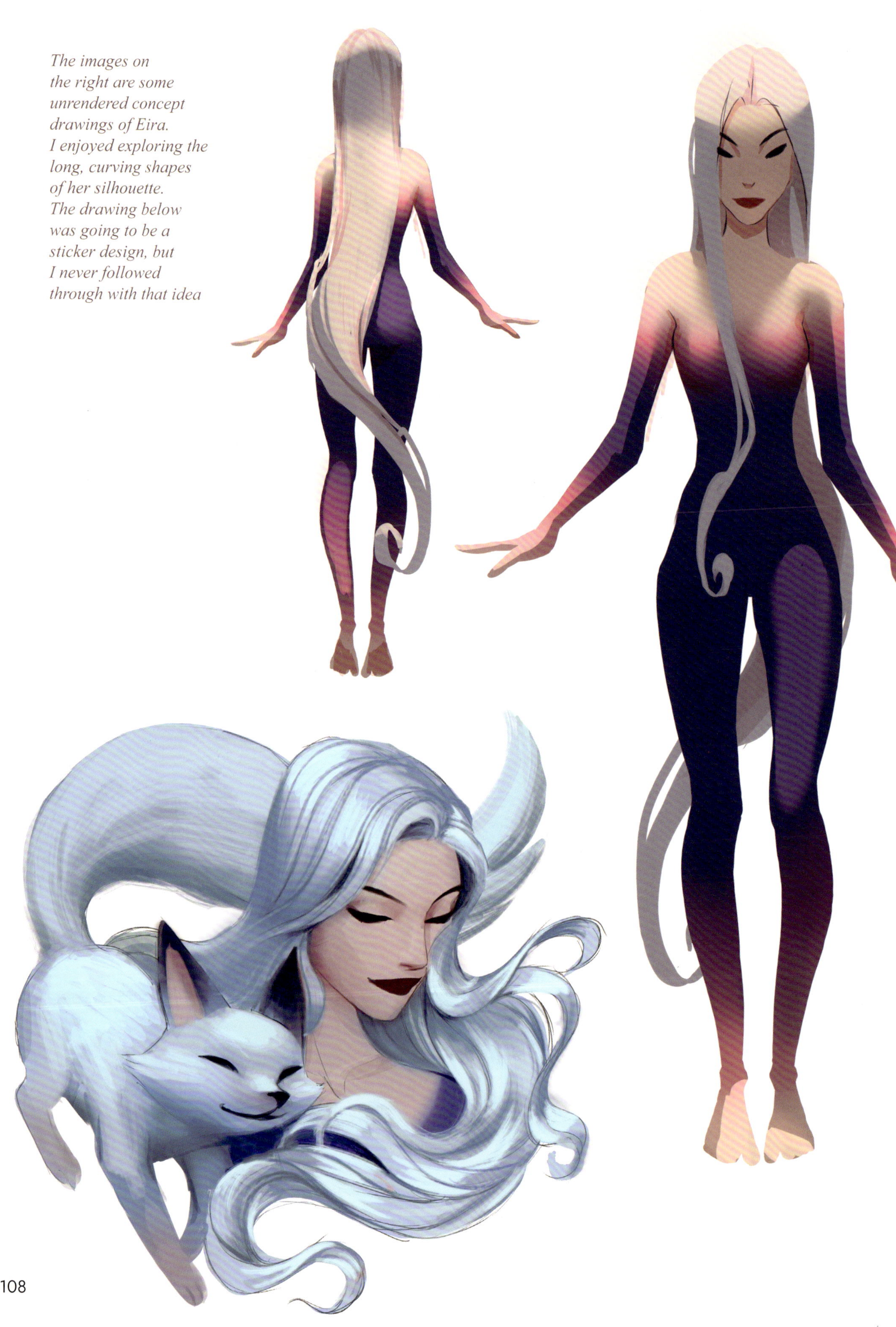

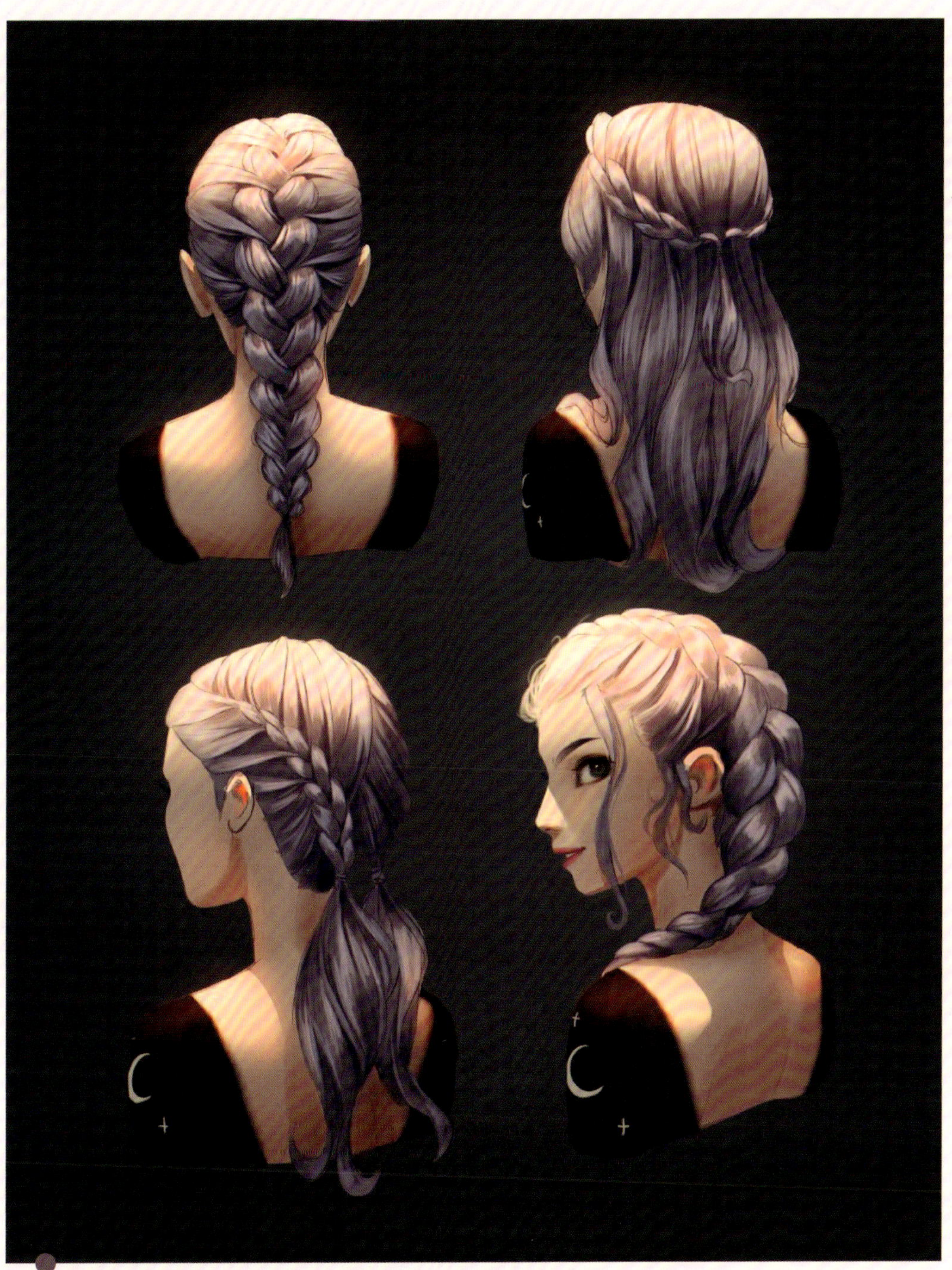

Even though I love to paint hair, I barely take the time to learn how to draw different types of hairstyles. I therefore looked up four different photo references, studied them, and recreated them on this sheet

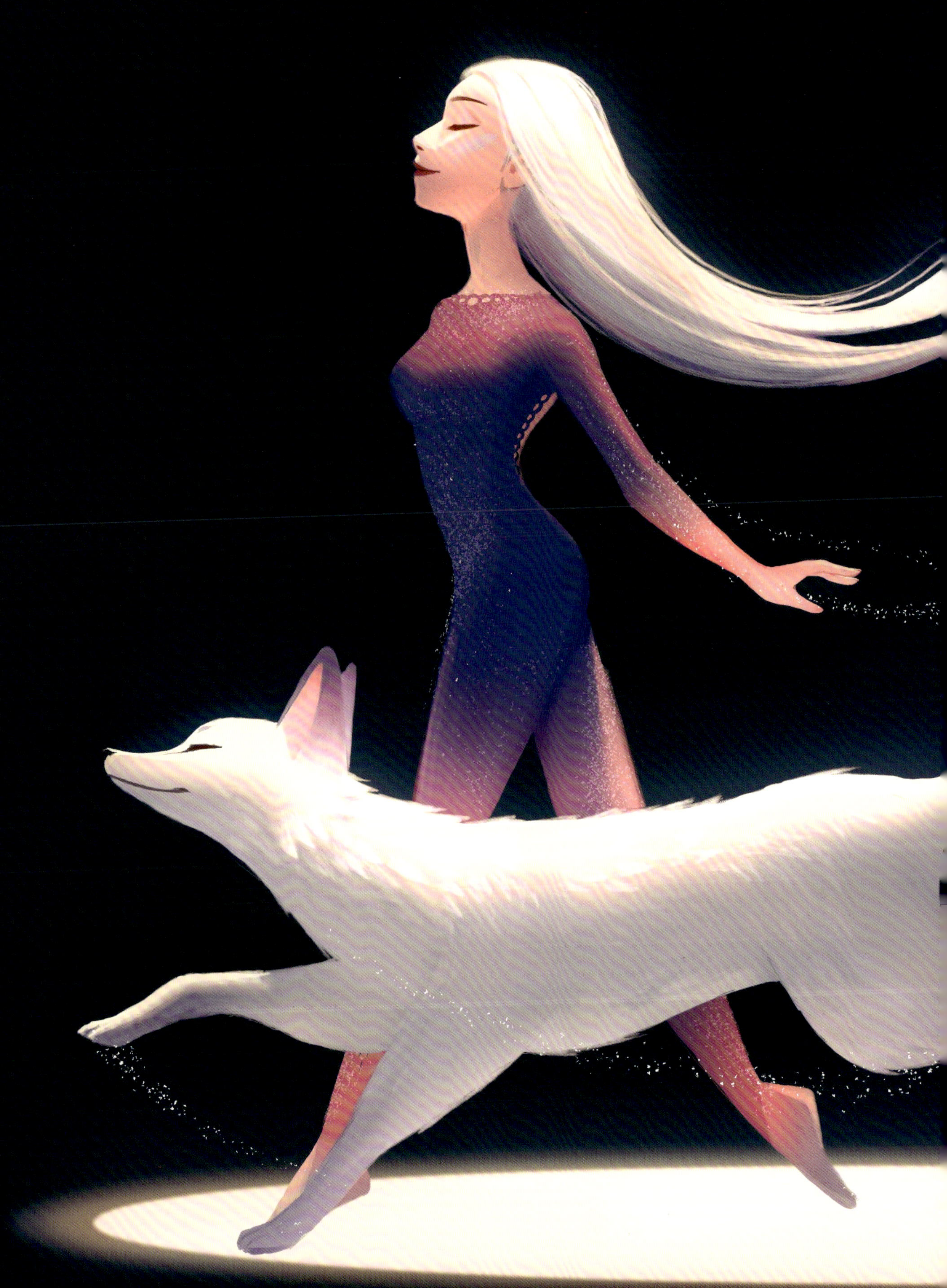

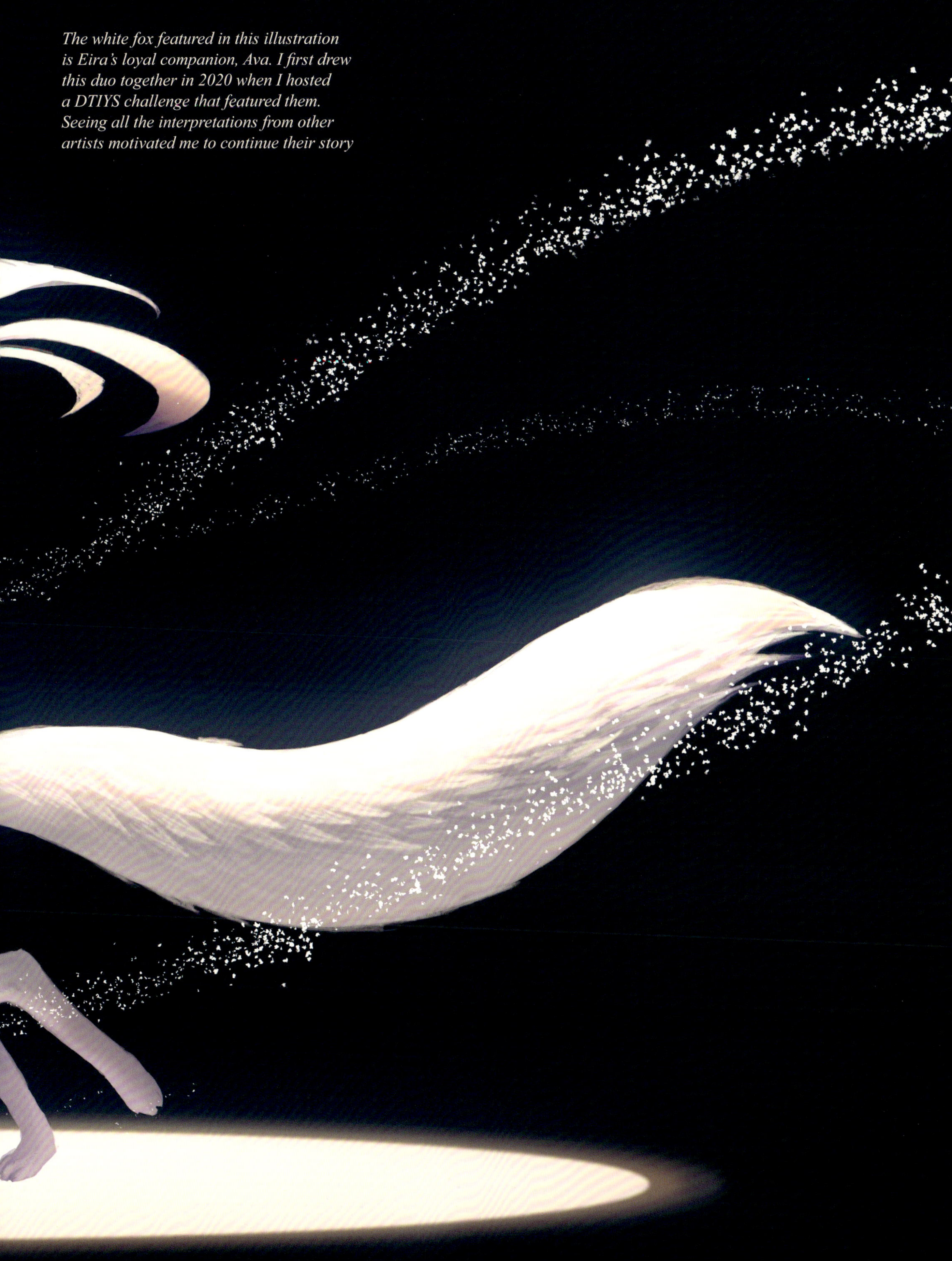

The white fox featured in this illustration is Eira's loyal companion, Ava. I first drew this duo together in 2020 when I hosted a DTIYS challenge that featured them. Seeing all the interpretations from other artists motivated me to continue their story

I wanted to capture a carefree moment, with Eira and Ava running down a mountainous slope, crossing a field of white flowers

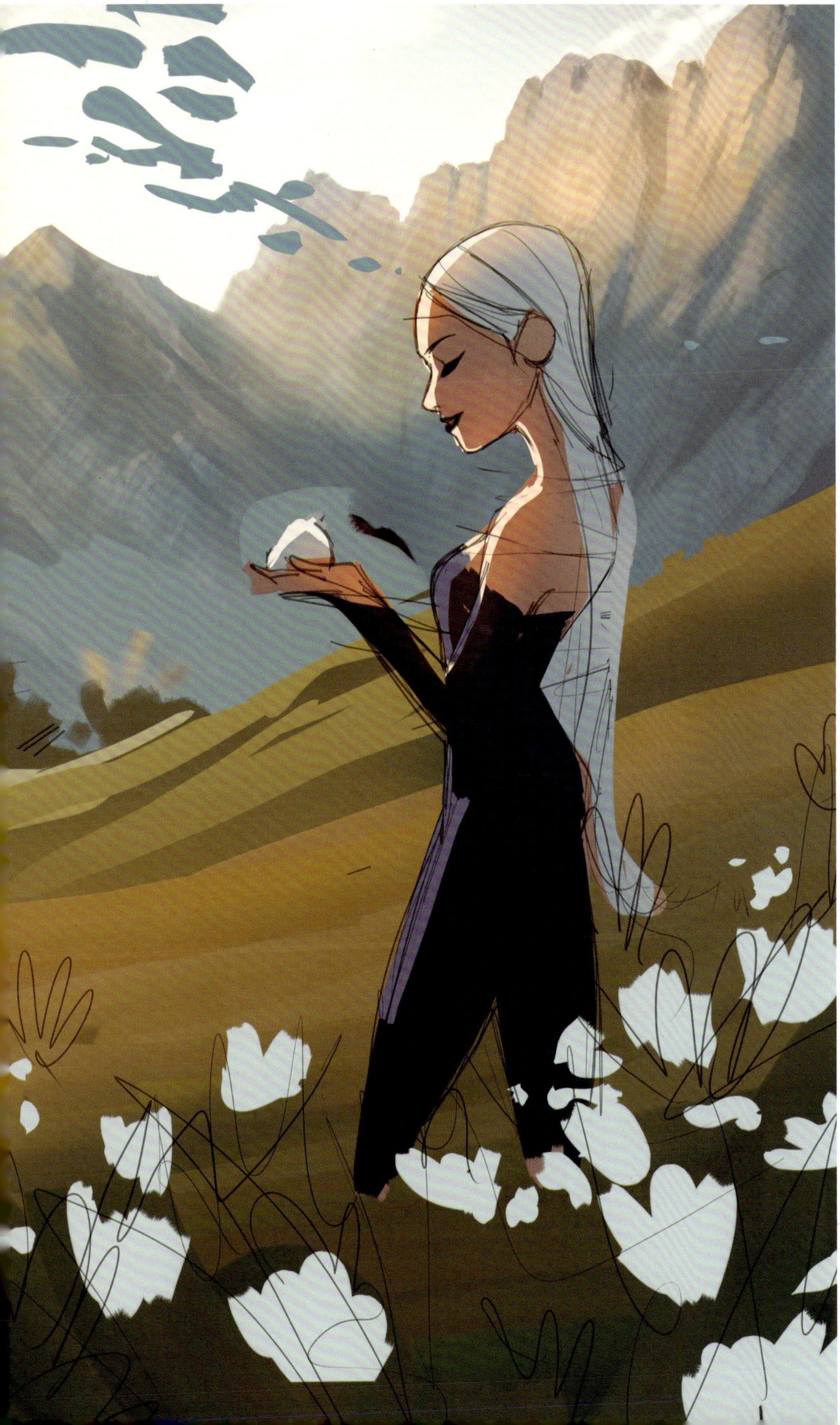

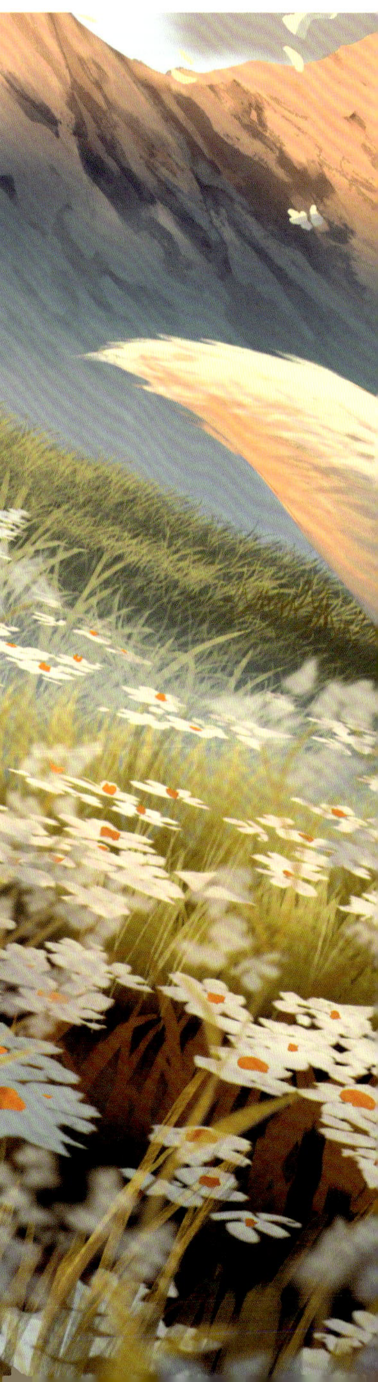

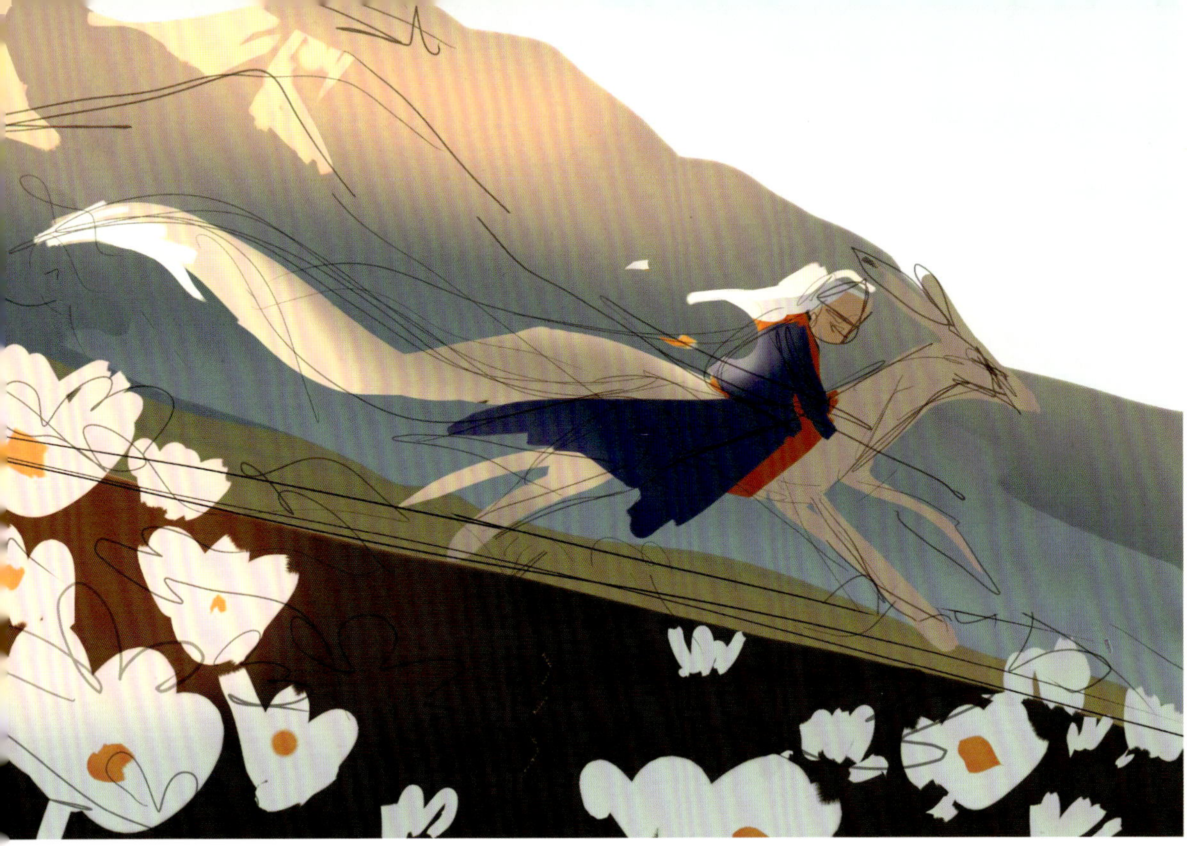

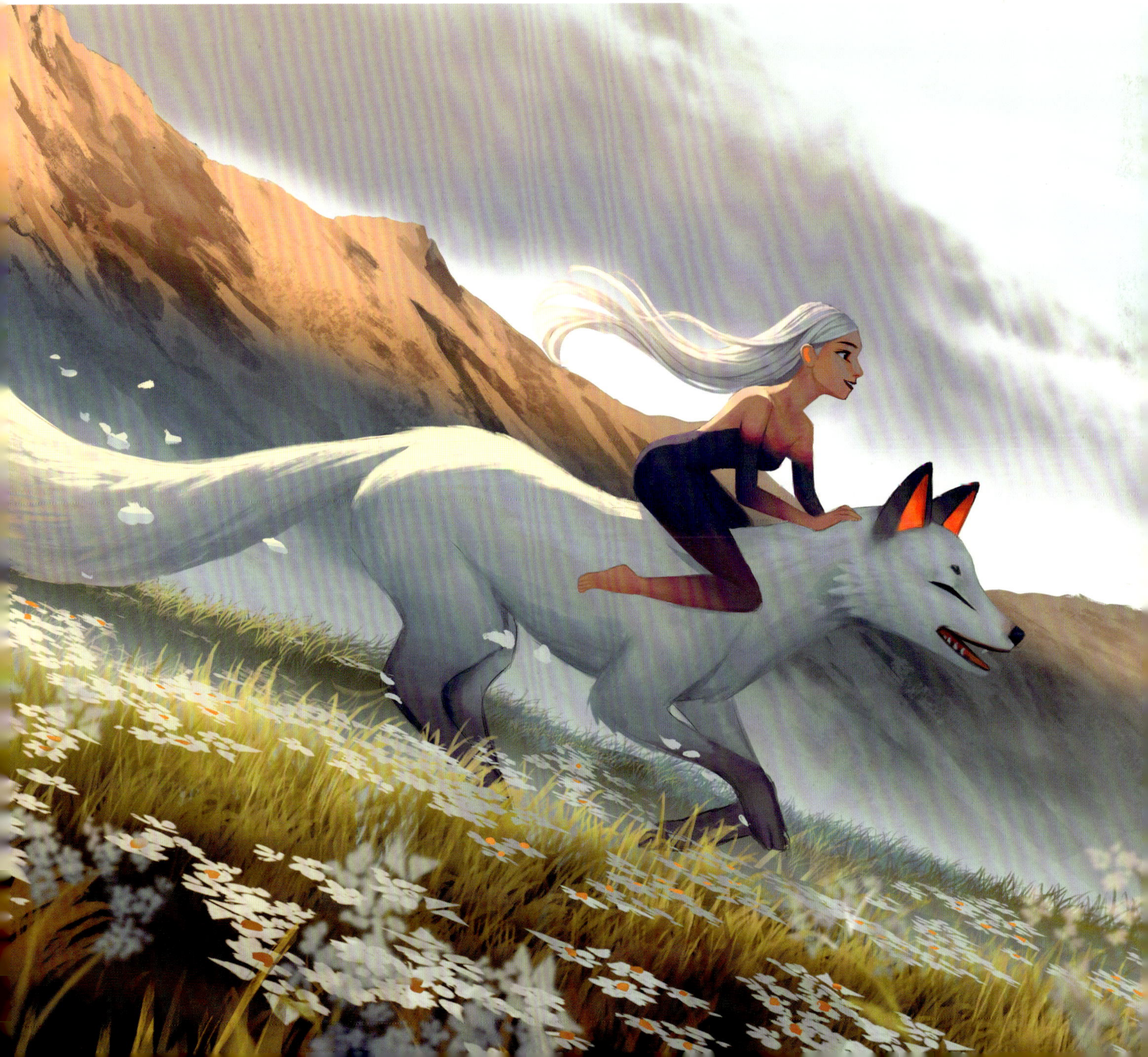

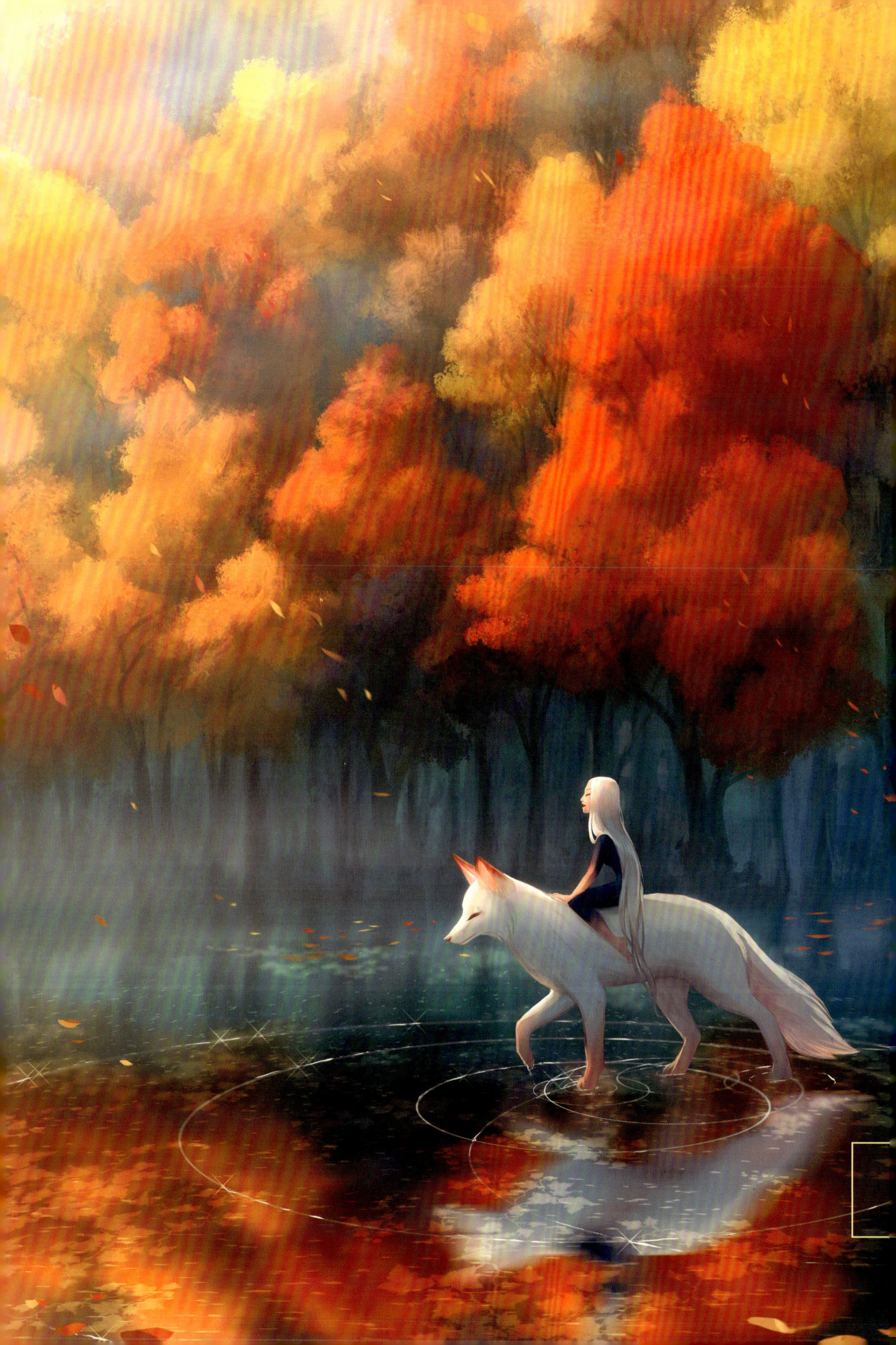

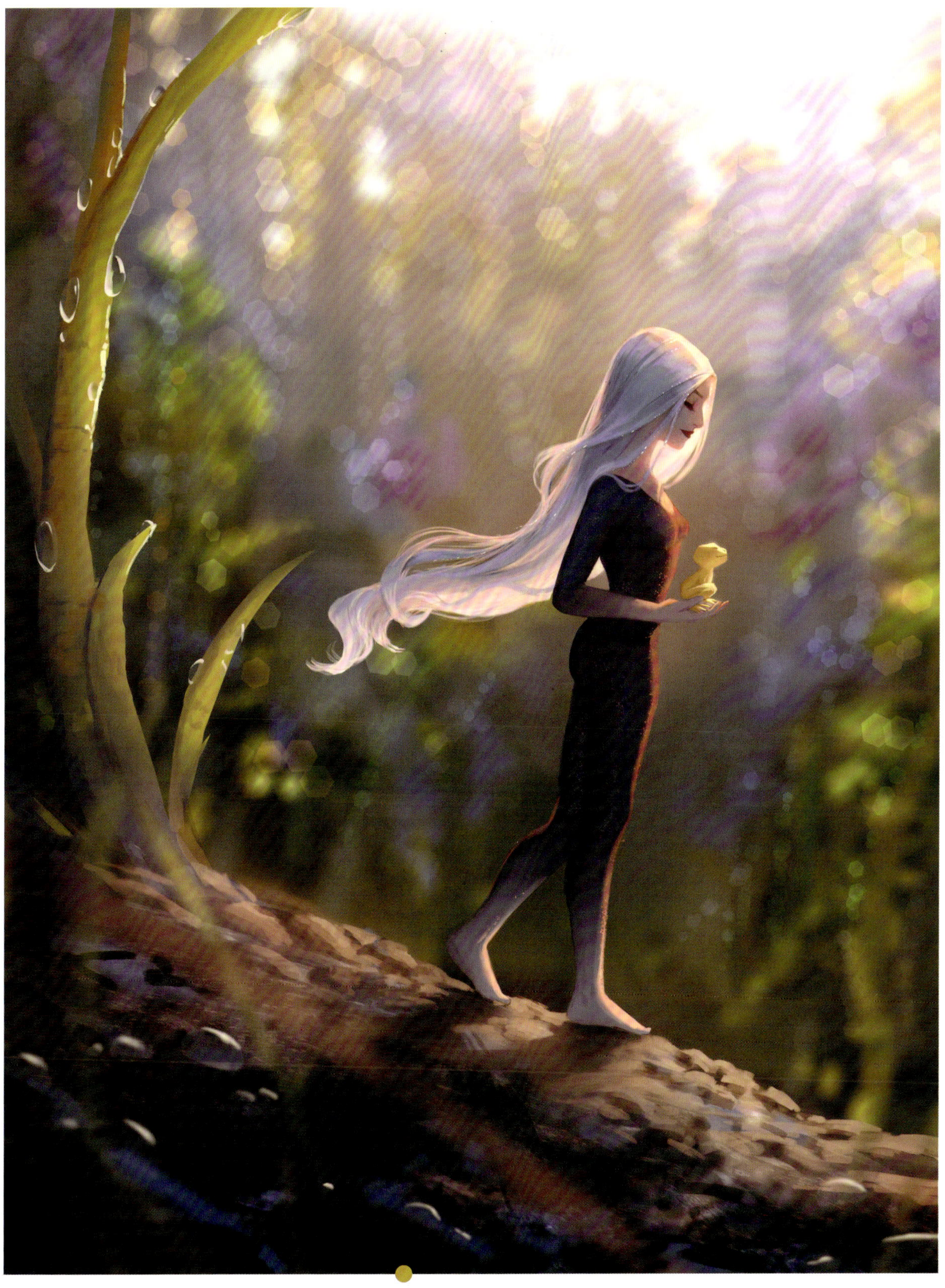

Here, Eira is holding a golden frog, which is one of my sister's original characters. We love mixing each other's characters and storylines!

This piece is one of my favourites! I think I managed to capture the beauty of this autumn landscape quite nicely

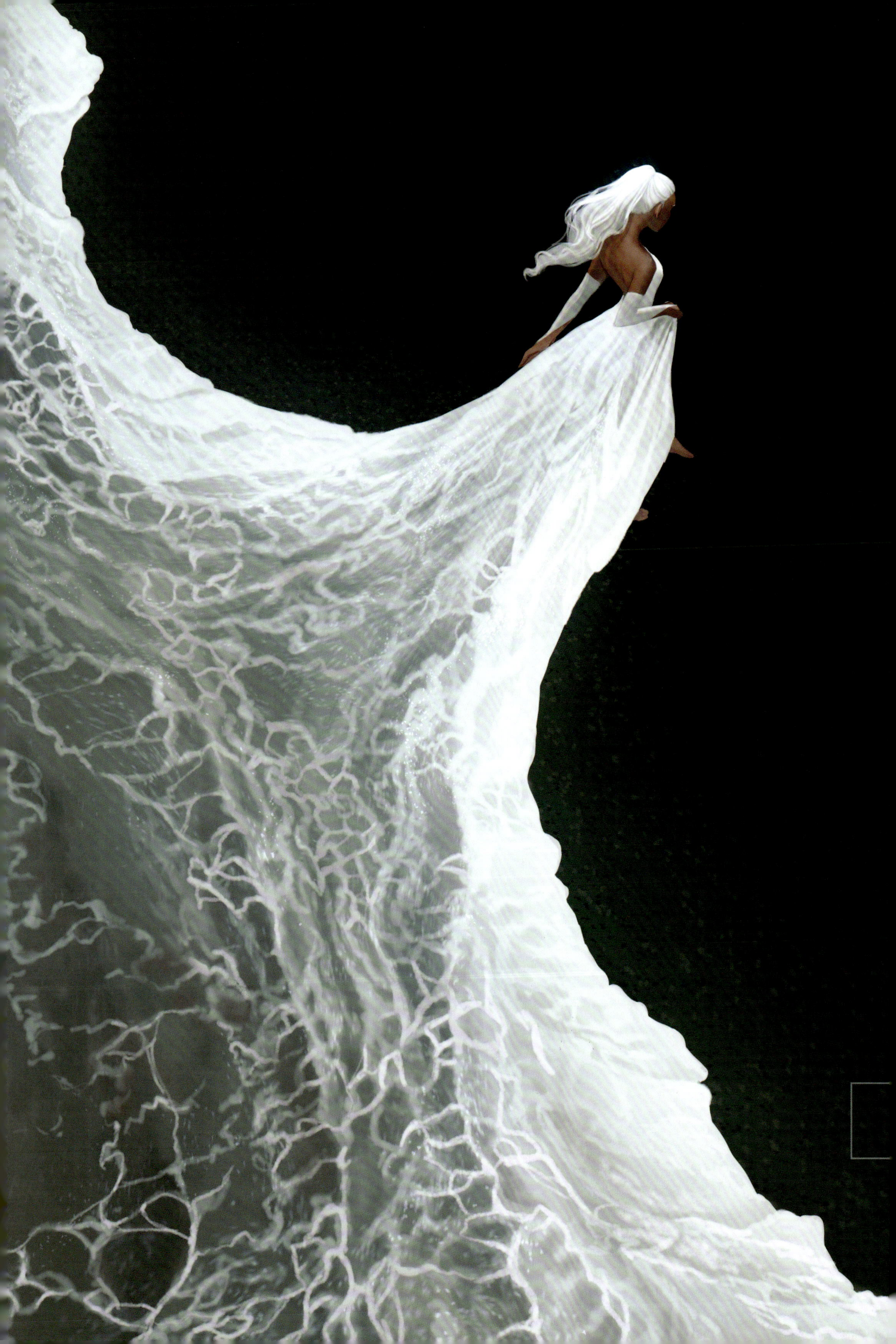

WAVE SERIES

As I explored more nature photography, I stumbled across the beautiful black beaches found on Iceland's coastline. I would love to travel to these places one day to experience this incredible environment with my own senses.

The striking contrast between the white waves and black sand was so intriguing to me, so I thought it would be fun to design a character based on it. I wanted to create a surreal illustration where the character's dress blends into the ocean, making it appear as if she's carrying the white-wash with her onto shore.

Initially, I had no plans to explore this concept further, but as I completed the artwork, I thought it would be a fun series of fantasy illustrations. I focused on exploring the character further while improving my skills in painting water.

In order to achieve some visual cohesion, the other illustrations in this series have the same colour scheme

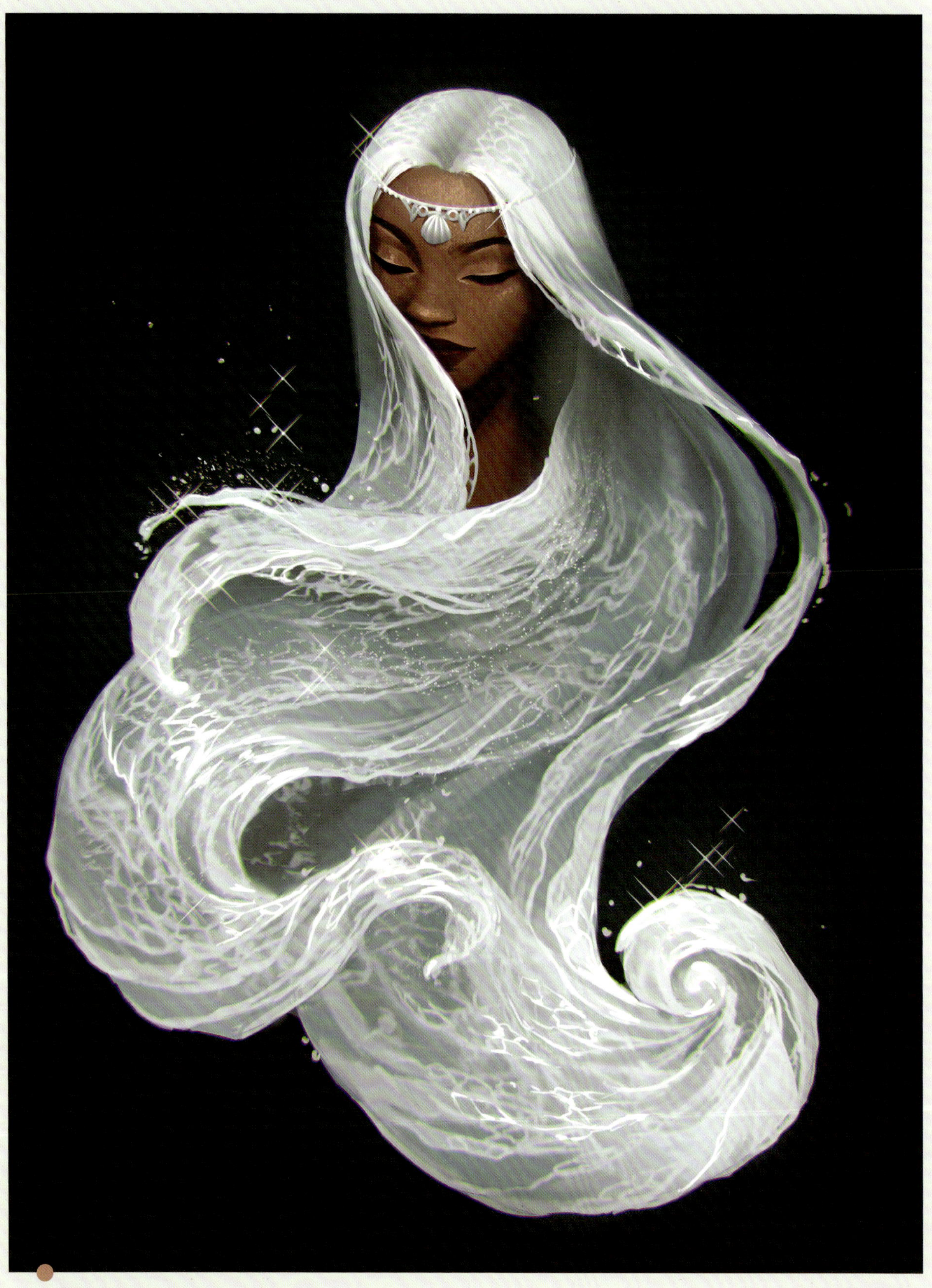

I love the idea of visualizing the ocean in an unusual way

This is the final piece of this short series. I explored a different iteration, showing the character in an underwater setting

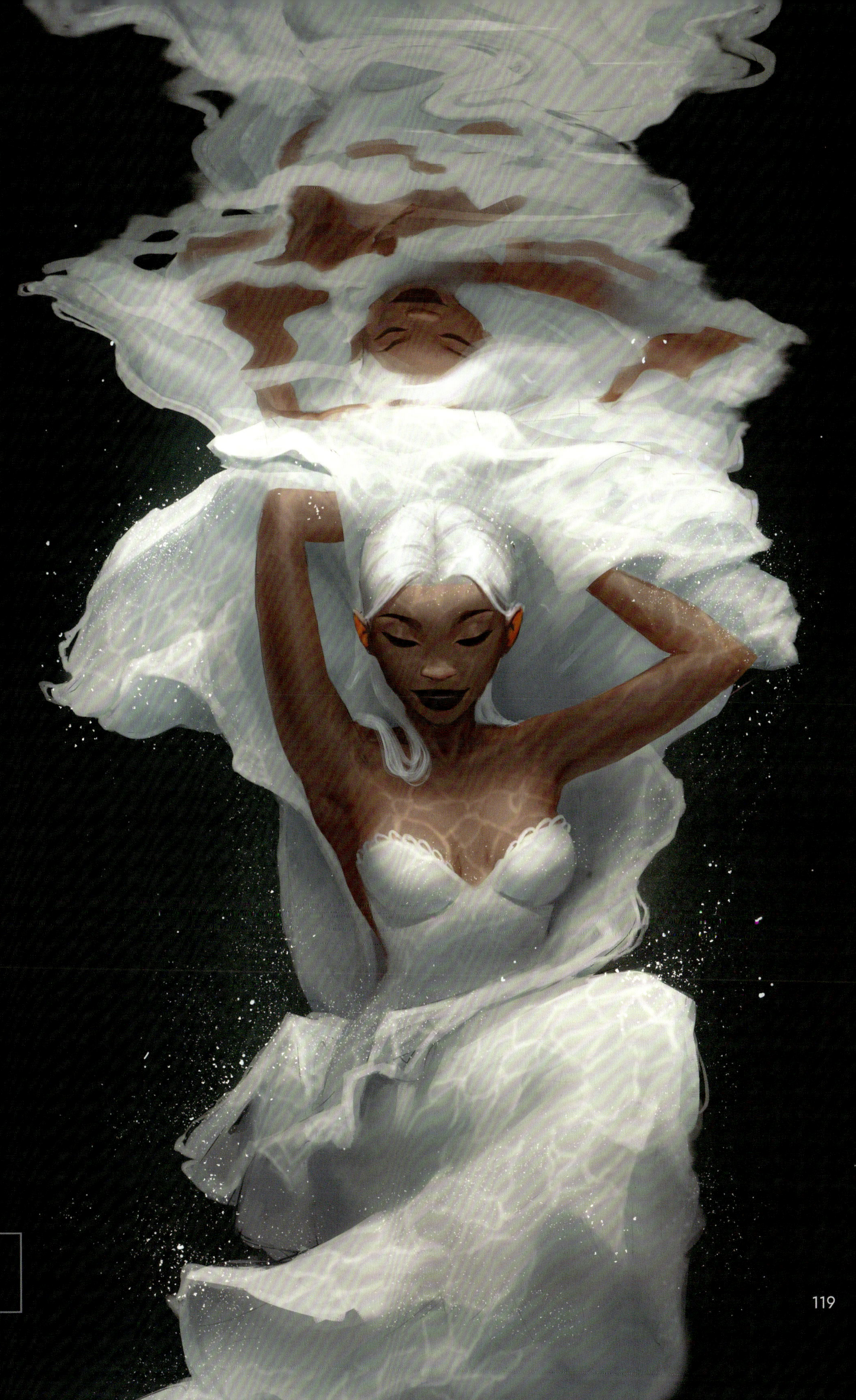

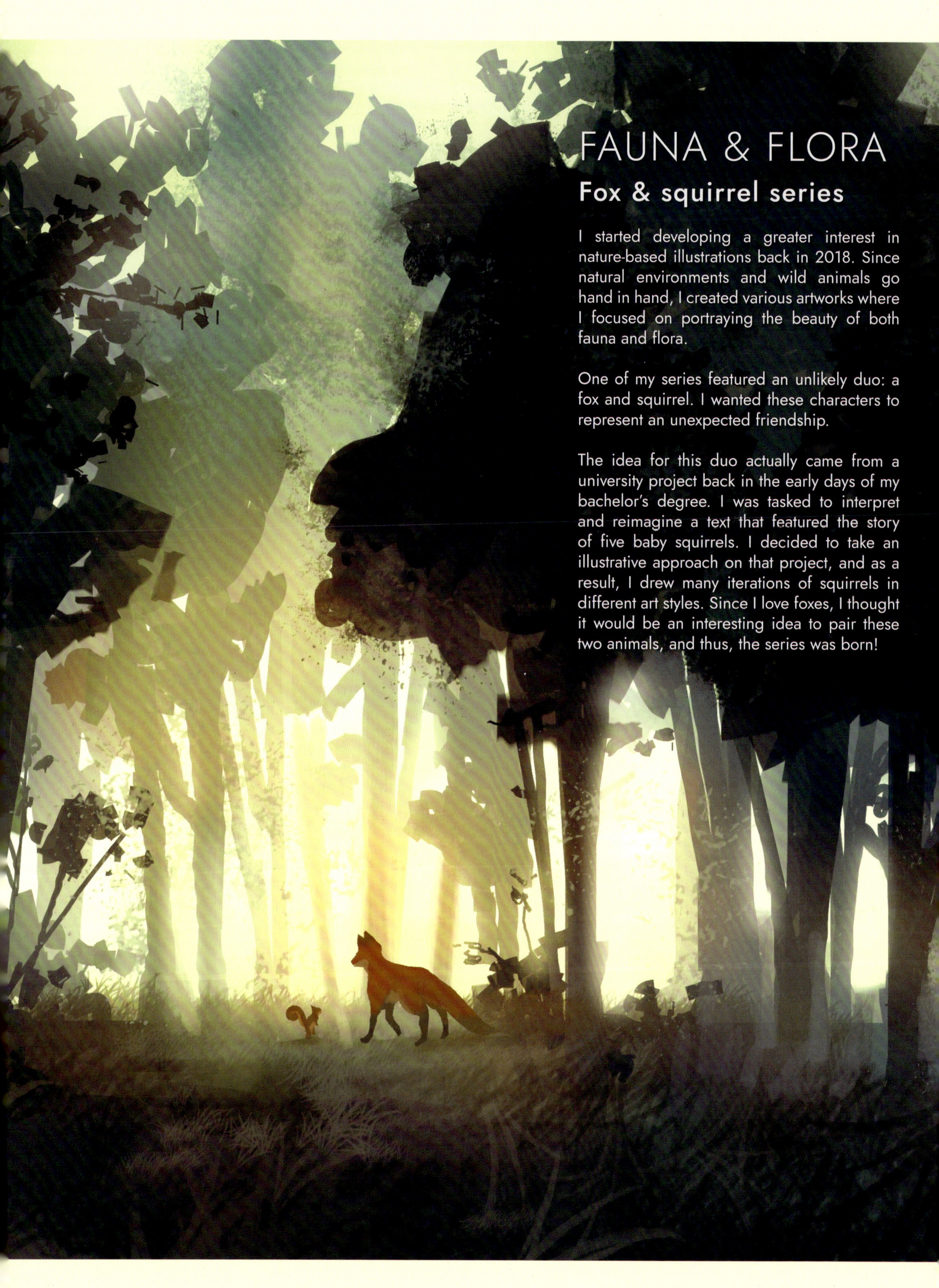

FAUNA & FLORA

Fox & squirrel series

I started developing a greater interest in nature-based illustrations back in 2018. Since natural environments and wild animals go hand in hand, I created various artworks where I focused on portraying the beauty of both fauna and flora.

One of my series featured an unlikely duo: a fox and squirrel. I wanted these characters to represent an unexpected friendship.

The idea for this duo actually came from a university project back in the early days of my bachelor's degree. I was tasked to interpret and reimagine a text that featured the story of five baby squirrels. I decided to take an illustrative approach on that project, and as a result, I drew many iterations of squirrels in different art styles. Since I love foxes, I thought it would be an interesting idea to pair these two animals, and thus, the series was born!

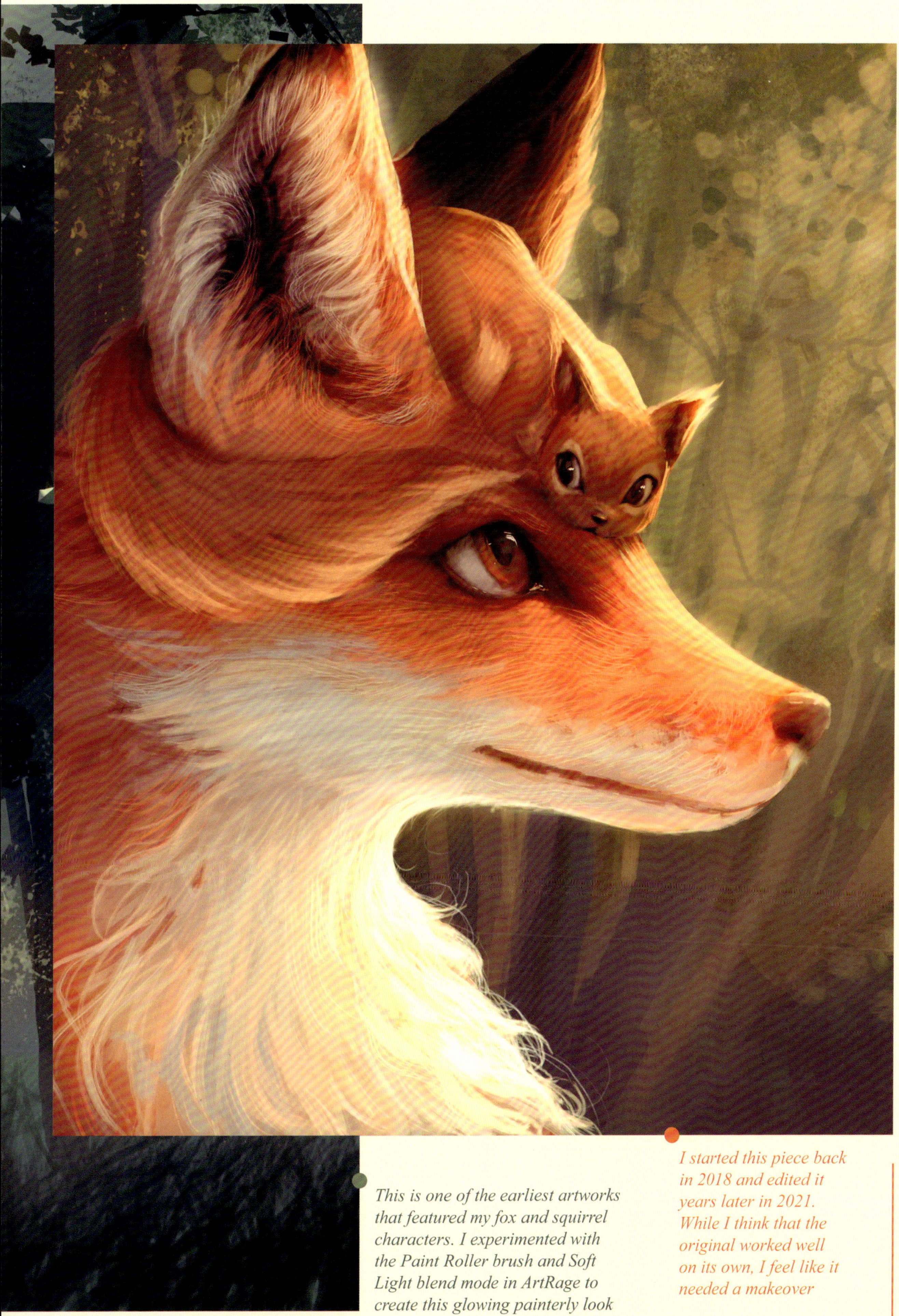

This is one of the earliest artworks that featured my fox and squirrel characters. I experimented with the Paint Roller brush and Soft Light blend mode in ArtRage to create this glowing painterly look

I started this piece back in 2018 and edited it years later in 2021. While I think that the original worked well on its own, I feel like it needed a makeover

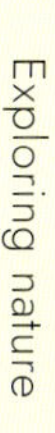

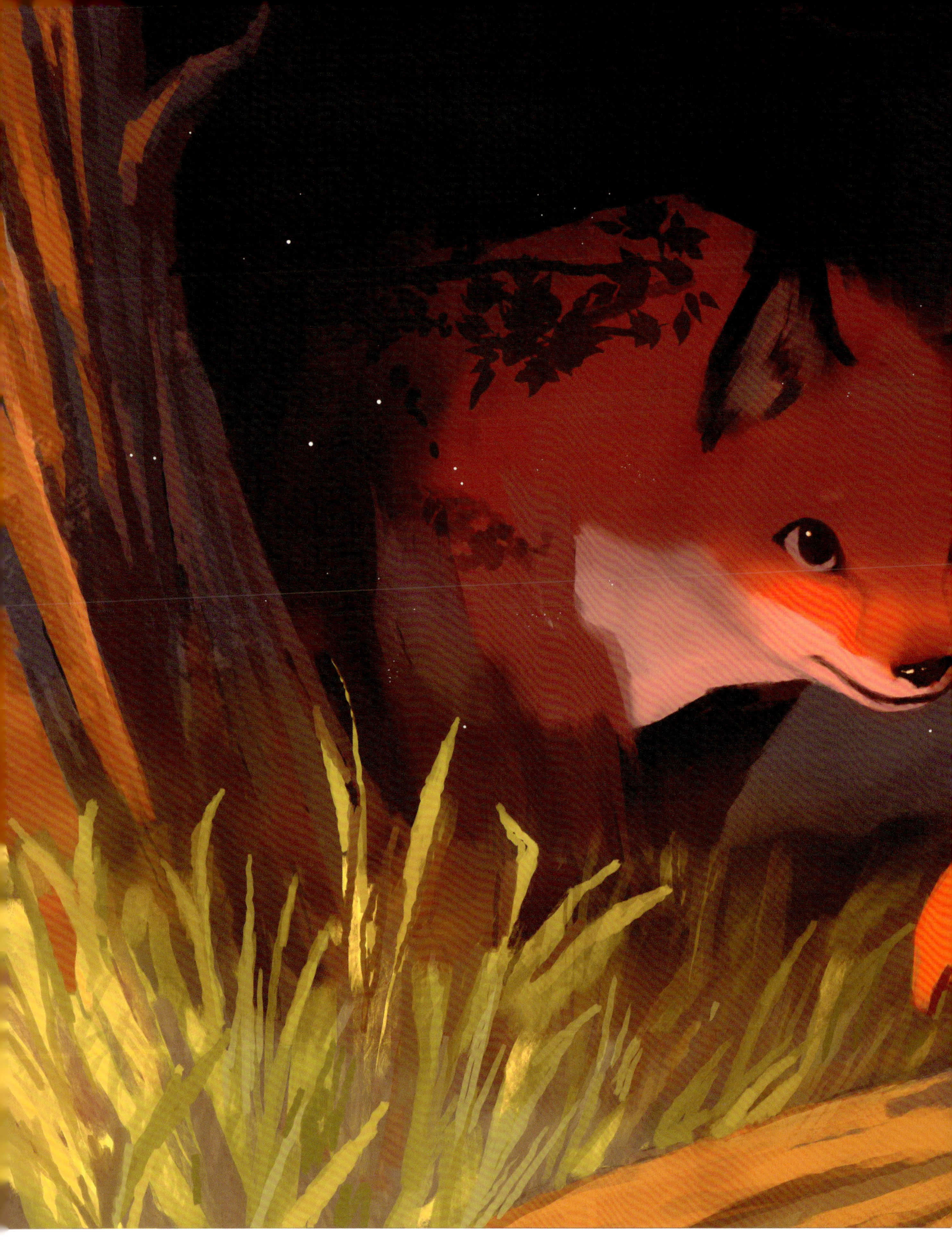

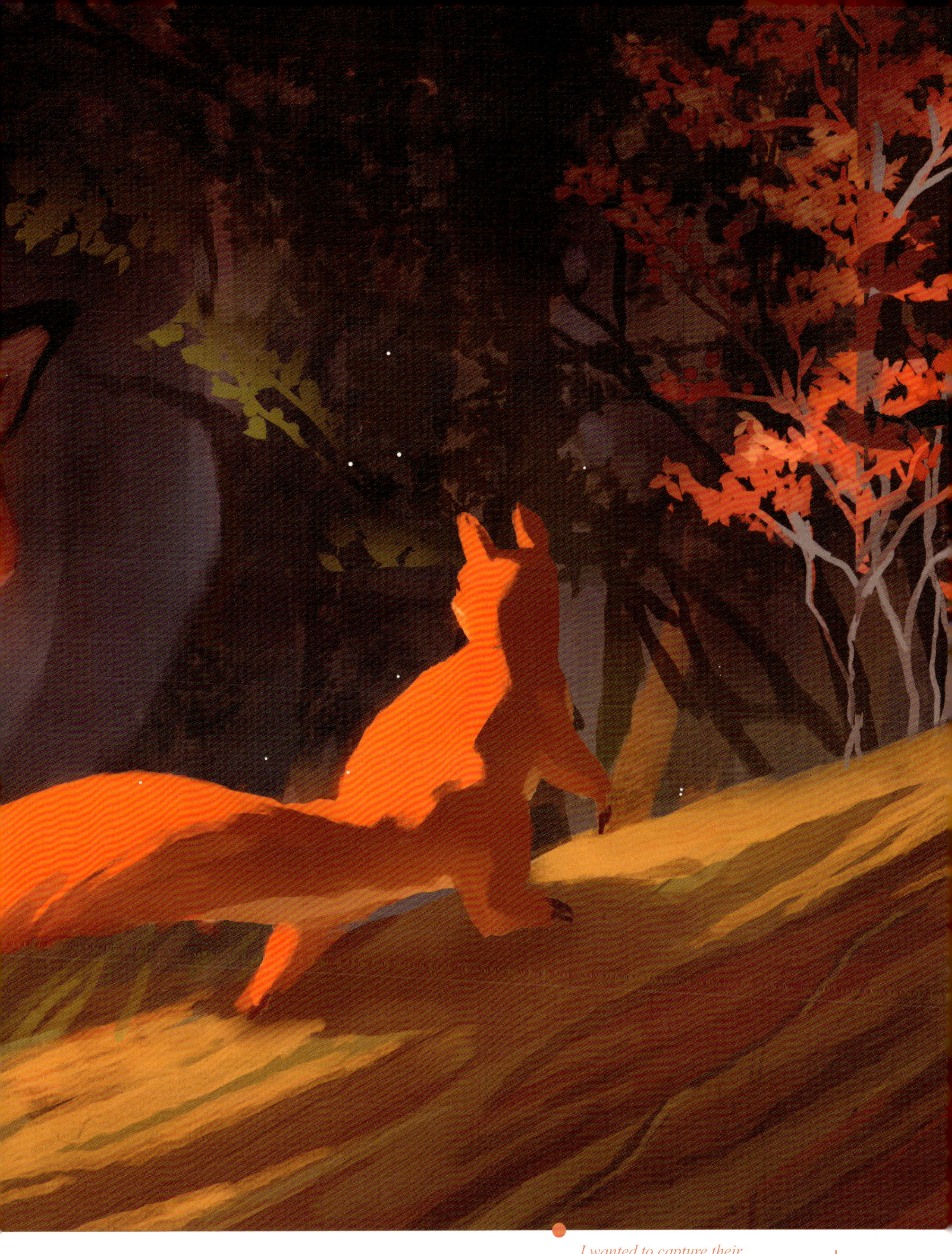

I wanted to capture their first unexpected encounter

Trees & flowers

I like to capture warm feelings in my work, either through a happy scene or comforting lighting. Flowers are an integral part of many of my nature illustrations; they make up the most beautiful patterns the world has to offer. I spend so much time studying the anatomy of various flowers, thinking of how I could reimagine them in different styles.

As a result of my many nature studies, I have created several custom brushes with which I can quickly recreate silhouettes of certain flowers and leaves. While using premade or custom brushes can save a lot of time, I'm always careful not to overuse them. Any brush that's repeated too many times without variation can give off a copy-paste look. Since I always aim for a natural look, I try to mix things up by using premade brushes as a base before adding custom-painted details like blades of grass or petals overtop. I find that this technique works wonders for me.

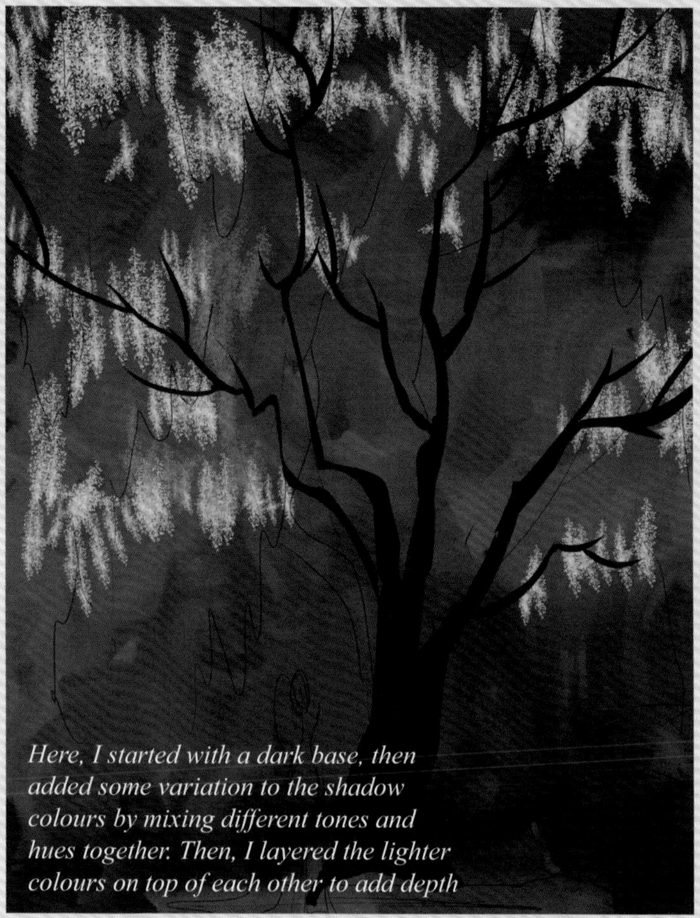

Here, I started with a dark base, then added some variation to the shadow colours by mixing different tones and hues together. Then, I layered the lighter colours on top of each other to add depth

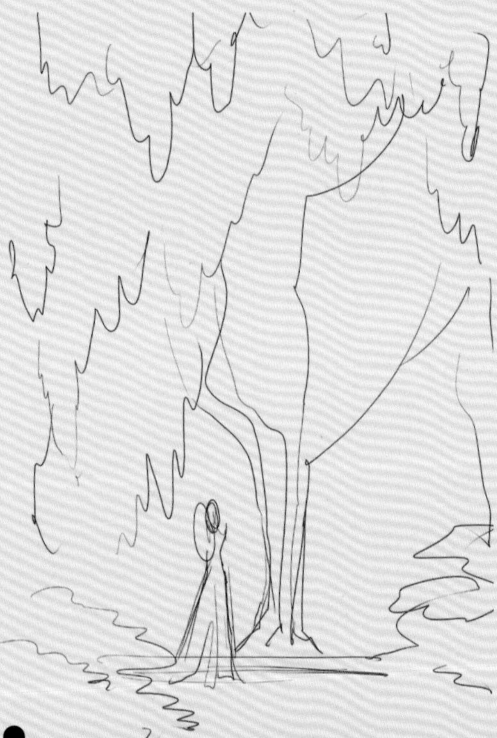

I usually start with a refined sketch to define the general outlines of background elements. However, since this illustration mainly featured blooming flowers and organic shapes, I wanted the painting process to feel natural and experimental. I created a very rough sketch as a base and painted freely without sticking to clean line art

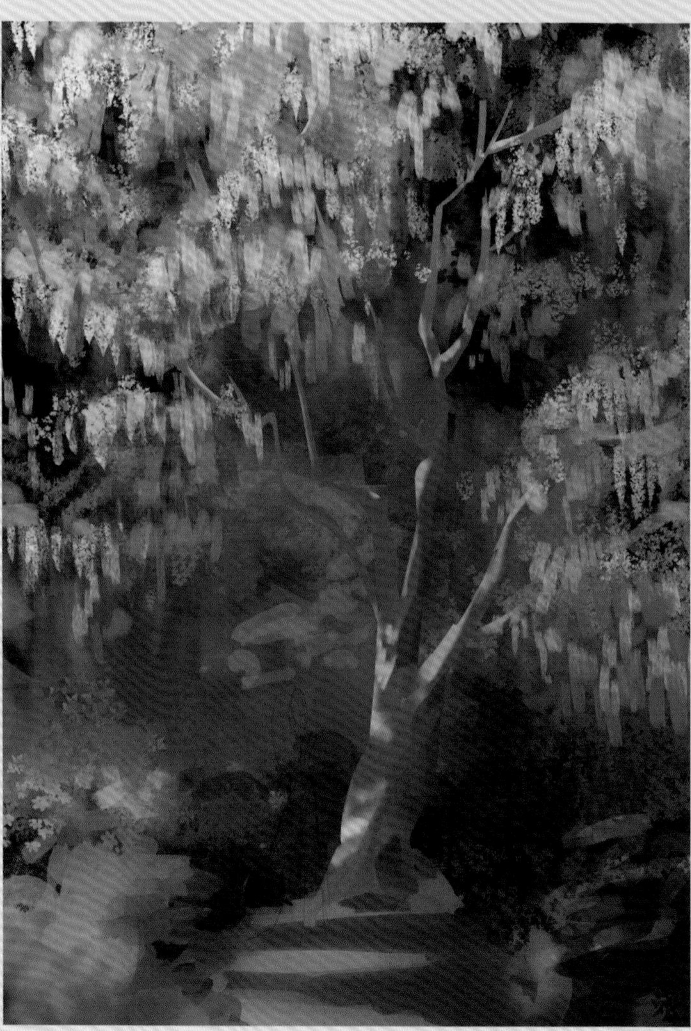

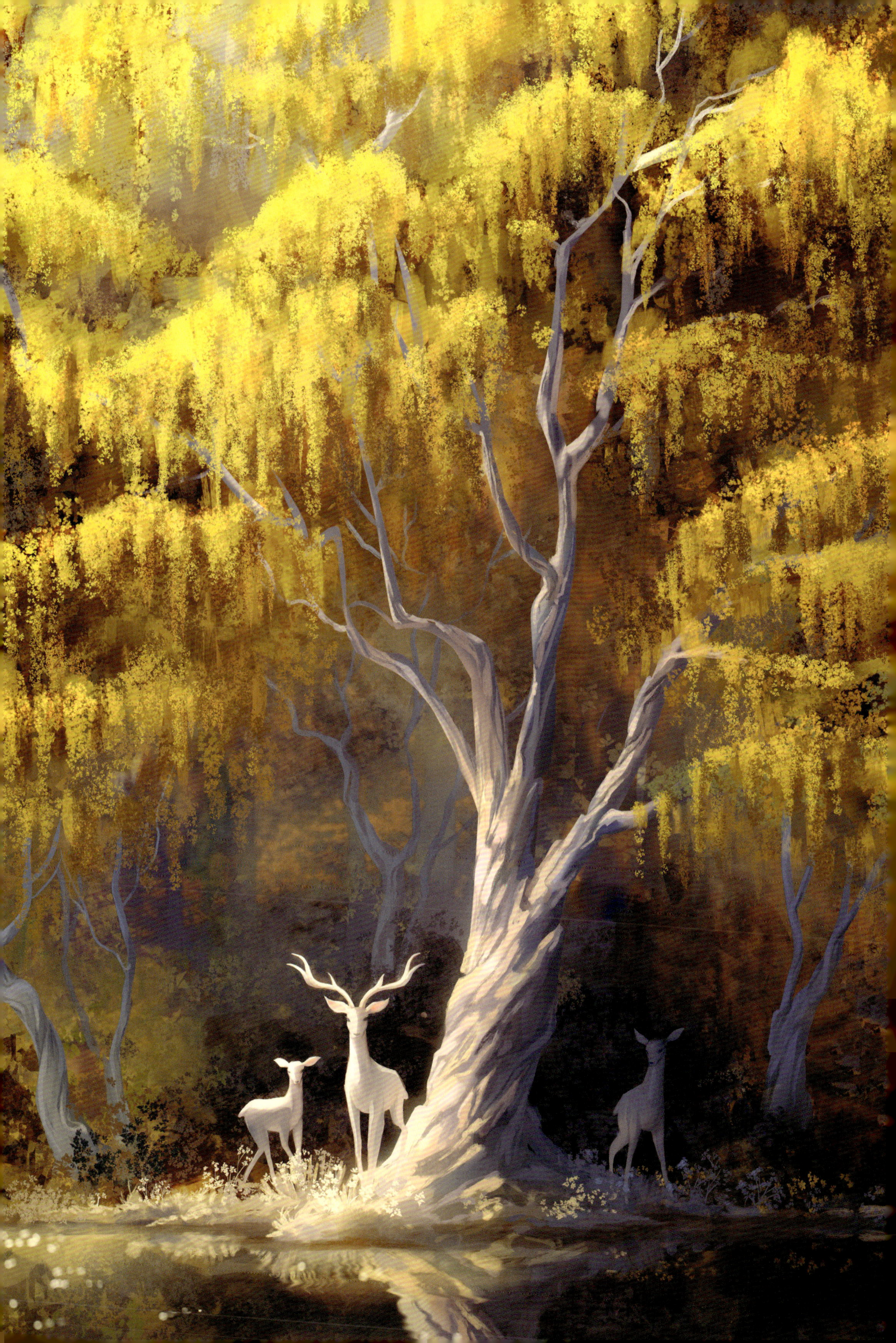

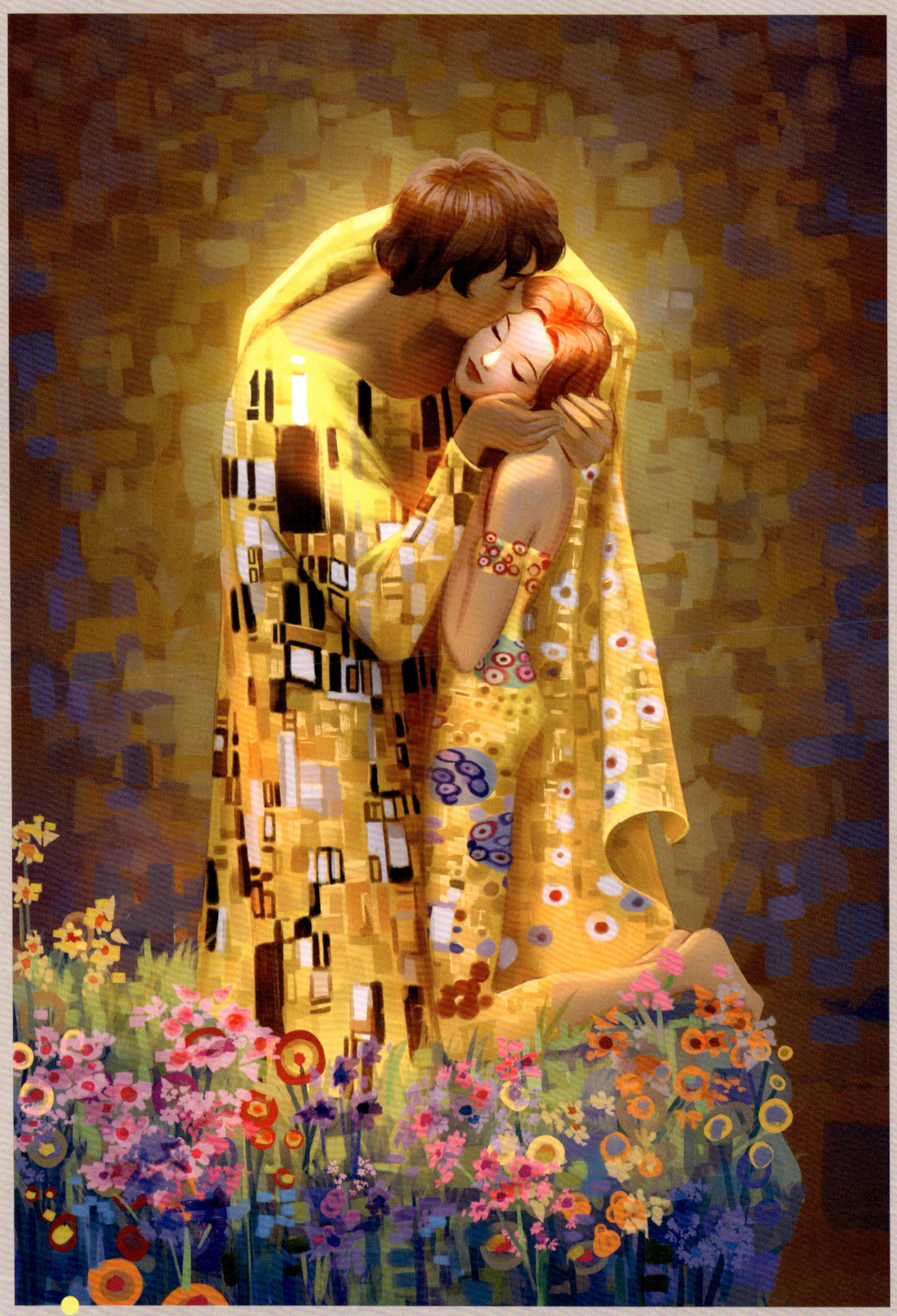

Studying the works of masterful artists really helped me improve my skills! This painting is my interpretation of Gustav Klimt's famous work, The Kiss. *I wanted to capture the scene's tenderness while also experimenting with the graphic style of the original. I found it intriguing to mix these flat, stylized flowers with the more realistically shaded characters*

Daisies radiate happiness and freshness. In this piece, I focused on studying these flowers and creating a character who would blend well into the scene

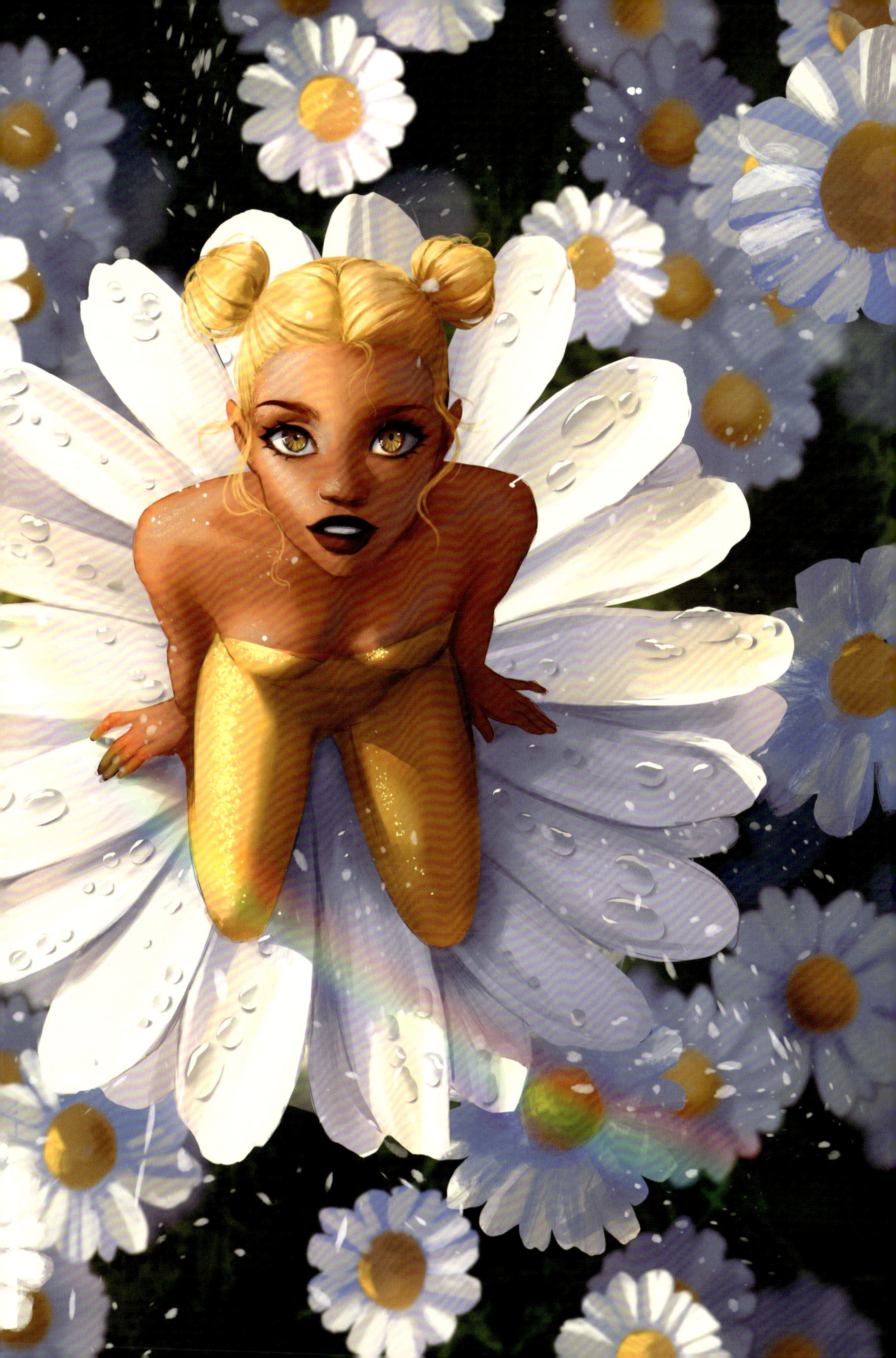

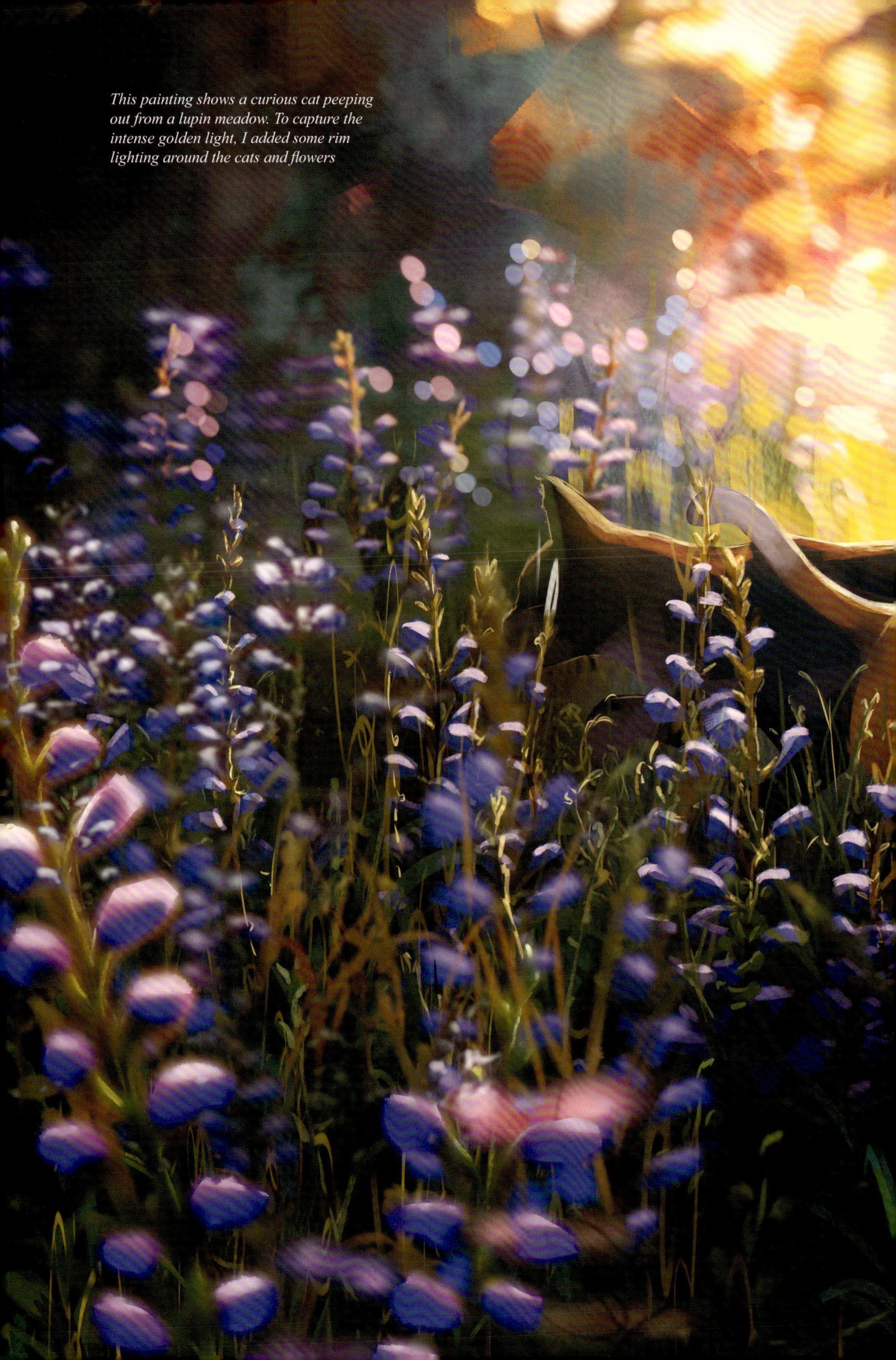

This painting shows a curious cat peeping out from a lupin meadow. To capture the intense golden light, I added some rim lighting around the cats and flowers

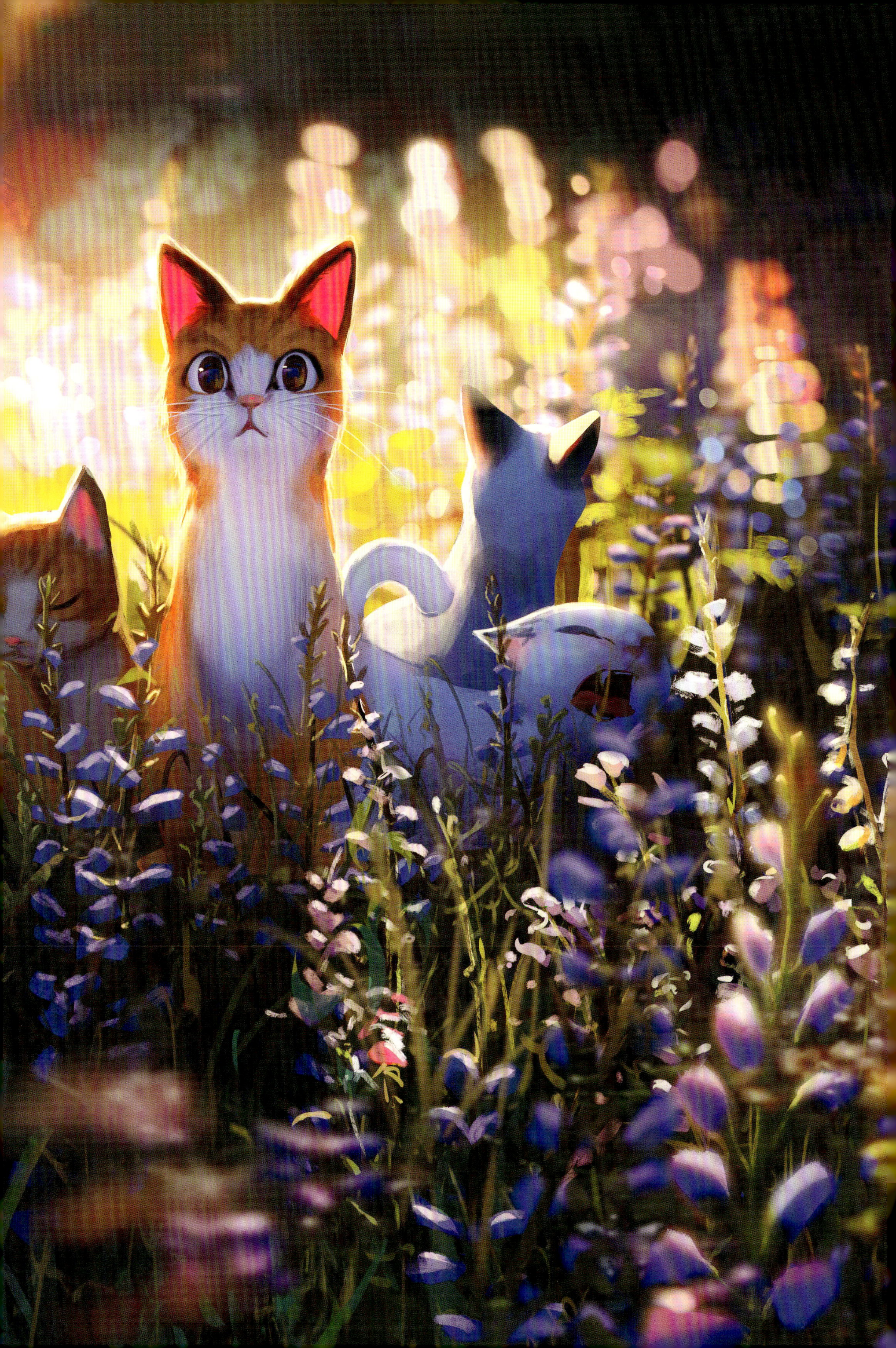

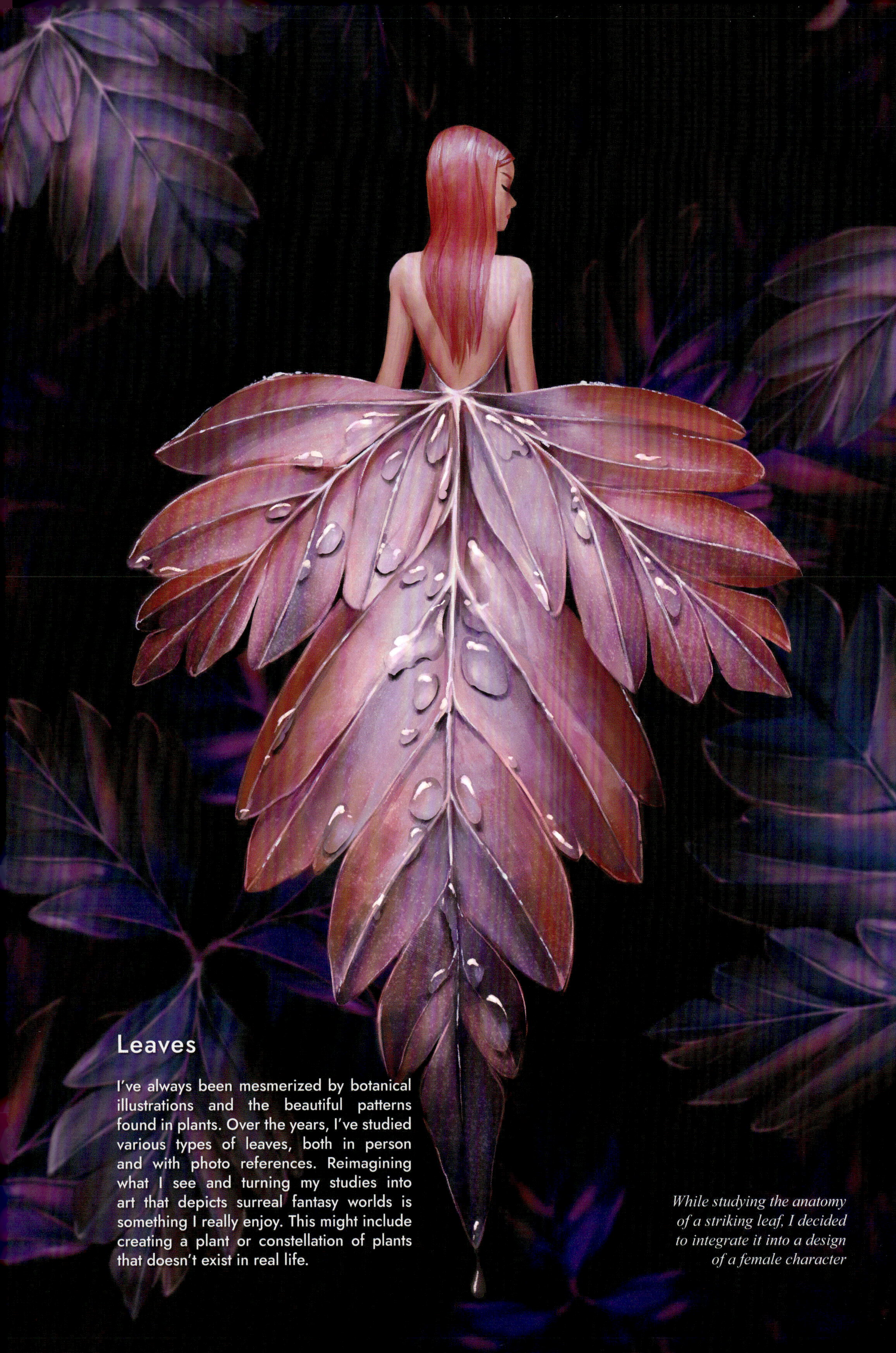

Leaves

I've always been mesmerized by botanical illustrations and the beautiful patterns found in plants. Over the years, I've studied various types of leaves, both in person and with photo references. Reimagining what I see and turning my studies into art that depicts surreal fantasy worlds is something I really enjoy. This might include creating a plant or constellation of plants that doesn't exist in real life.

While studying the anatomy of a striking leaf, I decided to integrate it into a design of a female character

Mixing traditional & digital tools

During my master's degree at the Hochschule Anhalt, I joined two short watercolour courses led by Mauricio Sosa Noreña that focused on illustrating botanicals. Before then, I hadn't worked much with traditional tools. While I absolutely love to work digitally, there was something captivating about picking up an actual brush once again.

Since I wanted to incorporate what I learned from the course into my digital workflow, I decided to create some custom brushes from my watercolour paintings. This is something I probably wouldn't have tried if it weren't for that course. I'm so happy to have gone outside my comfort zone to learn something new.

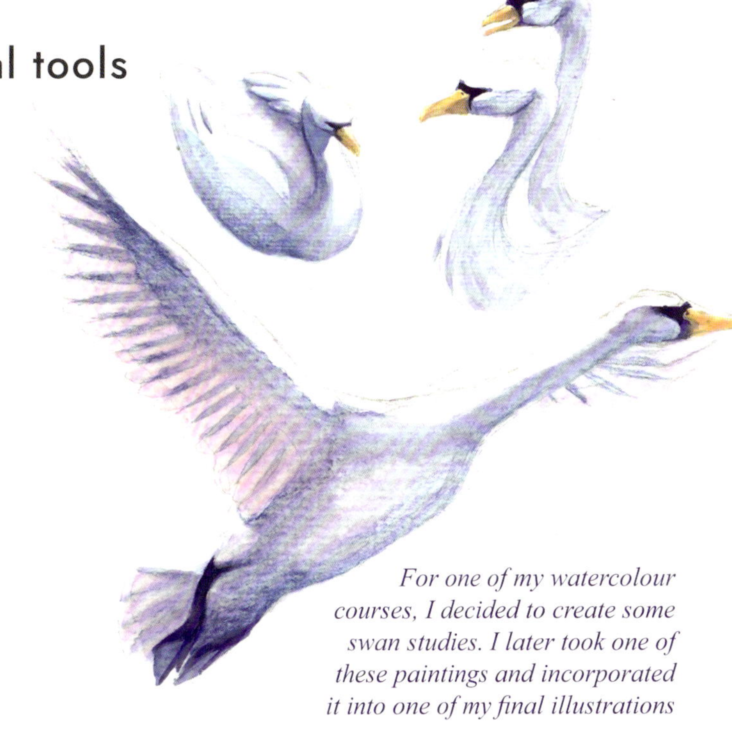

For one of my watercolour courses, I decided to create some swan studies. I later took one of these paintings and incorporated it into one of my final illustrations

These are some stylized watercolour feathers, leaves, and trees. I scanned these illustrations and used some of them as brush heads for new custom brushes

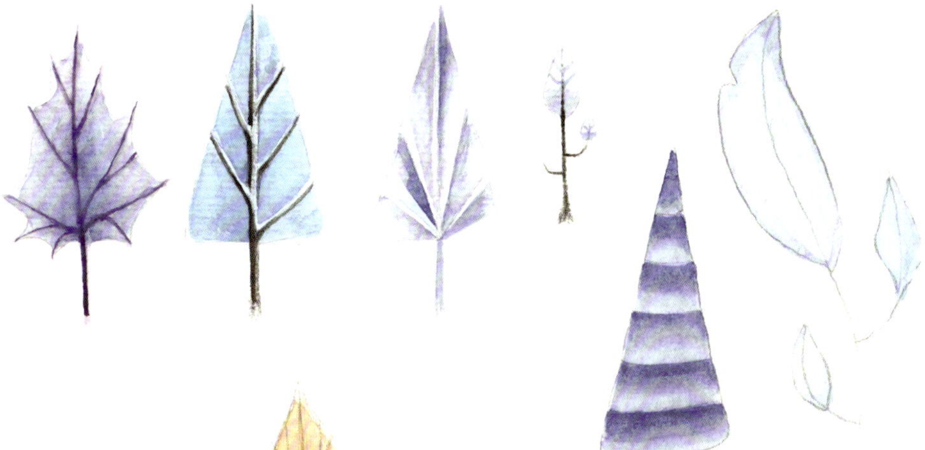

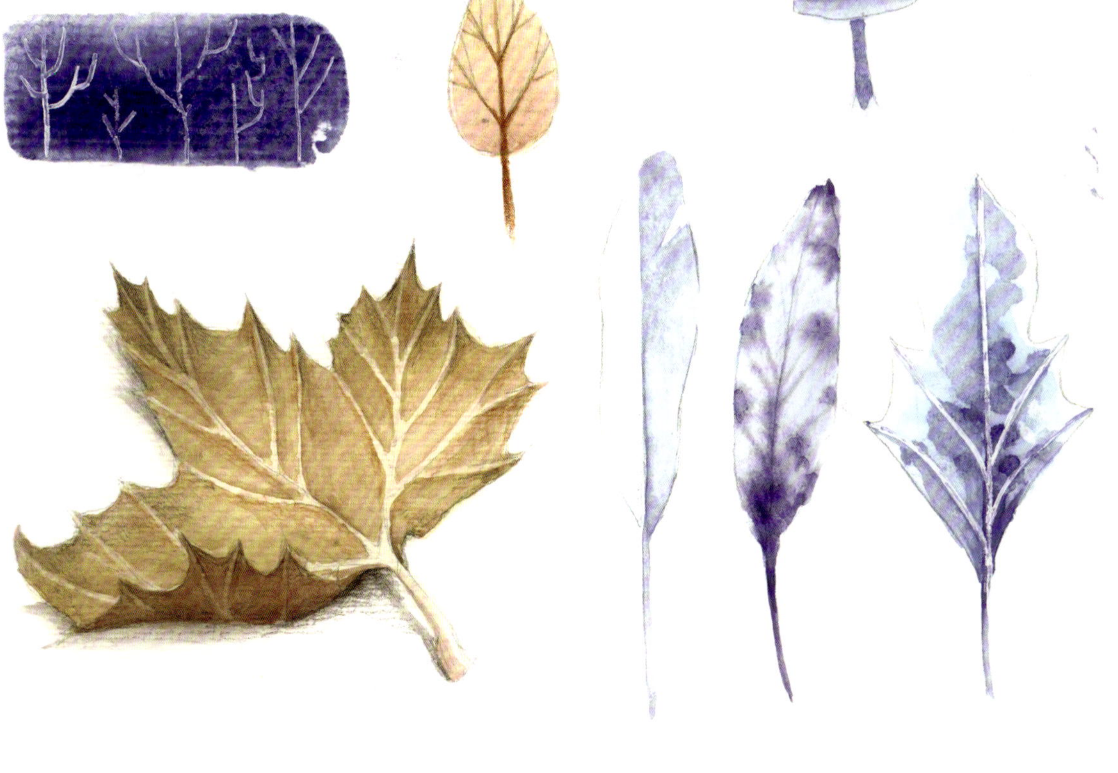

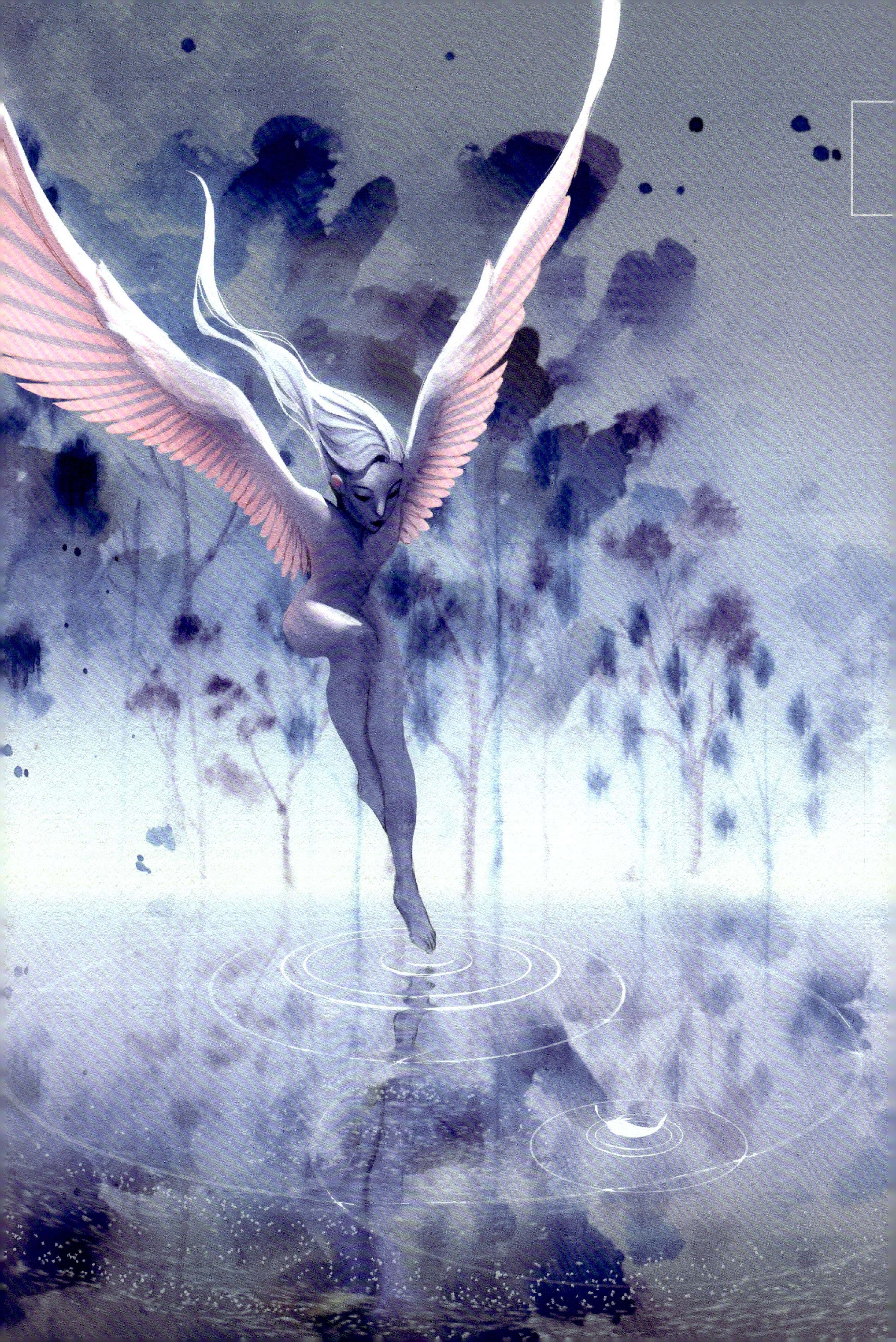

To round off this project, I created this illustration using the methods I'd learned on the short course

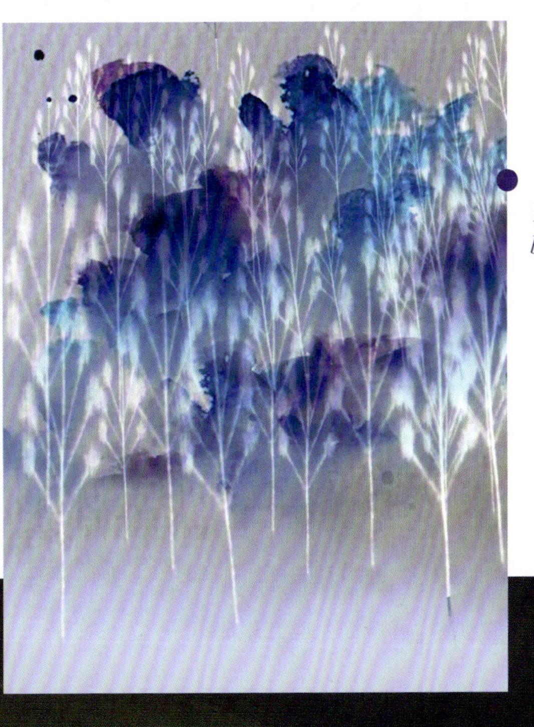

I tested out some of the custom brushes I'd created to see what types of textures I could make

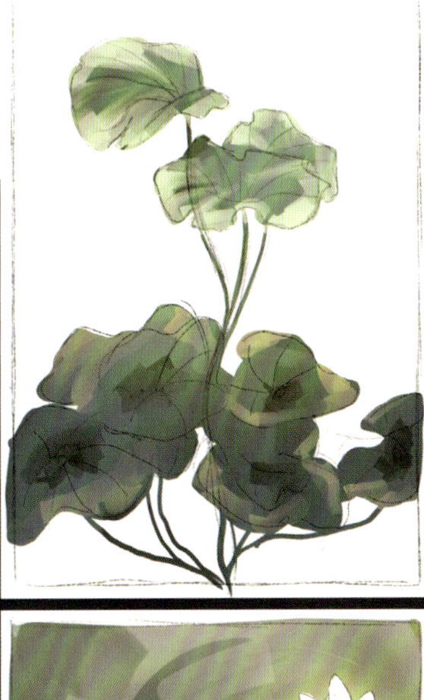

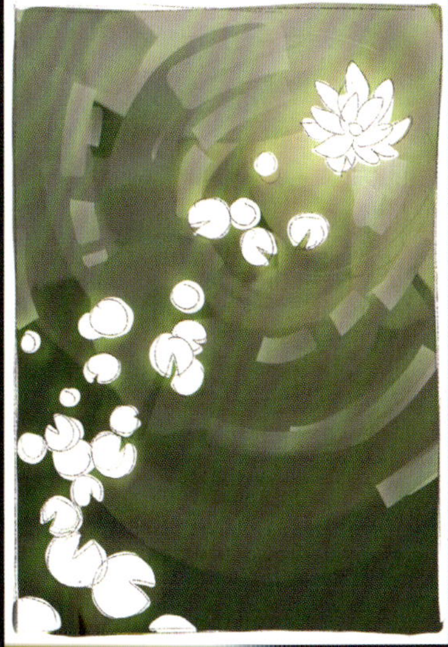

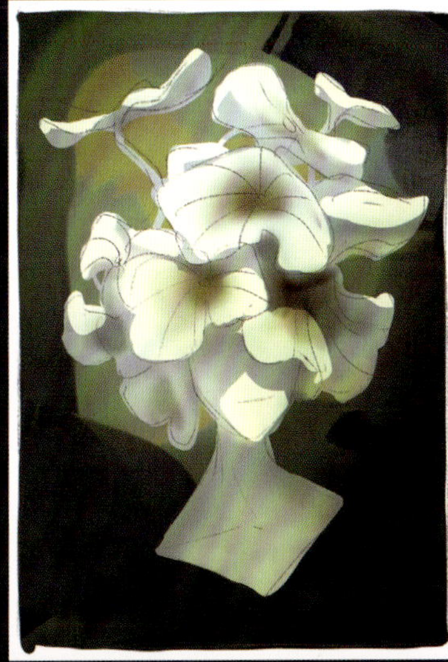

Here are some of the many sketches I created for my class project

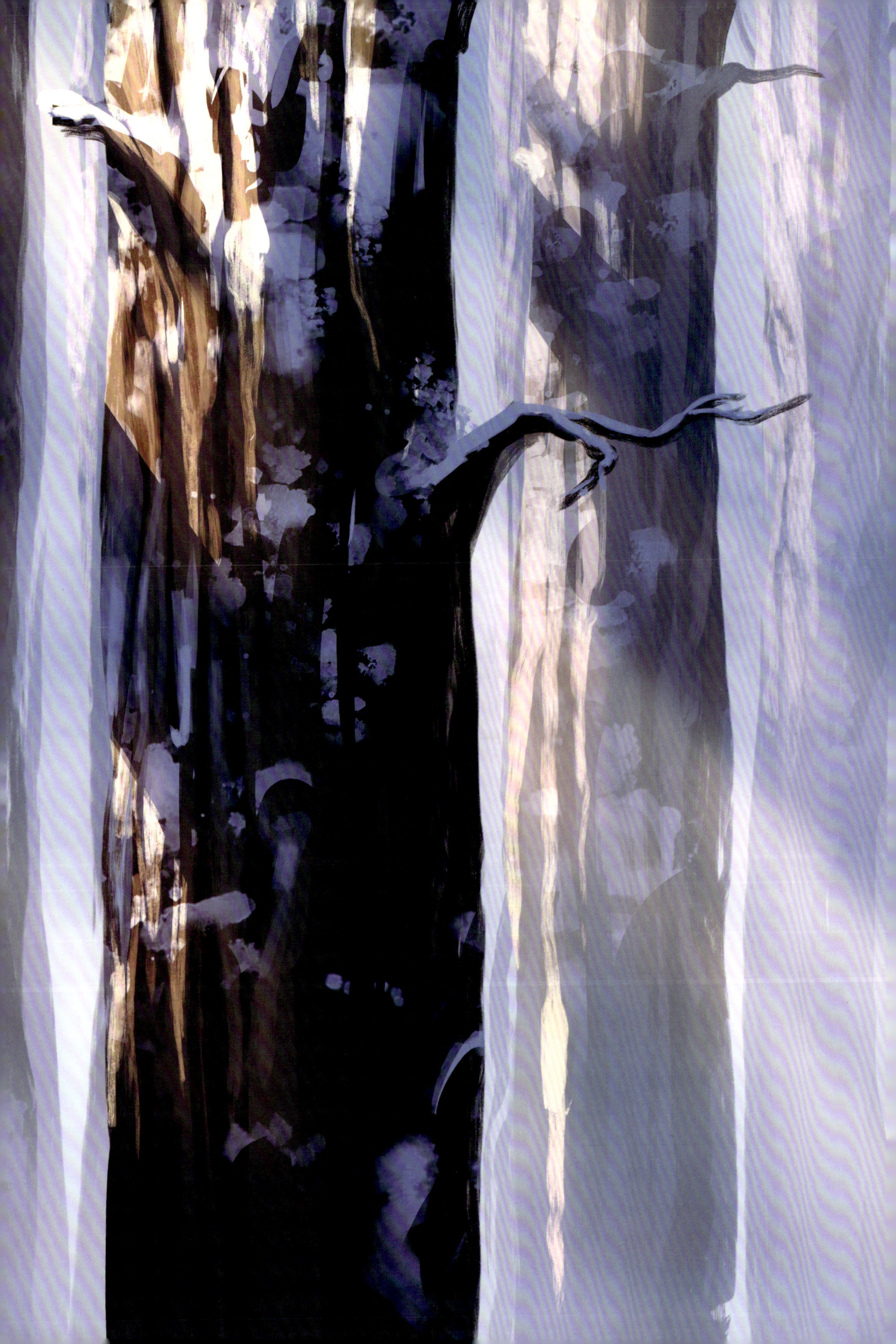

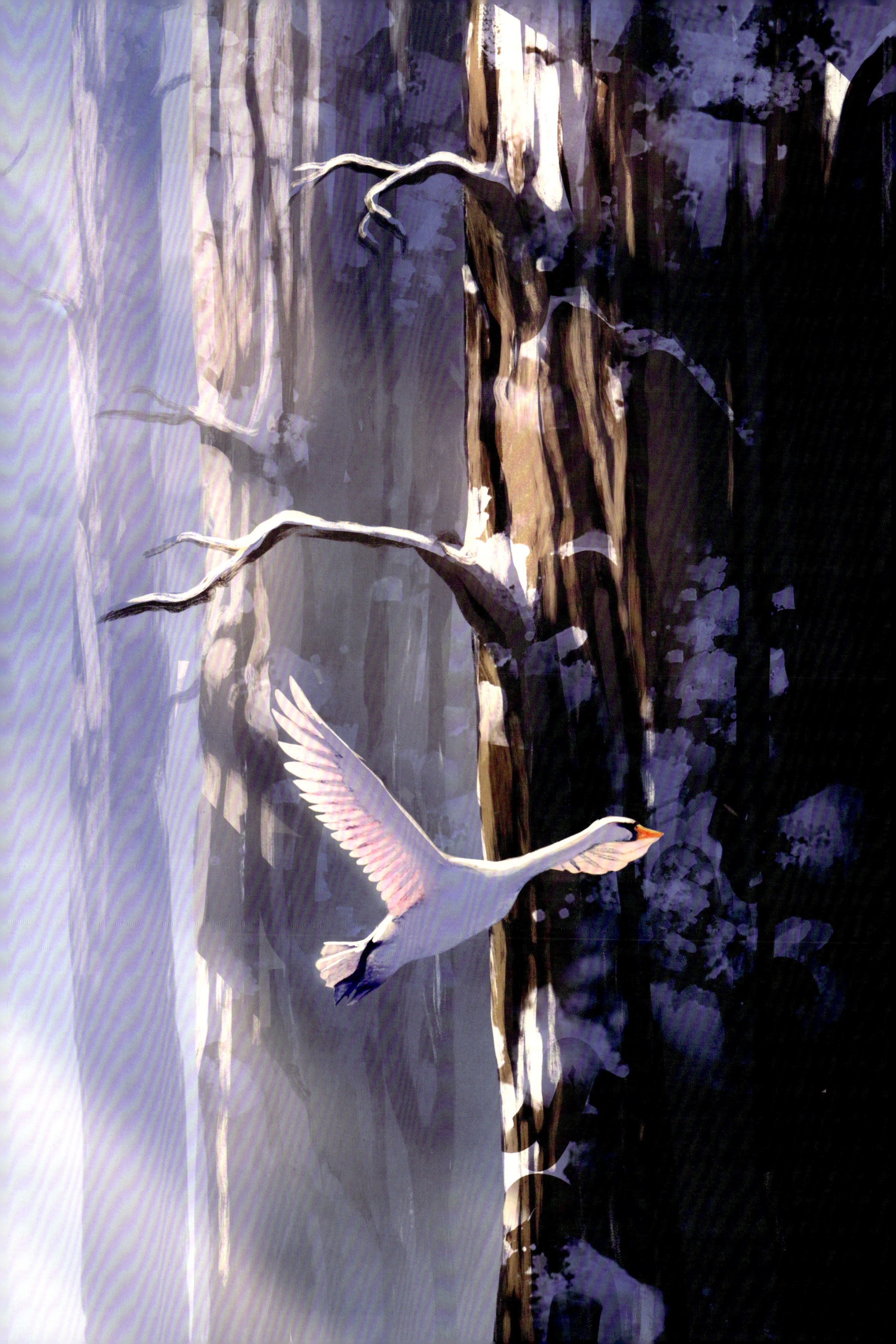

CRAFTING THE COVER

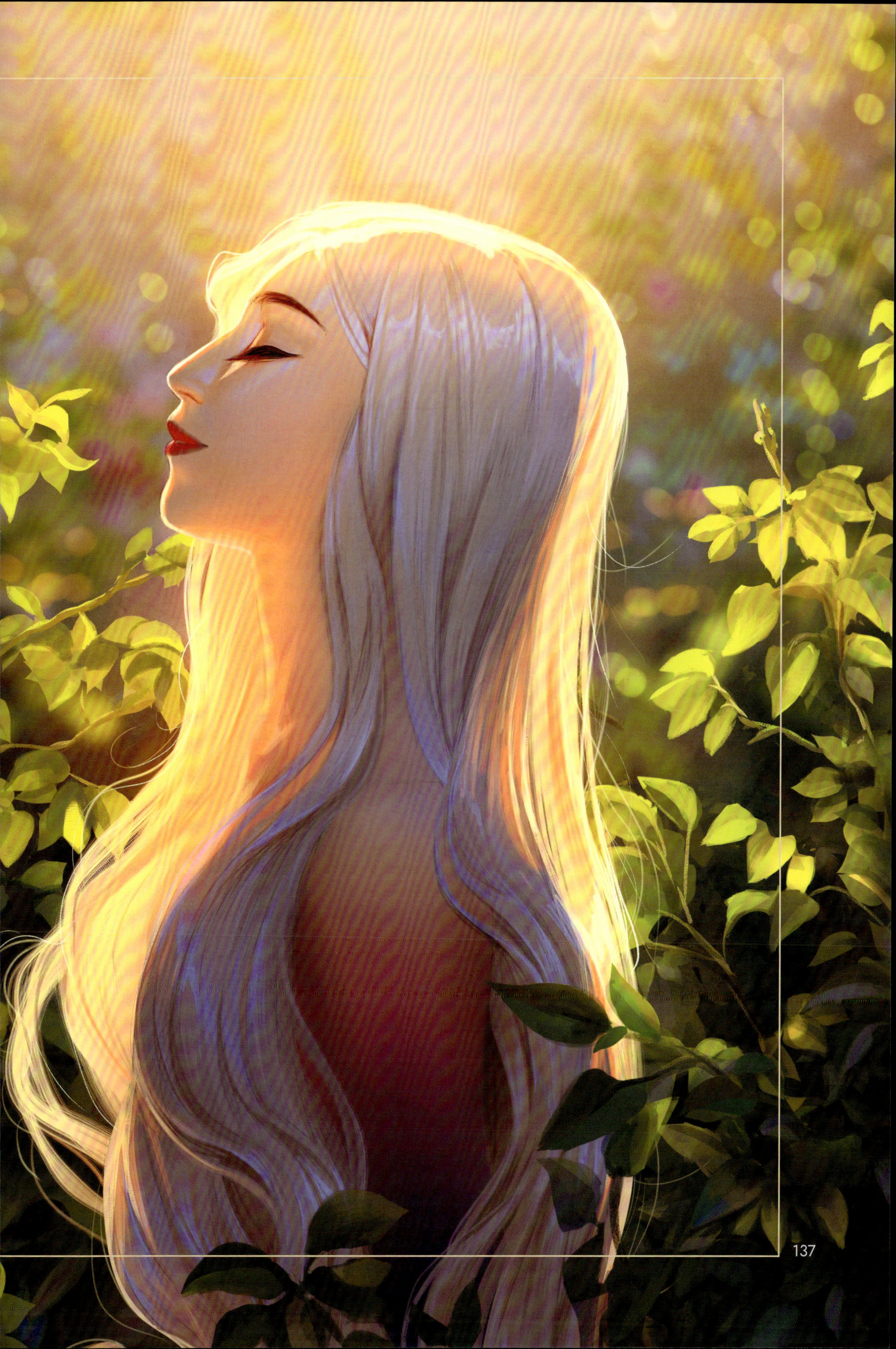

My favourite time of the day is golden hour, the short period in the mornings and evenings when daylight appears softer and warmer. As the name suggests, it illuminates everything in a gorgeous golden colour. As I often enjoy taking walks when the sun reaches these points, I thought it would be fitting to incorporate my admiration for this natural phenomenon into the cover.

While writing this book, I kept asking myself what I wanted the cover to look like and what I wanted it to represent. I started gathering ideas by simply jotting down some key elements that I felt defined my artwork. Terms like 'colourful', 'atmospheric', and 'illuminated' came to mind. At that stage, I already knew I wanted the cover to showcase my love for colour and light, so I listed potential titles for the book and organized inspirational images on a mood board. Finally, with a clear vision in my head, I started working on the illustration.

In the coming pages, I'll guide you through the process I took to create the cover artwork – from the first couple of thumbnail sketches to rendering and finalizing the artwork.

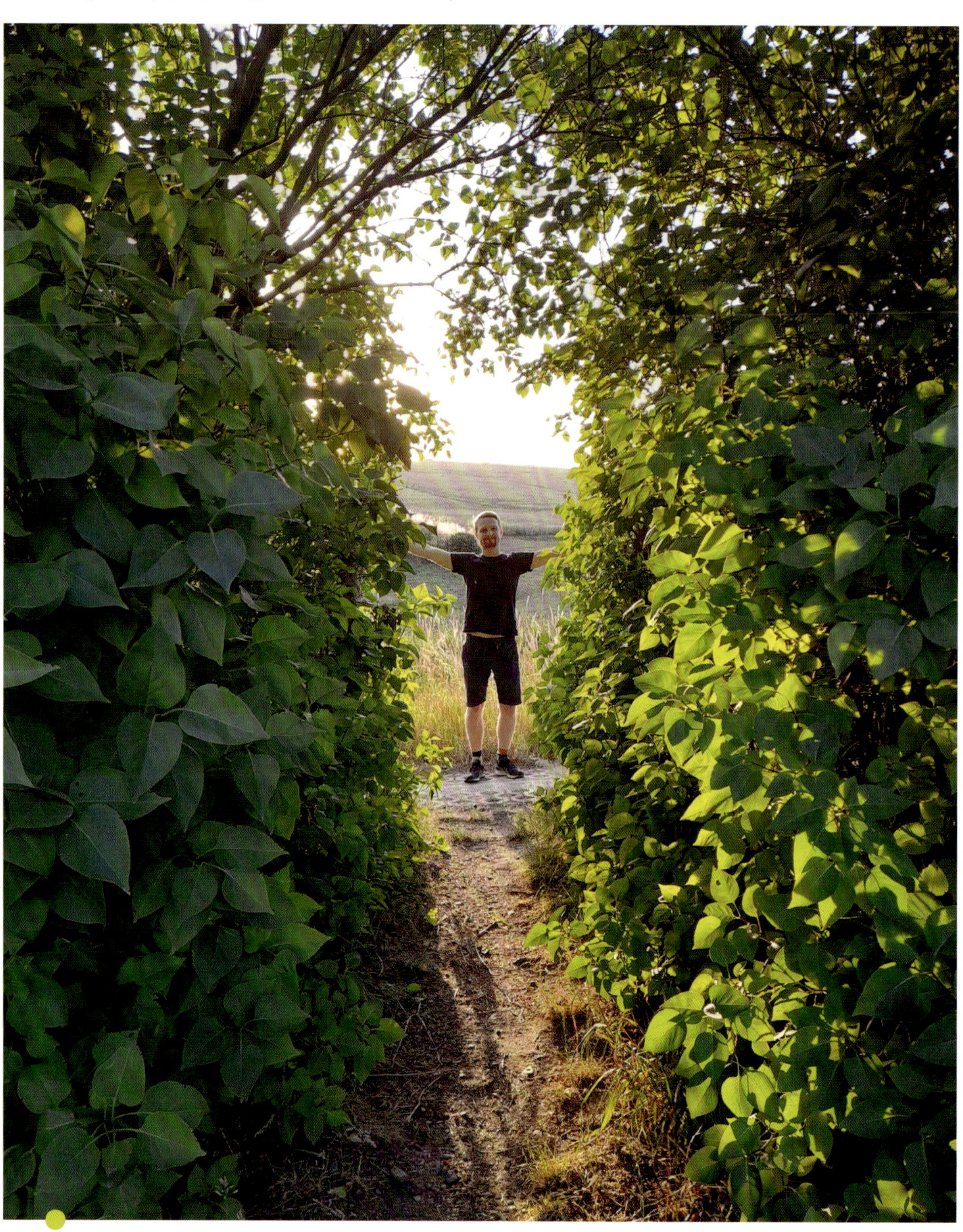

I took this photo during a summer walk. I was in awe over the golden sunlight shining through the leaves, illuminating them in saturated green tones. Since I was so inspired by the subsurface scattering effect, I wanted to include it in my cover illustration

Creating thumbnails

With the theme of 'golden hour' in mind, I sketch some thumbnails. Each thumbnail features a warm and bright light source. While I like each of them for different reasons, I decide to explore the sketch featuring my original character Eira. I enjoy the mix of the cooler blue tones with the warmer ones. Eira's backlit hair also adds to the warm mood.

This design didn't come without some doubt. I asked myself, 'Is it too similar to a piece I've already made?' and 'Shouldn't I go for something grander?' I decided to step back from the designs for a week to reflect on it. After revisiting them, it wasn't hard for me to make my choice: I wanted the cover to represent me.

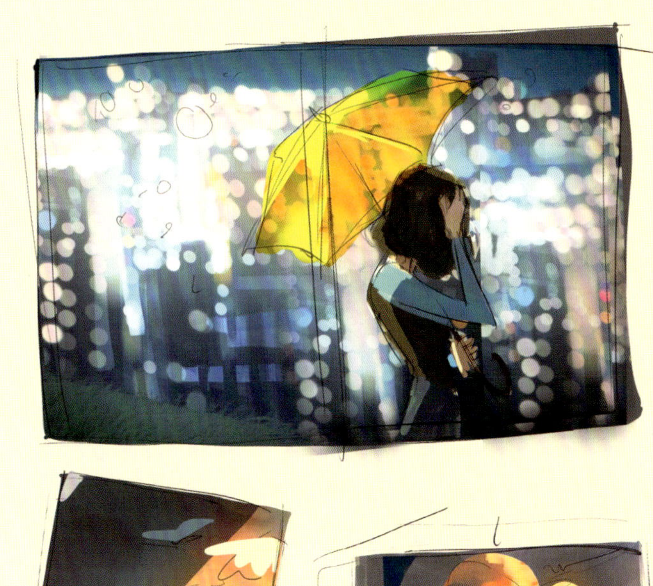

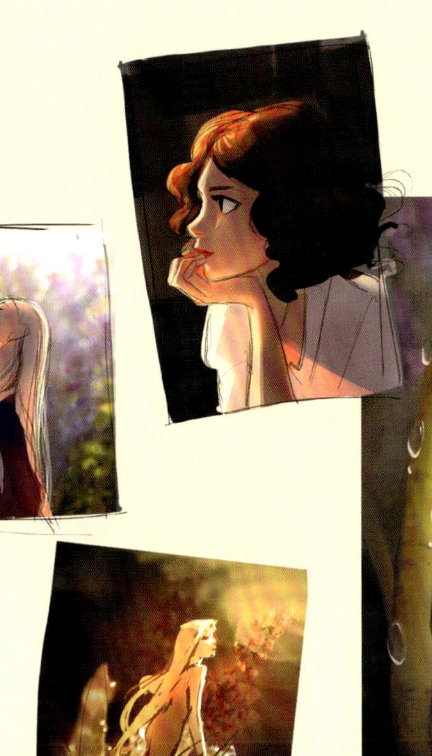

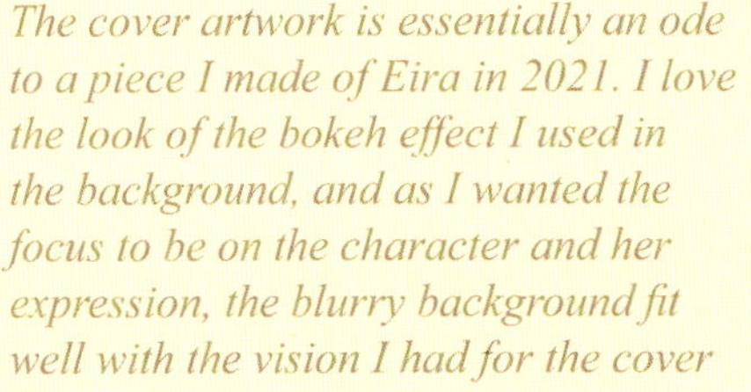

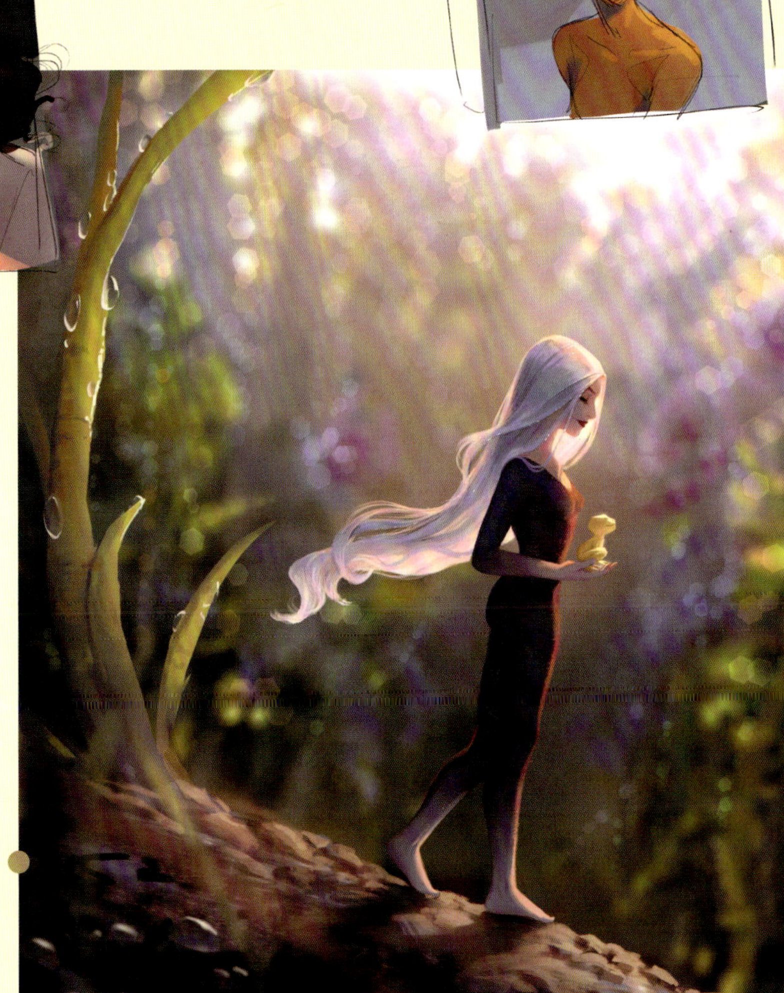

The cover artwork is essentially an ode to a piece I made of Eira in 2021. I love the look of the bokeh effect I used in the background, and as I wanted the focus to be on the character and her expression, the blurry background fit well with the vision I had for the cover

Sketching & adding base colours

Armed with a clear vision in my head, I load the thumbnail sketch as a reference to my cover file and start drawing the character. I also import the artwork I previously made for Eira as a second reference. Using both illustrations as a guide, I make a rough sketch, and on new layers I add both the line art and base colours with ArtRage's Ink Pen tool. I also add the gradient in Eira's outfit with a Square Canvas brush. In order to change the gradient shape later, I add it on a separate layer above the base colours and set the blend mode to Multiply.

Since Eira is standing in the shadows while illuminated by strong sunlight, I opt for relatively dark base colours. I want to add strong and bright colours later, so a dark base makes more sense for this particular illustration.

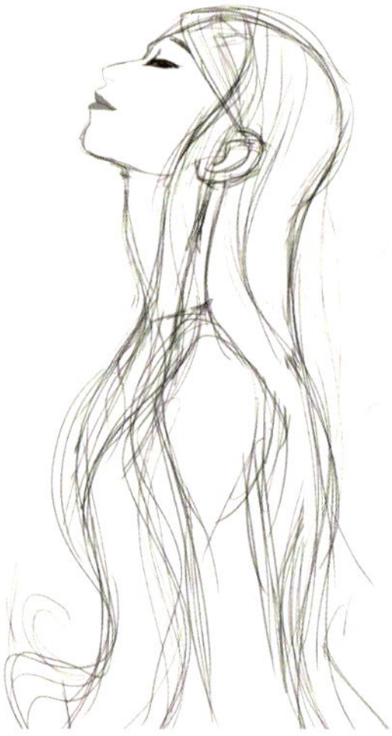

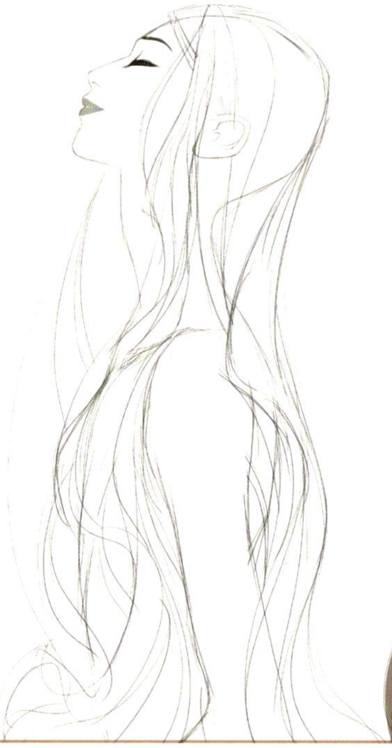

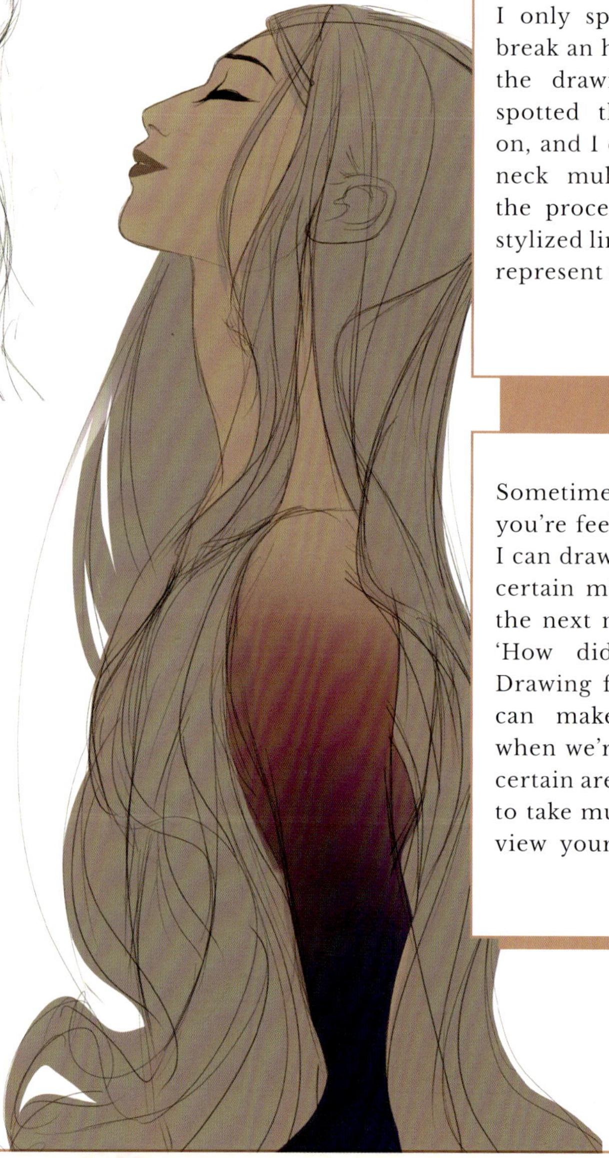

TAKING A BREAK

After drawing the line art and adding the base colours, I hadn't noticed her extremely long neck. I only spotted it when I took a break an hour or so later. I showed the drawing to my sister, who spotted the disproportion going on, and I ended up shortening her neck multiple times throughout the process. While I enjoyed the stylized line art, it didn't accurately represent my character and current art style.

Sometimes, taking a break when you're feeling stuck does wonders! I can draw all day without noticing certain mistakes, only to wake up the next morning and ask myself: 'How did I not notice that?!' Drawing for long periods of time can make us 'blind', especially when we're used to zooming in to certain areas. I would always advise to take multiple breaks in order to view your work in progress with fresh eyes.

CREATING A CUSTOM BRUSH

Since nature is a key element in most of my pieces, I thought it would be a nice idea to add in some plants behind Eira. To do this, I created a custom plant brush in ArtRage. After tweaking the settings to my liking, I saved the brush and added the basic leaf shapes on a new layer.

For the highlights, I added some cooler shadows and saturated greens. To capture the magic of golden hour, I wanted Eira's hair – and the leaves around her – to appear as if they're glowing.

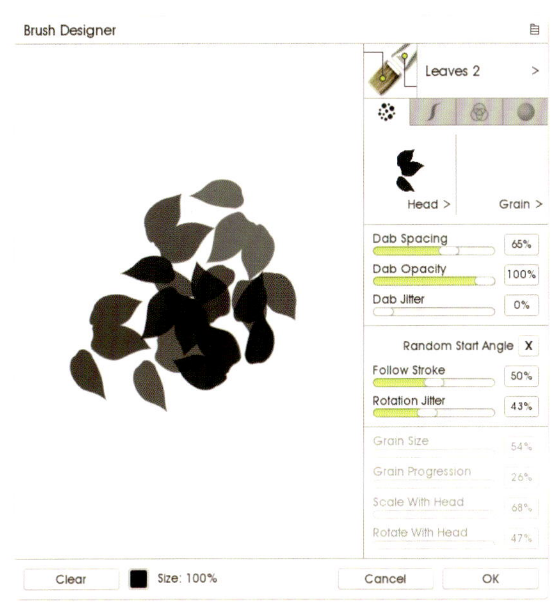

This is what the Brush Designer looks like in ArtRage. On the left is an area to test out the brush in its current setting. You can adjust the settings on the right. For this particular brush, increasing the rotation jitter makes the leaves randomly face other directions, creating a more organic look. The closer the setting is to 100%, the more the stroke rotation will jitter.

This is the head of my custom plant brush. I ended up rotating the head 270 degrees before loading it into the Brush Designer in order for the leaves to face downwards.

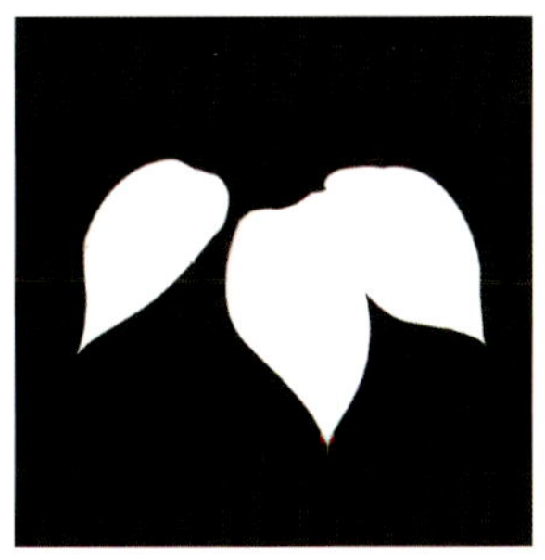

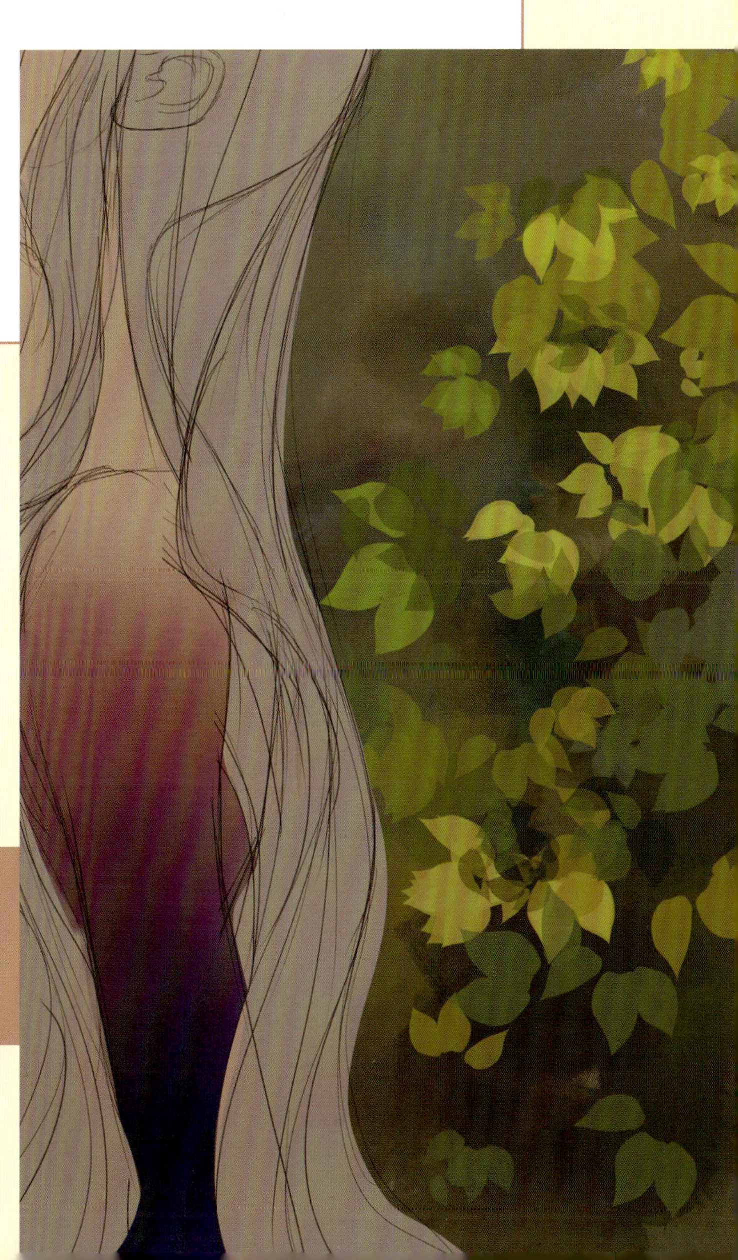

At this stage in the painting process, it's easy to see the shape of the custom brush that I used for the base of the plants. Next, I gradually changed the shape of some leaves and painted more variations on top.

Painting the background

Now that the character is set in the composition, it's time to start the background. I begin with the Paint Roller brush. I add small dabs of colour, slightly changing the hue and tone in order to add some variation. Once the background is filled with these dabs of colour, I use the Square Canvas 4 custom brush with the Color Pickup setting enabled in order to smudge the tones together. This results in a nice base for the blurry background.

To add more texture to the scene, I copy the leaves I painted, reducing their scale and blurring them by 19 pixels. I also add some dabs of purple and blue with the Airbrush in order to add more variation to the background, indicating the presence of some cooler flowers in the scene.

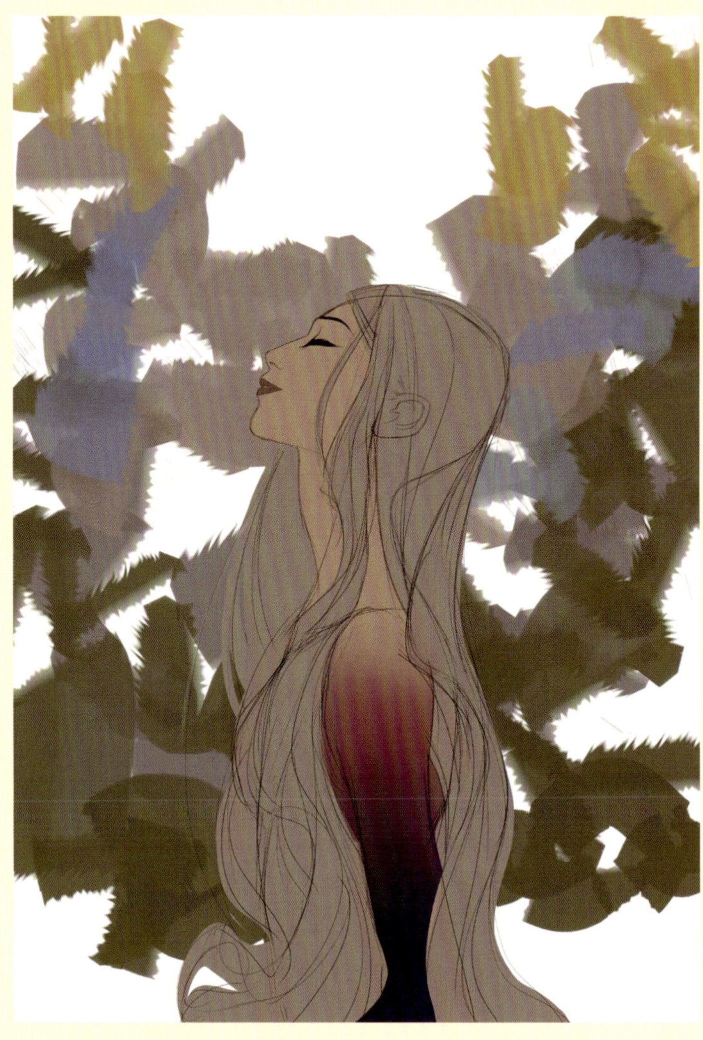

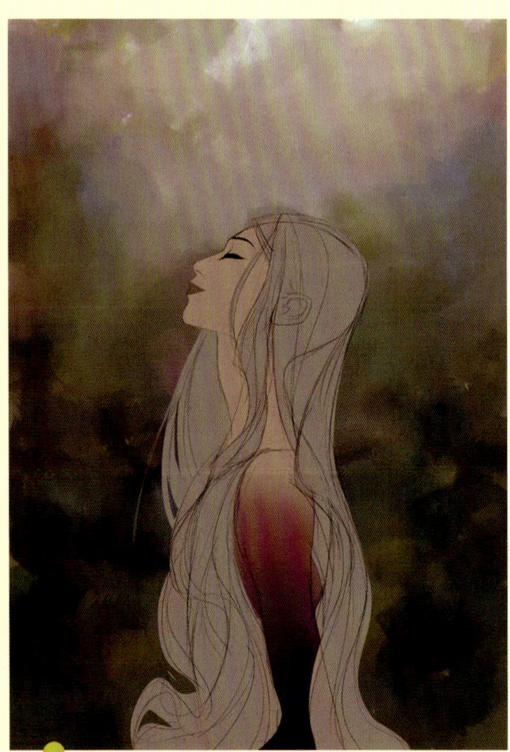

I added large dabs of colour and blended them together to create a smudgy background

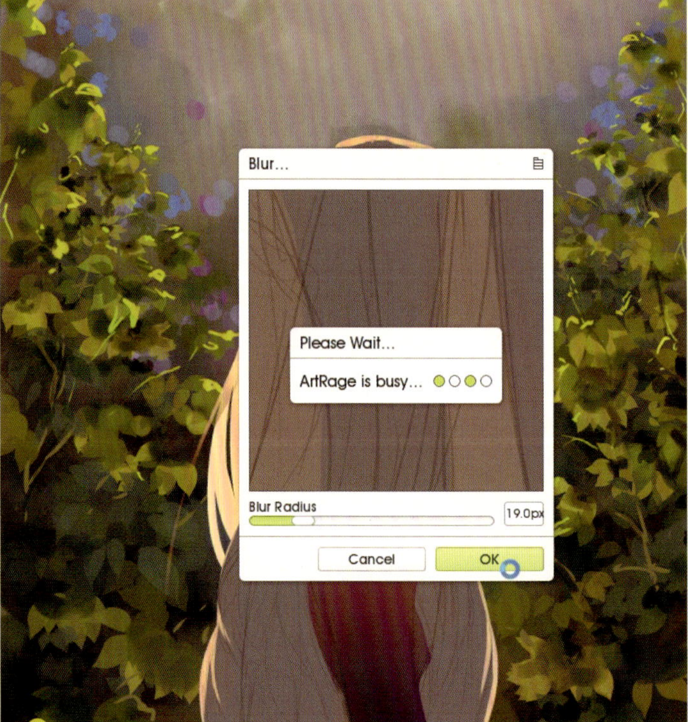

If I want to blur the contents of an entire layer, I use the Blur Layer option. This method allows me to control the intensity of the Gaussian blur by inputting a number of pixels for it to spread across

Adding rim light

Once the general mood and background colour scheme is set, I shift my focus back to the character. I would usually add some general soft shading at this stage, but since the strong, golden rim light is an essential part of this piece, I decide to add that first.

I add the rim light on a new layer, setting the blend mode to Overlay. I use a light-yellow colour and apply the lighting along the character's outline.

Rim lighting really helps set the mood of a scene

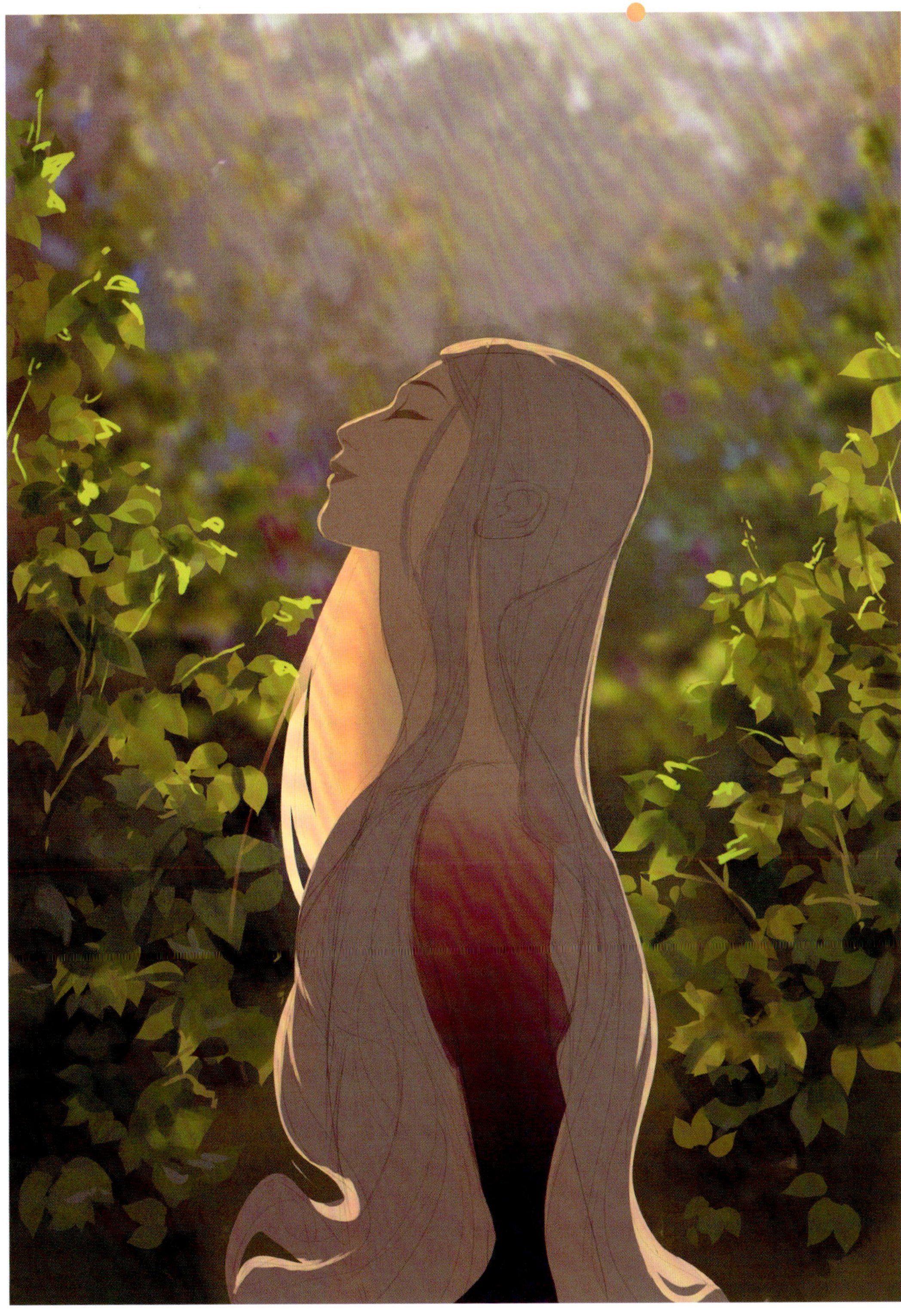

Adding shadows & highlights

Next, I darken the base colours even more. They needed to be a bit cooler in order for the warm lighting to stand out. To do so, I select the contents of the character layer and create a new layer on top of it, setting the blend mode to Multiply. I fill the selection with a light-blue colour, which shifts the base colours to a cooler, darker tone. This creates more contrast between the rim light and the base colour.

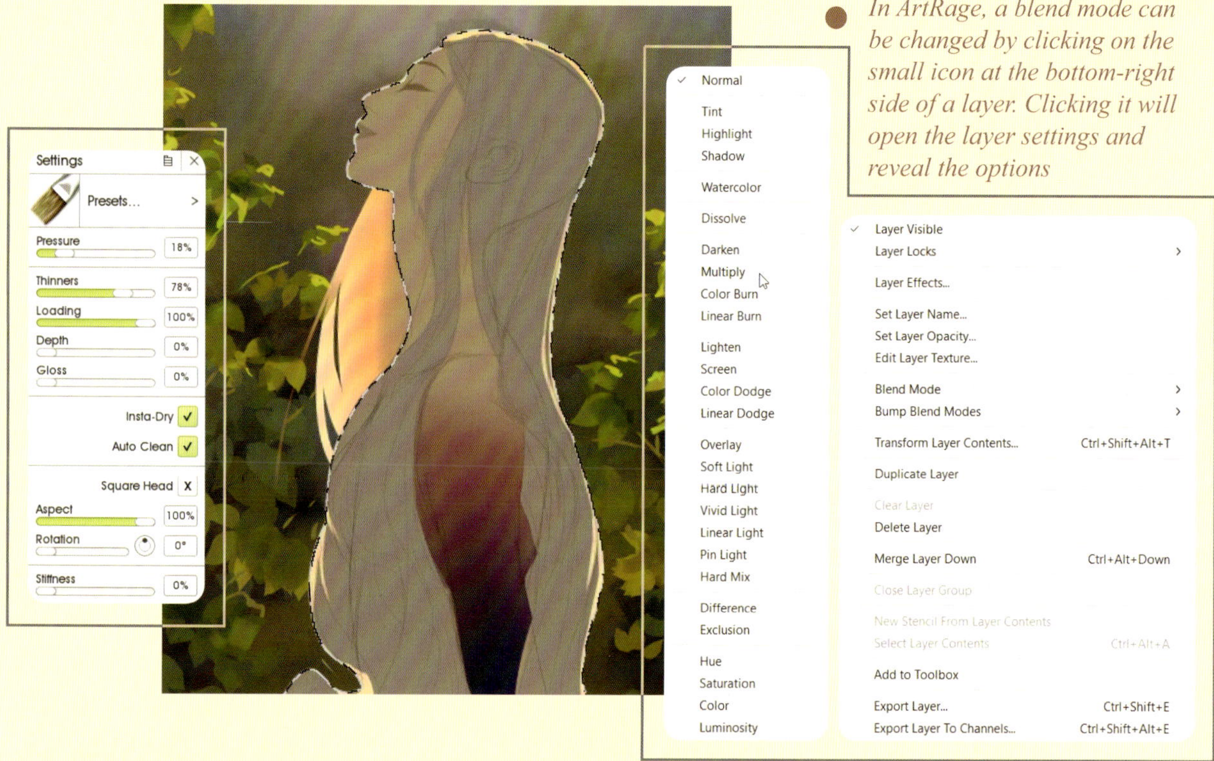

In ArtRage, a blend mode can be changed by clicking on the small icon at the bottom-right side of a layer. Clicking it will open the layer settings and reveal the options

At this stage, the character's general colours are set. Now, I move on to the shadows and highlights. I apply the warm shadows with the blend mode set to Multiply while the cool highlights are set to Soft Light. Once I am happy with these two separate layers, I merge them with the base layer.

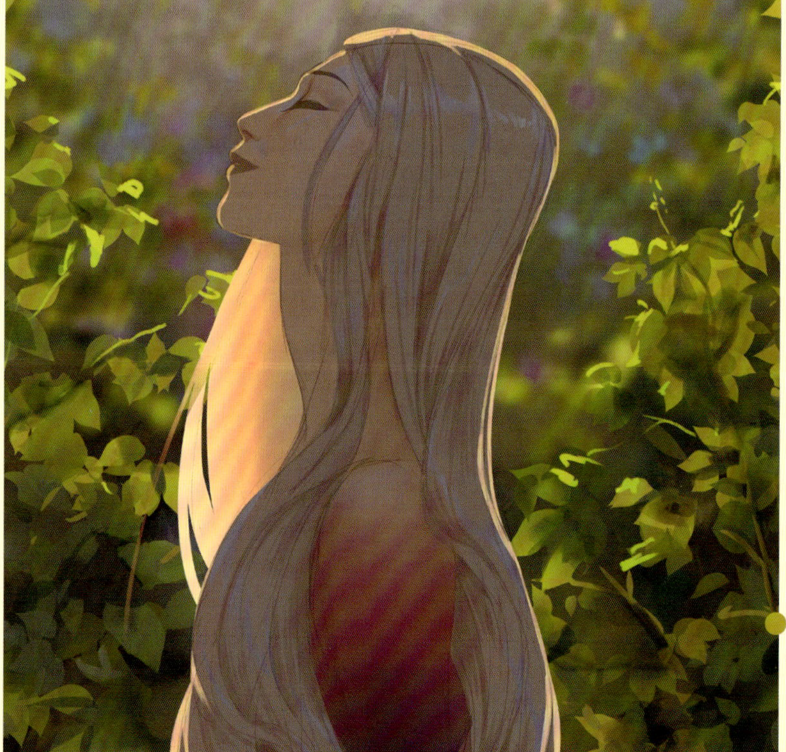

After adding basic lighting and shading, the portrait is taking form!

Rendering & adding details

With the character on one layer, I start the rendering process. I apply more contrast and details to the hair and face, and erase remnants of the line art. Gradually, I add and refine more details, including a saturated blue highlight along the waves of the hair.

At this stage, I work back and forth between the background and the foreground, taking multiple short breaks in between. This workflow helps me identify which regions need more attention and which are overworked in comparison.

In order to increase the gleaming effect, I also warm the rim-light edges with an airbrush set to Overlay blend mode.

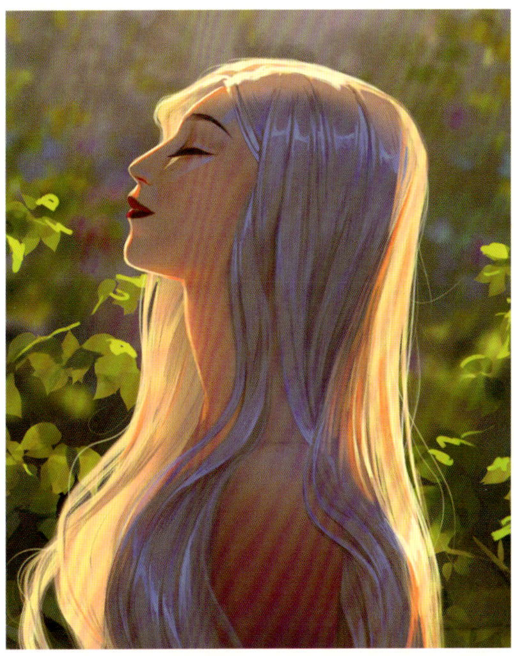

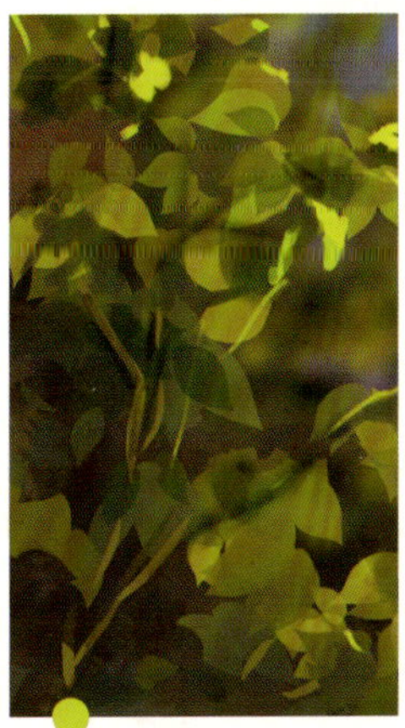

This part of the process is always the most time consuming. Listening to a calming playlist makes it even more enjoyable

SPEEDING UP THE PROCESS

I like to add in more lighting and details on a separate layer. Before merging the edits with the base layer, I work on one main layer for two reasons:

1. It speeds things up. When I'm really looking forward to a piece, I often find myself painting pretty fast. Having the character base on one layer feels more natural to me, and it speeds up the painting process even more. Of course, saving time is always a good thing!

2. It's easier to stay organized. I can't calculate how many hours I've spent searching through layers for that one specific brushstroke that was bothering me. Working with fewer layers makes my files more manageable. It also helps with saving time!

ZOOMING OUT

To get an overview of the composition, I often zoom out and observe the painting as a whole. I make no exceptions here! Looking at the image from far away allows me to discover proportional errors and to get a feeling for the overall look of the piece.

In ArtRage, there is a handy option to load the current state of the file as a little reference window. This can be found in the Refs window under the New View option. Clicking this will make a small new window appear that can be moved, rotated, and sized up or down. It is also possible to draw within the window. You can load multiple windows into your file.

Since I often find myself zooming and rotating the art as I paint, I always have the Canvas Positioner window open. This circular window allows me to freely move around the canvas. Some curved strokes are easier to draw at a certain angle, so I can't imagine working without this handy tool

Editing the colours & finalizing

Colour enhancement plays an important part in my artwork. In order to edit the colours in Photoshop, I export the illustration in ArtRage as a PNG file. I then open that file in Photoshop and use a Color Balance adjustment layer to edit the colours.

The separate layers I organized in ArtRage won't translate through the PNG-file format, so if I want to keep those layers separate, I can export the ArtRage file (PTG) into the PSD format, which will work smoothly in Photoshop. It must be noted that any effects, layer masks, and adjustment layers won't show up when you switch back to ArtRage.

To finalize the piece, I import the colour-corrected version back into ArtRage. I use Overlay and Soft Light blend modes to add a little more warmth to the piece. I really want to capture the whimsical beauty of golden hour, and adding that extra orange glow does the trick!

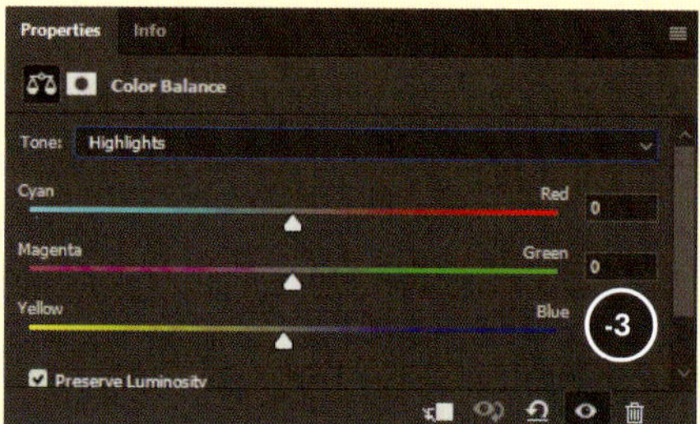

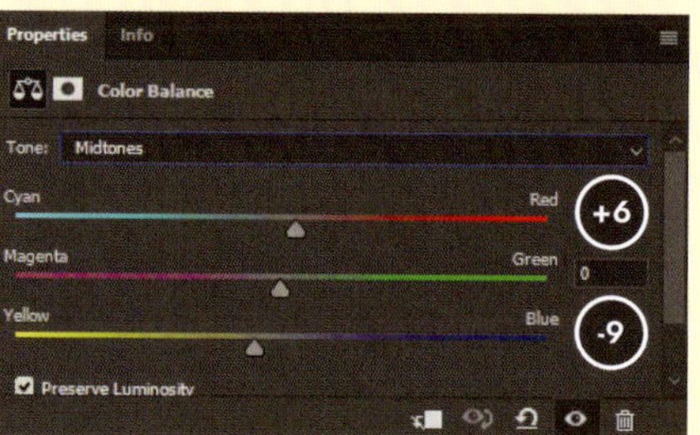

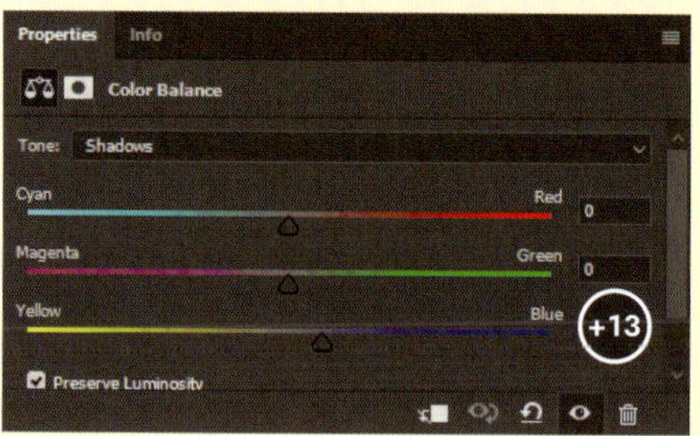

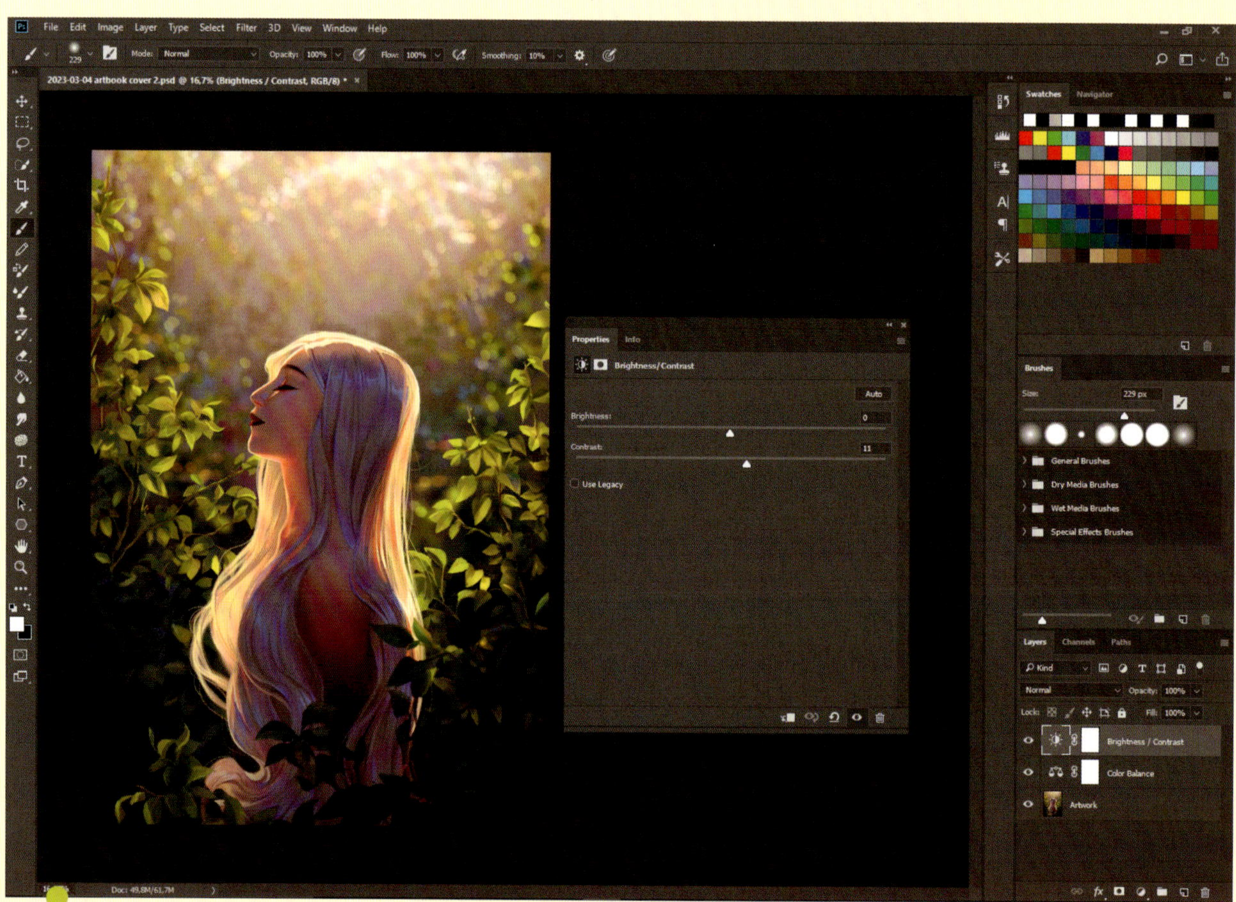

I make the midtones warmer and the shadows slightly cooler

Here is the final illustration!

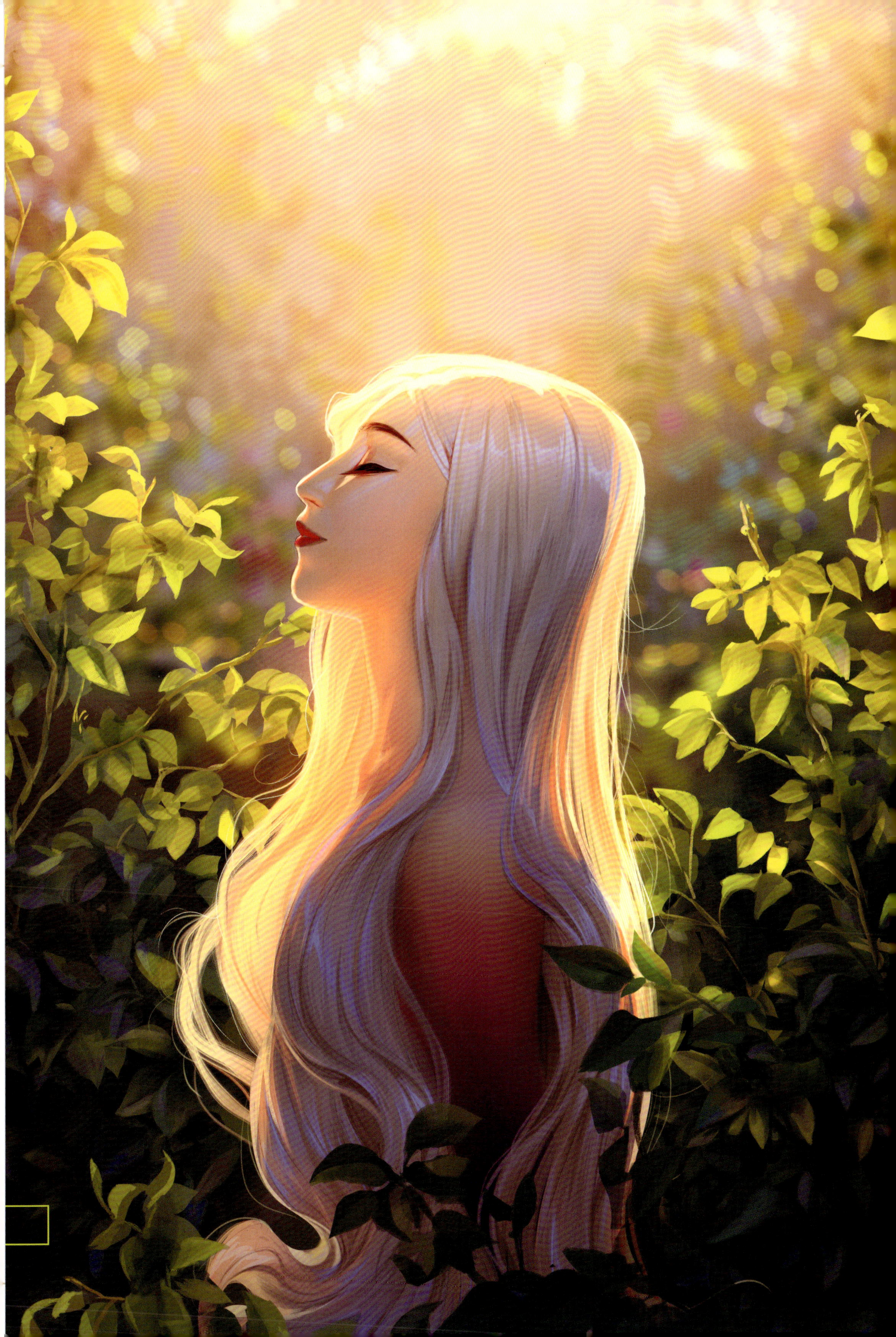

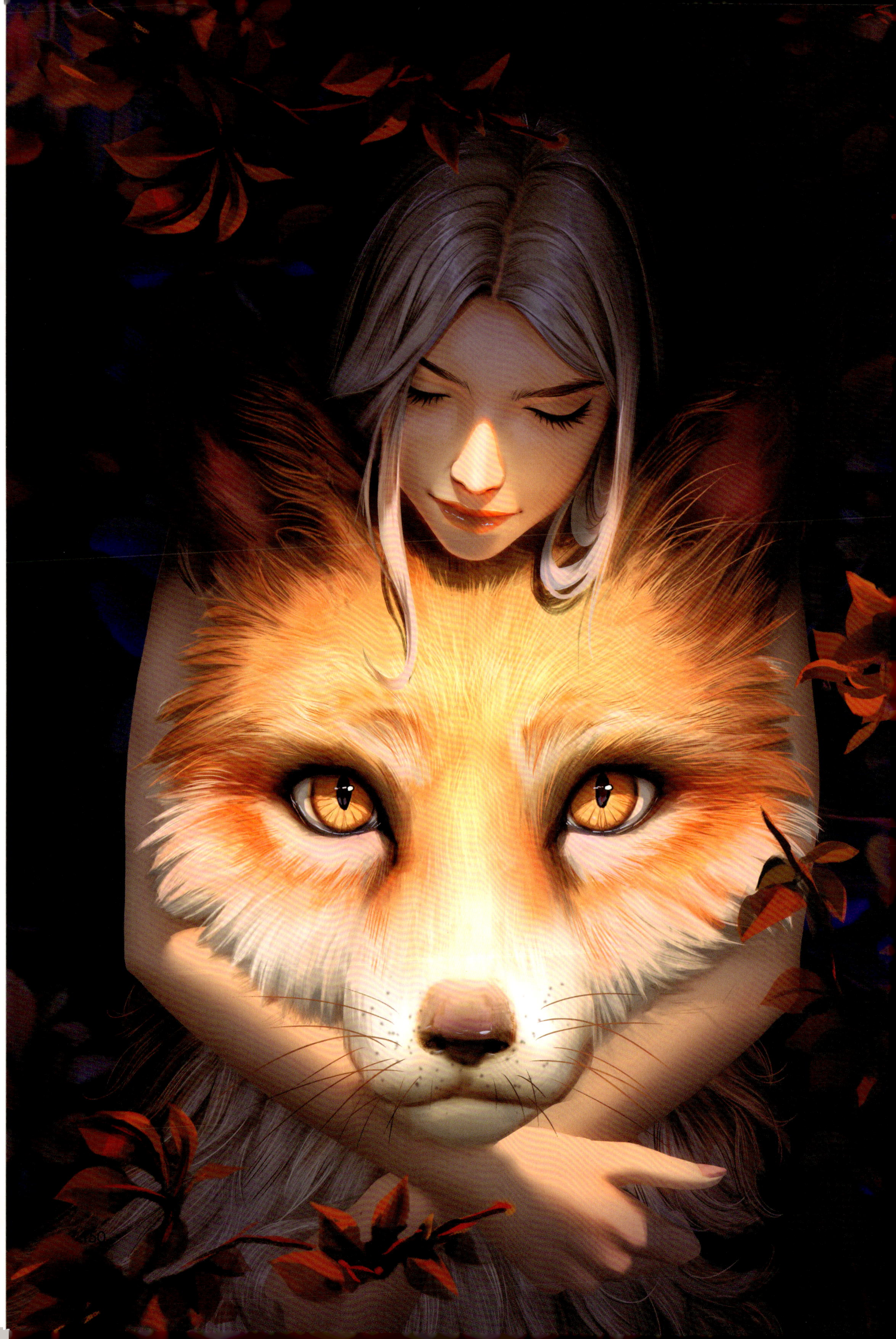

THANK YOU

I can't believe we've already reached the end of this little journey. It feels like a time lapse from the moment I created my first portraits to now, as I am writing the final few paragraphs of this book.

I'd like to take this opportunity to thank my supportive family and friends from the bottom of my heart. Without their help and unconditional support, I never would've been able to make it this far. Having a safe and warm space to work is essential for me, which I've only recently realized. I am incredibly grateful for them.

Big thanks to my professors and teachers who have critiqued my work and motivated me throughout the years.

I also want to thank my followers – you helped my art reach people all over the world. Special thanks to those who have been following and supporting my journey since I first set up my social-media accounts. Every single comment has motivated me to continue pursuing my dreams.

Thanks to the awesome team at 3dtotal and my wonderful editor, Rhee. Her feedback was incredibly helpful and it was a pleasure to work with her. The book is absolutely beautiful! Thanks for making this dream become a reality!

Last, but certainly not least, I want to say an extra special thank you to my lovely twin sister, Leffie. I'm so glad that we are both pursuing our dreams together, and I hope I will continue to inspire her as much as she's inspired me.

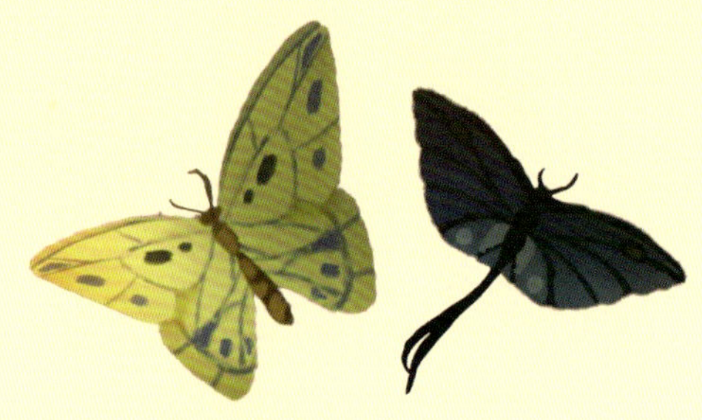

ABOUT 3DTOTAL

3dtotal Publishing is a trailblazing, creative publisher specializing in inspirational and educational resources for artists.

Our titles feature top industry professionals from around the globe who share their experience in skillfully written step-by-step tutorials and fascinating, detailed guides. Illustrated throughout with stunning artwork, these best-selling publications offer creative insight, expert advice, and essential motivation. Fans of digital art will enjoy our comprehensive volumes covering Adobe Photoshop, Procreate, and Blender, as well as our superb titles based around character design, including *Fundamentals of Character Design* and *Creating Characters for the Entertainment Industry*. The dedicated, high-quality blend of instruction and inspiration also extends to traditional art. Titles covering a range of techniques, genres, and abilities allow your creativity to flourish while building essential skills.

Well-established within the industry, we now offer over 100 titles and counting, many of which have been translated into multiple languages around the world. With something for every artist, we are proud to say that our books offer the 3dtotal package:

LEARN · CREATE · SHARE

Visit us at store.3dtotal.com

3dtotal Publishing is part of 3dtotal.com, a leading website for CG artists founded by Tom Greenway in 1999.